Separation, Assimilation, or Accommodation

CONTRASTING ETHNIC MINORITY POLICIES

Terrence E. Cook

Westport, Connecticut
London

Library of Congress Cataloging-in-Publication Data

Cook, Terrence, E., 1942–
    Separation, assimilation, or accommodation : contrasting ethnic minority policies / Terrence E. Cook.
        p.   cm.
    Includes bibliographical references and index.
    ISBN 0–275–97825–7 (alk. paper)
        1. Ethnicity—Political aspects.   2. Ethnic conflict.   3. Assimilation (Sociology)   I. Title.
    GN495.6.C69   2003
    305.8—dc21   2002033384

British Library Cataloguing in Publication Data is available.

Library of Congress Catalog Card Number: 2002033384
ISBN: 0–275–97825–7

First published in 2003

Praeger Publishers, 88 Post Road West, Westport, CT 06881
An imprint of Greenwood Publishing Group, Inc.
www.praeger.com

Printed in the United States of America

The paper used in this book complies with the
Permanent Paper Standard issued by the National
Information Standards Organization (Z39.48–1984).

10   9   8   7   6   5   4   3   2   1

Contents

Figures

Introduction

This is a book about conflicts of ethnic groups, defining "ethnic" quite broadly to understand racial, religious, linguistic, national, or kindred cultural categories other than those of class. By one definition, an ethnic group shares its name, notion of common descent, history, cultural traits, and sense of home place (cf. Gurr, 2000, 5; Smith, 1986, 22–28). Although I dwell on ethnicities, others may find that the book's analysis can be readily extended to other kinds of conflicts, such as those of class or gender.

Ethnic conflicts, often far more than other sorts of human conflicts, are prominent in everyday news, if only because they often result in highly destructive forms, taking many human lives as well as destroying much property. International wars have been sparse since 1990, whereas civil warring has become common, although the violence has somewhat subsided from about 1995. But Maya Chadda notes that "of the eighty-six conflicts recorded by the United Nations since 1989, only three involved armed conflicts between countries. The rest were internal wars caused by ethnic and intercommunal violence" (Chadda, 1997, x–xi). Metta Spencer offers a reinforcing observation of one year: worldwide, of the 40 wars fought in 1996, 38 of them involved conflict between rival ethnic groups, and one of the two remaining was a war among distinctive clans of what was essentially the same ethnic group in Somalia (Spencer, 1998, 18; also 38 notes 28 and 29). But more violence occurs in less spectacular forms, such as ethnic riots or individual acts of aggression. Ethnic animosity was involved in the terroristic destruction of the World Trade Center towers and part of the Pentagon, taking about 3,000 lives. Any theory about human violence must give a central place to ethnic group rivalries. These are humanly caused and potentially subject to human control.

Although there are many speculative theories of human aggression, we actually know very little about it, aside from good evidence that hotter climates, and the hottest seasons of temperate climates, correlate with more of it. But because we cannot air-condition mean city streets, that cause is not something we can control (Geen, 2001, 32–35).

Virtually all states have some ethnic diversity, and many of these states experience heightened forms of conflict among groups. Furthermore, it is impossible for a state not to have some kind of policy (or sometimes a set of policies) regarding its ethnic minorities.

For the sponsors of a given sort of policy, what are they *saying* they are trying to do? When can we take these self-reports for granted, and when should we consider the possibility of ulterior motives? What are the *implicit assumptions* behind those announced and unannounced policy objectives? What are some theoretical and practical *problems* with those policy initiatives, considering such possibilities as counterproductivity, unintended and unwanted and usually unforeseen consequences of implementation, should that succeed?

If a policy works at all at helping a problem, perhaps it is applied not enough when the problem is not being better managed or solved.

But a policy approach is being pushed too far when it (1) becomes counterproductive with regard to its own goal, or (2) does unacceptable damage to the effort to reach *other* worthwhile goals. Although one could arguably make an exception for moderation, literal "maximization" of any one goal is madness. Trade-off situations inevitably occur, but it is rarely clear how such tensions among worthwhile goals should be handled. Illustrations of such problems will arise during the course of this book.

OF HUMAN PSYCHOLOGY: IMMEDIATE, EMERGENT, SUBMERGENT

Some hold that any social science must be rooted in, or even quite literally reduced to, "microfoundations," or some allegedly simple propositions about human behavior at the *micro* (small) level that could permit the building of theories at the *meso* (middle) or *macro* (large) levels.

Perhaps this thinking supposes there are some very simple mechanisms at the small level that can permit deduction of behavior at middle or large levels. There may be some immediate and simple aspects of human psychology, such as drives for self-preservation or sex, that often are shared with nonhuman animals. There are also relatively simple mechanisms of learning or changing the relationship of stimuli and responses as through imitation, classical (Pavlovian) conditioning, or operant (Skinnerian) conditioning.

But sometimes forms of learning seem less helpful in predicting political behavior than are some cognitive weaknesses that limit our more complex psychology. As Herbert Simon and his associates knew, we are only "boundedly" rational at best. Consider some limits of our rationality. We tend to be *unable* to (1) discern many differences in what seems remote from us, such as in an ideological family removed from our own, (2) preference order too many things, (3) evaluate by very many standards, (4) grasp many options as a whole set rather than by pairs or serially, meaning one by one, (5) be more *logically* consistent than *affectively* so as in uncritically linking one thing pleasant with another, or what is painful with its like, (6) experience as much pleasure in an equivalent gain as pain in a loss, (7) avoid discounting what we could not get yesterday or what we could only get in the distant future, (8) recognize that the same input may not have a constant relation to output at all magnitudes, places, and times, (9) avoid the gambler's fallacy of exaggerating the overall probability of gain dependent on a series of really discrete events, (10) correctly see much higher risk when a specific case of low risk becomes repeated at many similar places or during many future episodes, or (11) avoid being mired into sunk costs, or throwing good money after bad, or (12) recognize that not all individuals will be alike in all of the foregoing.

By contrast, what would unbounded rationality look like? Probably inspired by a largely imaginary view of investor behavior, many economists would have us specify a relevant frame of identity (self-interest or other-regarding, where many have accented self-interest), a master motive or "maximand" (often taken to be economic gain), and a general model of how agents handle uncertainty (usually taken to be expected utility-maximizing). Although this rational choice paradigm increasingly penetrates other social sciences, including political science, I am growing quite skeptical of the view that speaks as if salient identity, dominant aim, and orientation toward uncertainty are some "simples" that preexist any situation.

On the contrary, I recognize rather complex human psychological repertories in personal identities, goals, and postures toward risk, differently mobilized in adaptation to the situation of choice. Further, without meaning any personification, I hold that the situations of agents often largely determine what is selected from such repertories, or can literally shape these repertories, as in adding or subtracting motives, and so on. That is, I recognize the reality of "emergent properties" and "submergent properties," as defined next.

First, let us address emergent properties. Mario Bunge, although conceding that wholes are built up of parts, has denied the position (called "methodological individualism") that social behavior must be reducible to primitive axioms and hypotheses of human behavior (let alone to chemistry or physics), or that large-scale movements of matter must be accounted for ultimately by subatomic theories, perhaps ending with superstring theory. What the methodological individualists fail to grasp is that there are *emergent properties* in many phenomena, such that, say, a scaling up will reveal behavioral properties that could never be discerned by looking at the parts (in the social sciences, individuals) alone, even if a systemic analysis would include attention to parts (Bunge, 1996, 51). He goes on to say, "the individual approach to society cannot account for the emergence, maintenance, or breakdown of social systems" (Bunge, 1996, 247). For "every system possesses (emergent) properties that its components lack" (Bunge, 1996, 251). Citing physicist Philip Anderson, K. C. Cole similarly notes, "The universe is full of things that cannot be understood—ever—simply by understanding smaller and more fundamental parts. Each time you go from quarks to atoms to chewing gum to life to galaxies, new things emerge that cannot be explained or predicted by goings on at lower levels" (Cole, 1997, 62). To Anderson, the big is not the small writ large, but "More is different." What is true in physics may also be so in social sciences: "In the same way, individual people behave quite differently than crowds. One person cannot have mass hysteria any more than one illness is an epidemic" (Cole, 1997, 63). So emergent properties recognize that observable events at lower levels may not permit prediction or explanation of what happens at higher levels.

But arguably it is also true that sometimes what happens at higher levels, or larger situations, *can* predict or explain what happens at the lower levels of analysis. Often innovative thinking in all sciences involves conversion of assumed "constants" into "variables," sometimes after observing anomalies, or unexpected events. Particle or subatomic physicists have long believed they were unraveling laws that are constants, able to ultimately explain what happens in mass movements of matter as studied by solid-state physics. But some solid state physicists, yet a minority movement among physicists, wonder if that is reversed. Mavericks such as Robert Laughlin (Stanford) or David Pines (Illinois and Los Alamos) argue that far from needing perfected subatomic physics to understand gross movements of matter in the universe, it may be true that gross movements of matter may predict or explain what happens in subatomic physics, *perhaps even causing changes in the "laws of nature" one may observe there.*[1] Many anomalous observations arise from recent studies of space. Thus, as I was writing this, scientists report finding a new kind of extremely dense stars, apparently of quarks packed tightly in ways not previously observed or thought possible.

Similarly, what happens at the human individual psychological level may be affected far more than we think by the patterns of larger masses of human behavior, which constrain choices of individuals. I concede that our biogenetic endowments, or hard wiring, may be thus changed only in long courses of time, but I suspect that our soft wiring varies far more readily than is usually believed.

As a term for this sort of reversal of methodological individualism, I coin the term "submergent properties" and speculatively suggest some illustrations. In the application of the concept of merely *emergent* properties to social science, often individual psychologies at best offer the potential for a pattern of behavior that would not appear unless one scaled up to include large numbers of persons in an interactive mode. But it may be true that patterns in wholes not only *select from* psychological repertoires that are already there but actually *shape them*. If *selecting* from already available repertories speaks to emergent properties, the actual *shaping* is what I am trying to address under the rubric of *submergent properties*.

That is, the structured framing of our situations may sometimes dominate how we cognitively frame our choices within them. Gross patterns of human behavior, such as a normatively guided and reproducing (hence "institutionalized") marketplace or a political order, could precede present choices and also dominate some choices regarding any individual's (1) posture toward uncertainty or what most of us call risk, (2) interest identity, and (3) aims. When this is so, larger patterns of human behavior addressed by macrotheories or at least mesotheories may quite literally shape micro-level psychology. Apart from some relatively primitive autonomic processes, there is little human psychology that is not situated. Game theorists like to remind us that slight shifts in our *situations* may cause greater shifts in our *expectations*, which in turn could cause very large shifts in our *behavior*. All of that recommends close attention to situations, often in part patterned or structural, as likely to cause shifts in human psychology and behavior.

Consider *risk aversiveness or acceptance*. First, imagine a spectrum of choice models ranging from almost pathological caution ("minimax," which is to choose as if preoccupied with avoiding the worst possible outcome) to reckless boldness ("maximax," or choice as if totally preoccupied with the big win, not even considering the odds). One wonders whether structural settings and more immediate aspects of situations not only dominate selection from someone's existing repertory but also subtraction from or addition to that repertory.

The situation need not always be defined in large scale. Suppose a bat landed on your face, and you learned that on average one bat per hundred would be rabid. Further, not only a bite but a bit of its spit on one's eyeball could transmit rabies, a fatal disease. One could background all other choice models but minimax, taking the antirabies vaccinations, as did my son, who is otherwise a too incautious mountaineer and kayaker.

As for novel additions to repertories, could any preliterate people not yet familiar with *investments in markets* have imagined the economists' "expected utility-maximizing rationality," which assumes one has some cardinal measures comparable to prices and discounts the values of possible outcomes by subjective probabilities of gains and losses? Did utility-maximizing rationality precede and shape markets, or did the situation of markets construct approximations of that psychology?

Now consider *identity*. As many have argued, we all form multiple identities, and our situations as well as our aims and postures toward risk may dominate which among them are selected for emphasis, becoming merely emergent properties. Thus, after destruction of the World Trade Center towers, many of us in the United States predominantly identified as Americans.

Or salient identities could shift to the subnational level. One could have identified more as a Yugoslav before evidence that Yugoslavia was falling apart.

Then one could accent instead one's identity by one of the principal ethnic groups, but under extreme duress the frame of identity could shift to the narrow frame of one's family or only oneself.

But identities can also be submergent, actually created by situations. As David Laitin tells us, many russophones, not all of them Great Russians, were left marooned in new countries such as the Baltics outside Russia when the USSR fell apart, and similarly situated Russians, Ukrainians, and so on, began to identify by a *novel* category, "Russians in the near-abroad," focused on such shared goals as having Russian-language schooling (Laitin, 1998). Although quite aware that other identities are far older, Stuart Kaufman similarly observes such a new identity in a russophone (but more Ukrainian than Russian) slice of Belarus:

The fact that Transnistrians are not an ethnic group is not critical: identities are frequently made and remade in the crucible of ethnic conflict, and it is not unusual for ethnic mobilization of one group to prompt the creation and mobilization of a diverse opposing "group" whose identity may well fade away as soon as the conflict is over. (Kaufman, 2001, 130)

Or one reads that relevant residentially segregated ethnic minorities in England resist hyphenation with the British in defining themselves as "Afro-Caribbeans" or "Asians." Yet could development of the European Union evolve a more-than-verbal identity called "European," which may ultimately eclipse both national and subnational group identities?

Now similarly consider *goals*. Even rational choice theorists sometimes recognized that goals could be more or less given by the situation of the actor. Thus William Riker knew from business management literature that often there is an "agent-principal" relationship, such that the appropriate goal is not left to the discretion of the agent but is predefined by the employing principal: the CEO of a firm is *expected* to aim at maximizing profits. A general is *expected* to maximize less survival of commanded troops than damage to war-making capacities of the enemy. A professor is *expected* to stimulate thinking, as I am trying to do with you now. As the older sociological role theory taught, some situations virtually rule in or out specific goals.

But regarding the subject of this book, I am saying that it is a fool's errand to look for one maximand, or overriding goal (what used to be called "the spring of action"), underlying all ethnic conflict, because distinctive situations may elicit varying emphases among possible goals. Thus, perhaps inspired by Thucydides, Hobbes believed that agents, for the most part, variously pursue "safety," "gain," and "reputation" as main aims in life, seeing "power" only as a present means to those goods.

Some emphasize safety or physical security anxieties as the main motive. Like hostile states in international relations, domestic ethnic groups may get caught up in a security dilemma when looking for safety in the absence of a common authority: When one group mobilizes soldiers or acquires more weapons for protection, to another group it looks like potential aggression, and a vicious circle may ensue (e.g., Hardin, 1995; Posen, 1993). It is plausible enough that some may come to fear another ethnic group out of concern for likely crime or even genocide from that quarter. In the second round of the presidential election in France in May 2002, 18 percent of the French voted for an extreme xenophobe, Jean-Marie Le Pen, whose program centers on boosting reproduction of those he thinks truly French (subsidize childbearing, ban abortions) and discouraging immigration of the ethnically different (ban immigration, block them from jobs). Explicit attention to crime and an implicit attention to adverse economic opportunities were central to his appeal.

Others may emphasize gain or economic rivalry as often central, especially in struggles where one group wants to leave a nation along with its local territory, usually expecting if often not attaining better economic opportunities (e.g., Cook, 2001; Cook, 2002, esp. 67–70; Horowitz, 1985; Woodward, 1995). Often ethnic bigotries can arise from a sensed threat to one's economic opportunities, as when the highly unemployed region of the former East Germany shows the highest xenophobia. But no evidence indicates that ethnic hatred or hate crimes neatly correlate with economic destitution by subregions or by individuals. Far from always emerging from a slum, these impulses and acts can arise from any level of regional or personal economic standing.[2]

Yet others may see "reputation" or group status as the master motive, often rather irrationally bound up with emotionally charged ethnic myths or symbols, as argued by Stuart Kaufman (2001). Kaufman is misguided in discounting security or economic goals. Agents sometimes act counterproductively with regard to them, but that can also apply to status seeking. Surely status anxiety is often part of ethnic animosity, although often linked to concerns for security or economic position.

I have heretofore avoided discussion of the correct theory of ethnic identity (e.g., Stack and Hebron, 1999, esp. 33–45). My position is pluralist: there may not be one correct theory, because validity may vary with the group in question, as well as by whether one speaks of why the group loves its own or why it may feel hostile toward another specific group. There are three main directions in ethnic identity theory, which, when arrayed by decreasing stability of identity, are (1) primordialist, (2) rational choice, or (3) constructivist, which, respectively, tend to give top emphasis to (a) physical security, (b) economic benefit, or (c) status symbolics. Although not supplied, the implicit nine-celled matrix of theory types and relative goal emphases would be helpful in analyzing specific group identities.

Bases of identity or enmity may even shift over time, which could also frustrate any tidy theory of identity. Thus to the extent we are confident of our physical security and our economic position, many of us could shift emphasis to status symbolics.

Bigots can be born of various personal motives. Perhaps most agents in ethnic conflict, whether leading elites or masses, are mixed in motives. Also, the weights of these motives may vary by the context, including the kinds of ethnic policies pursued. But imputing motives has many difficulties. We can never directly observe motives but at best make weak inferences from what we can observe. In part we may want to look at what they say. But among other problems, actual motives may not be publicly admitted, and some that are publicly stated may be insincere, as inferred from what may be said in private to their intimates. Or should we look at what agents do? Motives may be inferred from what would make overt behavior intelligible by the assumptions of bounded rationality. It is little help to look at actual outcomes, because intended ones may not be gotten at all, due to misjudgments, as when agents pursue the goals of security or economic advantage but end up worse off on either head. In other cases, wanted results may be just lucky accidents. When addressing possible resolutions of ethnic conflict, especially in chapters 5, 6, and 7, we must reluctantly return to the complex issue of motivation.

For now, my point is that we should *not* regard the laws of individual psychology as if simple and constant, but regard them as *complex and even changing variables*. As in all other systems, a psychological system has more complexity if it has many parts, many relations among the parts, much change in the parts, and much change in the relations.

In passing, I concede there can be some postures toward risk, identities, or goals that *resist* current environmental shaping. These may have been learned early amid some shock that becomes an obstacle to relearning, or at least causes lags in that. Thus Ronald Inglehart argues that many of those who came of age in the Great Depression may be economically cautious and preoccupied the rest of their lives, unlike their children who have experienced better times (Inglehart, 1977, 1990). Or as I was writing this, I discovered there were Chicano adults who not only do not know Spanish but have a block against learning it because their parents had very early punished them for speaking any Spanish words as children, wanting them to master only English for better assimilation.

In Hans Gadamer's hermeneutics, the art of interpretation of a text, he recommended going back and forth between the part and the whole of the text, and perhaps we must do something like that in interpreting human action, moving between individuals and their contexts. But rather than thinking we must first get the individual psychology right, social science may get more traction through a more structural approach, for although social systems can also be complex, we can describe social settings quite well for purposes of understanding strategic choices of boundedly rational agents. Besides, social settings can select from or shape the repertories that constitute individual psychological states. When so, we should look for the "springs of action" more in the structures of agents' situations rather than in individuals as if isolated from any such situations. Again, apart from certain autonomic processes, or the resistances to new learning as already mentioned, there is very little "unsituated" human psychology.

In looking at motivation, one could speak more positively of human *hopes*, but it often seems to me to be more revealing to speak in the negative frame of human *fears*. We do not seem to know enough about our fears, as evident when we can find sharply opposed statements of how fears impact our choices. Thus in his *Leviathan*, Thomas Hobbes explains how recognition of mutual vulnerability to death at the hands of others in a state of nature leads us to look for ways out of such a nasty condition into ordered civil society. He quips that "fear powerfully concentrates the mind." But Edmund Burke argues that death, "the king of terrors," makes us act very irrationally: "No passion so effectually robs the mind of all its powers of acting and reasoning as *fear*" (*A Philosophical Inquiry into the Origin of Our Ideas of the Sublime and Beautiful*, II, ii). This begs some sorting out, even if it may be wrong to think that apparent inconsistencies will always sort. Perhaps one can make this intelligible by holding that each is right, but under different conditions. Among other things, fears may concentrate the mind to the extent of prior experience with them, whereas they may scatter the minds of those with no such experience. Another plausible possibility: fear tends to make the wise even wiser, but it makes the foolish even more so.

Let us loosely follow John Dewey in supposing that *rational behavior*, however bounded, is situationally adaptive behavior, normally instrumental in the way of getting one's goals. Thus if I want to split a block of wood with an ax, I follow proven rules of thumb: pick a line that does not fight a knot; strike first on the eye; strike next on the distal side; strike last on the near side, with a bit of twist at the end. That works. If a bolt is all knots, it is your chopping block. In contrast, irrational behavior tends to either extreme, total *rigidity* or literally *random* change, when nonrigid and nonrandom behavior would have improved attainment of their goals.

I concede some very special cases when it could be rational to seem to be or even to be rigid or random, as when Ulysses bound himself to the mast or when von Neumann demonstrated that random but equal choice was optimal in playing the children's game of scissors, paper, and stones. Such special cases do not concern us here, because most of our normal choices must be more adaptive.

Although, as noted, I doubt that agents really think like an idealized investor following utility-maximizing rationality, our hunter-gatherer ancestors were not stupid. If they chose foraging locations either *randomly* (with no regard for where what is wanted would be more likely found) or *rigidly* (with no regard for a thinning harvest at one spot), they would have starved to death—and you and I would not now exist to think about such things.

Someone has noted that a fear is rational to hold when better information or argument would lead us to carefully avoid the danger, such as avoiding smoking. Hobbes's *Leviathan* argued that another instance is avoiding anarchy.

Locke's *Second Treatise* rather emphasizes avoiding tyranny, saying that even anarchy can be less dangerous than life under tyranny, where the tyrant has a whole state apparatus to kill us. Thinking of life and death under Hitler or Stalin, I give that one to Locke, who preferred limited government over either anarchy or tyranny.

We rationally respond to a fear when we seek out a good means to avoid the danger. Perhaps this is easier when the threat is more remote, the fear is not yet all consuming, and we have more time for deliberation, including any relevant past experience, or where in default of our own reasonings, we have time to recognize leaders wiser than ourselves.

In other cases, however, even if a fear is rational to hold, the fear can block rational processes, perhaps when it comes upon one suddenly, is unfamiliar, burns at white heat, and permits neither we ourselves nor better leaders to find a way out. A crowd psychology may reign (cf. Le Bon, 1968). One thinks of deadly panics in stadium stampedes into a closed gate. Or another crowd facing fire in a packed building may suffocate those at the front against a locked door before succumbing themselves.

Leaving aside such speculative reflections on the opposed propositions of Hobbes and Burke, I here merely note that I intend to say a few words near the ends of chapters about the kinds of fears that may motivate choice of ethnic policy.

ETHNIC POLICIES AS ALTERNATIVE STRATEGIES/ TACTICS

As the literature on ethnic minority policies keeps growing, one looks in vain for a good map through this thicket, a guide to the varied forms of policy. A clear classification of the kinds of policy strategies seems needed, and the present study in part attempts to supply it in a synoptic way. A good classification is especially needed to put this policy domain into clear comparative perspective. We cannot compare cases until cases are well defined.

Another weakness of the abundant literature on ethnic politics is that it offers little analysis of the very contrasting logics and illogics of the main alternative positions. Looking back on my principal publications, I find that a recurrent pattern is exploration of strategic-tactical alternatives through an exercise in comparisons and contrasts (e.g., Cook, 1991, 1994, 2000, 2002). Such analysis, I think, takes us to the roots of what people are doing by unearthing the often hidden presuppositions of their thinking.

In assigning term papers on ethnic conflict in introductory comparative politics, I have taught my students that the three main alternative moves in ethnic minority policy could be called (1) separation, (2) assimilation, and (3) accommodation. The first accents differences only, usually with some distancing; the second, similarities only, often with some convergence; and the third rejects mutual exclusivity, giving due moral recognition or even institutionalized legitimation to both similarities and differences, accepting also a mix of keeping apart and coming together.

More importantly, each of the main policy moves of separation, assimilation, or accommodation looks different depending on whether a socially strong or dominant ethnic group sponsors it or whether some subordinate ethnicity sponsors it. That is, each strategy of a dominant ethnic group has, as it were, a *doppelgänger,* a German term for a ghostly double, or here a near-double, in a strategy of a weaker ethnic group. As illustrated in chapter 1, in Figure 1.1, each of the three principal directions has two immediate subtypes, the option when deployed as a strategy of the stronger ethnic group, often a social majority, and the option when initiated by a weaker ethnic group, usually a minority. There are exceptional cases where the politically stronger group is an ethnic minority in the context, such as when whites yet ruled Rhodesia or South Africa, in Iraq where the minority Sunni Muslims ruled over the majority Shi'as, or within the Indian-controlled portion of Kashmir, where Muslims outnumber Hindus, or in Rwanda, where military government Tutsis currently dominate the majority Hutus.

Although most of the main policy modes have subvariants that I define for further analysis in the relevant chapters, it is important to grasp six broad categories of ethnic minority policy.

As I review the various stances on ethnic minority policy, it will become increasingly clear that just who backs a policy and what others think can make much difference in outcomes. I will sketch some things to be thinking about, because they are highly important.

First, a given group, whether a dominant group in the setting or a weaker one, may share a broad consensus on the main direction to be taken, whether as separation, assimilation, or accommodation. Yet reviewed more closely one may see they may not quite mean the same thing, as when one segment of the group favors one subform of the policy direction while another segment favors another. Nevertheless, sometimes small differences can be viewed as complementary rather than antagonistic.

Second, should the group be found to be fully on the same page, it can be an added bond of identity for the group, because the similarity could be taken as if implying complementary goals. Third, it is rare for the ethnic minority policy consensus of one group to be identical to that of another, and it is quite common, for example, for a dominant ethnicity to favor segregation while the weaker group wants a more egalitarian assimilation, or for the dominant to favor an aggressive kind of assimilation that erases group identity, while the weaker group then turns to secession, or taking themselves and a patch of territory out of the political community.

Often the action of one group in pursuing a policy causes a reactive choice of a policy by another group, not only when it pairs a dominant versus a weaker group (even the choice of one weaker group could influence imitative or competitive reaction by another weak group). This again shows the importance of understanding choices as situationally embedded.

When ethnic minority policy projects entail incompatible goals, it can lead to some of the nastiest intercommunal conflicts, having little saving grace but for their not having to watch their own backs for fear of attacks from their own group members, unless they are divided between moderates and militants.

Fourth, sometimes a given group may be intensely divided against itself, such that it can see their difference of preference as implying antagonistic goals. When this divergence seems important enough, it can sometimes even cause members of the group to attack other members of the same group. They may even kill them for allegedly selling out or betraying the group's interests.

Fifth, the targets of such violence may often tend to be the moderates of either the dominant ethnic group or the weaker one, or those most likely to be willing to turn to some kind of accommodation to resolve any group conflict.

Thus Mohandas Gandhi (1869–1948), a Hindu, was assassinated by a fellow Hindu, a fanatical disappointed office seeker who believed public jobs and other good things should be reserved for Hindus, not shared with those of other religions such as Muslims, Sikhs, or Christians. President Anwar Sadat of Egypt, shortly after 1978–1979 negotiating and signing a peace treaty with Israel, was in 1981 assassinated by ultramilitant fellow Muslims of his own armed forces, who broke out of a parade being reviewed by him.

Or again, Yitzhak Rabin was assassinated in 1995 by a fellow Israeli Jew, a militant of the Kach religious group who thought Rabin had conceded too much in the 1993–1994 negotiations concluding peace with Jordan and promising political autonomy for the West Bank and Gaza, to be led by Yasser Arafat of Al Fatah. Arafat has himself survived several assassination attempts, often launched against him by more immoderate Arab groups. In 2000 he rejected a peace offer from Ehud Barak with the quip that if he accepted its terms, his own people would kill him. He may not have been wrong.

This leads to a sixth suggestion that often if the more moderate forces of each side are to have a chance at accommodation, they may need to take protective action against the fanatics of their own side. That, too, can sometimes become violent.

If life is full of such paradoxes, it is well to recall that a true paradox is only a seeming contradiction. It need not imply any incoherence in what we are thinking about the world, which remains a sometimes dangerous place, often over ethnic groups in conflict.

The three principal directions of minority policy as separation, assimilation, and accommodation, each distinguished by sponsorship either by the strong or by the weak, frame six units of discussion.

Chapters 1 through 6 successively address separation as segregation, separation as emigrating or secession, assimilation as aggressive homogenization for control, assimilation as integration for expanding opportunities, accommodation as minimalist concessions, and accommodation as maximalist demands. The subforms of each policy direction emerge in subsections of the chapters. Together, these chapters cover much of the ground of ethnic minority alternatives, including attention to when dominant and weaker ethnic groups are or are not (more often true) pursuing the same ethnic policy, as well as when either group divides against itself over ethnic policy. Chapters 7 and 8 explore some fresh ideas about how to get out of dangerous games of ethnic conflict.

I view the primary contribution of this book as analytical, not intending any rivalry with far better analysts of the case studies of ethnic conflict in the world. This book was written with the aim of being intelligible to any reasonably intelligent reader. But failures in communication can sometimes occur against the best of intentions, if only because the author may be yet developing some concepts, such as situationally submergent psychology as mentioned earlier or transformational game theory as addressed in chapter 8. All other concepts, I think, should be relatively easy to grasp. If you cannot understand my analysis, or if you detect any errors in case studies mentioned, please feel free to contact me: *tcook@wsu.edu*

NOTES

1. See George Johnson, "New Contenders for a Theory of Everything," *The New York Times International*, Dec. 4, 2001, D-1, D-2, D-5.

2. See relevant comments of Princeton economist Alan B. Krueger, *The New York Times International*, Dec. 13, 2001, C-2.

CHAPTER 1

Separations as Segregations: Strategies of the Stronger Ethnic Group

> We are not only most interested in not unifying the population of the East, but on the contrary, in splitting them up into as many parts and fragments as possible. But even within the ethnic groups themselves we have no interest in leading these to unity and greatness, or perhaps arouse in them gradually a national consciousness and national culture, but we want to dissolve them into innumerable small fragments and particles.
> —Reinhard Heydrich, Hitler's SS head of the Security Services (Gestapo)

Nature seems to sort itself out into similar and dissimilar things (Schroeder, 1991). As impersonally done by the rest of nature, people seem fond of sorting things as dissimilar and separating them, or else aggregating them as similar, and we do this to members of our species by widely varying criteria. The way individuals may sort themselves need not always match how those who govern may sort them. Sometimes this governmental sorting and separating can get ugly. As cited in the epigraph, in this top secret memorandum forwarded from Himmler to Hitler on May 25, 1940, Gestapo chief Heydrich was yet talking of mass deportation rather than mass destruction of the Jews. With reference to Slavic peoples, he announced his intention to enslave the "subhuman people of the East" by means of elaborate divide and rule and blockage from education (Bauer, 1982, 352).

The first of three principal strategic directions in policy toward an ethnic group attempts separation of the group in question. First, it may separate the target group from a more favored ethnicity. Second, when it is the most convenient means to weaken the target group, it may also separate them from each other. Third, sometimes this is reversed when a dominant ethnicity wants to concentrate the ethnicity, whether to make use of their skills (e.g., the alien trading communities of Constantinople/Istanbul or Venice), to control them, or to kill the members of the weaker group, turning to genocide.

The first move normally involves (1) accent on real or imagined *differences* of the group, and (2) use of such supposed differences at least partially *to separate* the group from the dominant group. The main mental acts consist in deepened differentiation, often accompanied by physical operations of distancing.

If sharing differentiating and distancing, one may readily identify two subcategories of the separation strategy, the one as often pursued by the dominant group and the other as sometimes favored by the weaker.

I illustrate such main forks in ethnic minority policy in Figure 1.1.

In the present chapter, I look only at the first sort of separation policy, that initiated by a dominant ethnicity. It has varied gradations from mild social segregation to at worse rather aggressive *exclusions*, from certain roles, from the state, or even from life in its extreme form of *physical genocide*, as in the Holocaust and other twentieth-century slaughters. The segregationists, such as Hitler with respect to Jews, often hold that not only the culture but perhaps the very biogenetic endowment of the weaker ethnicity are inferior.

The dominant group needs stereotypy to vindicate its separation of the subordinate group. It usually means a sort of homogenization of the weaker ethnicity, which is by no means a sort of arithmetical mean of objective traits of that group. On the contrary, to heighten the contrast of the stronger and weaker ethnic groups, they must inflate any real positive traits of the former as well as any real negative traits of the latter. Further, stereotypy normally will include outright invention or fabrication of other positive traits of the former, negative traits of the latter.

Sometimes the differentiating and discriminating uses only some blunt category for the weaker ethnicity, not bothering to sort out any additional differences among them.

But if a number of cultural groups are to be differentiated, distanced, rank-ordered, comparable operations will be put into place at all of the required levels, as in the classic three and ultimately four *varnas* of India (Brahmins, Kshatriyas, Vaisyas, Sudras), undergirded by the untouchables (who now call themselves *dalits*) as a very distanced fifth rank.

Perhaps another citation of Reinhard Heydrich, Hitler's SS head of the Security Services for both party and state, illustrates the tendency to segregate: "I shall have to isolate the Jew so that he won't enter the German normal routine of life" (Levin, 1968, 88).

When the dominant deploy such a policy of separation, as the Nazis did toward the Jews, the Romany, and other ethnic minorities, it normally involves a more emphatic assertion of the differences of the weaker group in question, often but not always claiming even difference in underlying human

Figure 1.1
Six Main Directions in Ethnic Minority Policy

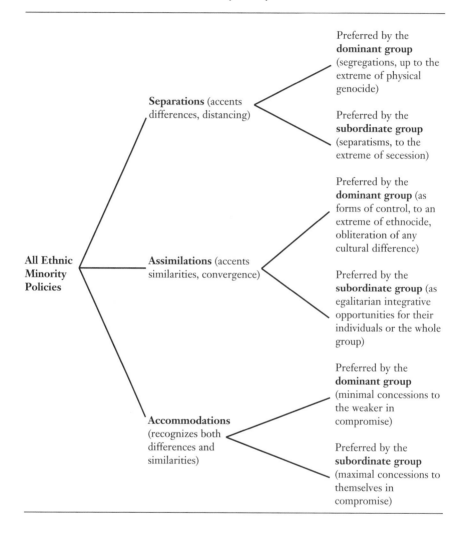

All Ethnic Minority Policies

Separations (accents differences, distancing)

Preferred by the **dominant group** (segregations, up to the extreme of physical genocide)

Preferred by the **subordinate group** (separatisms, to the extreme of secession)

Assimilations (accents similarities, convergence)

Preferred by the **dominant group** (as forms of control, to an extreme of ethnocide, obliteration of any cultural difference)

Preferred by the **subordinate group** (as egalitarian integrative opportunities for their individuals or the whole group)

Accommodations (recognizes both differences and similarities)

Preferred by the **dominant group** (minimal concessions to the weaker in compromise)

Preferred by the **subordinate group** (maximal concessions to themselves in compromise)

nature. If that suggests what is somehow genetically endowed, it is normally understood to be beyond any possibility of being changed by human artifice.

At least in Eurasian thought, here leaving gender aside, one can see changing emphases in how people were sorted as biologically unequal. Was it castes, classes, individuals, races, or cultures?

Sorting by castes as in India was most severe in rejection of all intermarriage of the *varnas*, with more sortings by subcaste categories focused about occupation, the *jatis*. To this day, Hindu men in quest of wives in India may post newspaper advertisements to interview prospects of the appropriate caste background as well as language.

Often assertions of biological inferiority were originally more of classes than of ethnicities. As discussed by the author elsewhere, traditionalist or landed aristocratic elites had codes that required clear ranks. For beyond irrigation and other limited measures, there was no view of expanded social production to meet any growth of aggregate wants. It was a zero-sum world where by definition more for some meant that much less for others. While imperial expansion suggested one possible resolution at the expense of other peoples, if that was unattractive it was imperative that the lower orders limit their aspirations to what their parents had enjoyed before them. The alternative could threaten class war (Cook, 1991, esp. 25–52). Differences of strata were good and supposedly justified unequal consumption. Medieval "great chain of being" theory even held that lesser orders became ever less divine and more like merely animal, plant, or mineral (Lovejoy, 1936). So Dante depicted the fallen angels, and his stony image of the devil was repeated in Alexander Solzhenitsyn's *The First Circle*, where Satan was Stalin. But as Ernest Gellner observed, if agrarian elites in premodern societies insisted on the differences of the ranks, elites of modern or industrial society would tend increasingly to concede important similarities, including aspects of shared human nature, shared capacity for learning, and shared nationhood, wherein the root term *natio* accents the idea of the same "birth" (Gellner, 1983).

Sometimes, however, modern societies could intermix class and ethnic rankings, as when the Hispanic New World often had sharp distinctions of *peninsulares* (born in Spain), creoles or *criollos* (born in the New World of Spanish parentage), *mestizos* (of mixed Hispanic and Indian blood), freed blacks, Indians or indigenes, and black slaves.

As noted, up to the nineteenth century it was argued that classes were biogenetically unequal, with the nobility claiming distinctively superior genealogy. Even the middle classes sometimes got into it, speaking dubiously of the lowest classes as if a distinctive breed of Homo sapiens. But already in the eighteenth century, radical liberal critics refuted such thinking, sometimes even turning it about, as when Tom Paine claimed that the nobles were if anything biologically inferior due to their extensive inbreeding. For thinkers such as Thomas Jefferson or even John Adams, the notion of class biogenetic inequality is replaced with the idea of biogenetic inequality of *individuals*, some of whom constituted a "natural aristocracy" as opposed to the one of hereditary titles. With a celebration of individual competitions, this accent on only individual biogenetic differences is continued into leading Social Darwinists such as Herbert Spencer (1820–1903) or William Graham Sumner (1849–1910).

But almost simultaneously, a new assertion of whole group inequalities then arises about racial or other ethnic categories. Thus a French count, Joseph de Gobineau, publishes his *The Inequality of the Races* in 1859. Houston Stuart

Chamberlain, a British-born resident of Germany and son-in-law of the composer Richard Wagner, produces his *The Foundations of the Twentieth Century* in German in 1899 and in English translation in 1910.

Much of such broad writing about unequal "races" seems to have grown out of European colonization of the world. Often the ideas do not take full wing until the native populations are decisively defeated: the Anglos penetrating the Great Plains or Hispanics moving into southern Chile could not speak with contempt of the Sioux or Araucanians when yet quivering in fear of their fighting prowess.

Typically, such biogenetic theory claims that subordinated "races" were not only biologically distinctive but also inferior. A problem of such biogenetic arguments was that most asserted genetic endowments were not directly observed or even observable but only built on vulnerable pseudo-inferential reasoning, which at best takes its departure from what *can* be observed. There are major pitfalls in biogenetic argument (cf. Cook, 1983).

Often claims of distinctive "natures" have been but indicators of prejudice, which generically consist in inconsistencies of thought that have the consistent result of always dignifying the favored group and discrediting the disfavored one. Bertrand Russell once quipped that "a philosopher's inconsistencies are the clue to his passions." But this is usually even more transparently so of the nonphilosophic. If there is a concession of any common nature at all, the nature of the group that is the target of prejudice may be viewed as evil, or it may be analogized to the least admirable kinds of animals.

Unconscious choice of animal metaphors may be especially revealing. Highly favorable groups may roar (like lions), soar (like eagles), and so on, whereas disliked groups are given unfavorable animalistic referents, as suggested by Frantz Fanon of white colonists in Africa:

[T]he terms the settler uses when he mentions the native are zoological terms. He speaks of the yellow man's reptilian motions, of the stink of the native quarter, of breeding swarms, of foulness, of spawn, of gesticulations. When the settler seeks to describe the native fully in exact terms he constantly refers to the bestiary. (Fanon, 1968, 42)

When not demonizing or animalizing the other, at least this viewpoint may assert gross immaturity of the humans who must be differentiated and distanced. Or it may be mixed. Thus Kipling described the white man's burden as "your new-caught sullen peoples, half devil and half child." But the more the emphasized difference is ascribed to immaturity only, especially if accompanied with an emphasis on the importance of new learning, the closer it gets to a tipping point, perhaps pointing toward an aggressively assimilative strategy as addressed in chapter 3.

E. S. Bogardus classically identified some central measures of prejudice in what he called the "social distance" variables. Purporting to measure "the degree of sympathetic understanding," the scale descends though willingness to marry, have as close friend, have as neighbor, work in the same office, speaking acquaintance only, visitor of nation, or debar from one's country (Bogardus, 1959, esp. 7, 31). That scale cannot apply to all dimensions of stratification, not working for inequalities of the sexes.

Yet it may work for sexual or marital relations crossing some ethnic frontier. For bigots, fear of taint of blood gets added. Recall that many bigots regard certain other humans as if an altogether different, inferior species. Marriages between the dominant and the dominated ethnicities may be made impossible, whether by social obloquy or by legal punishment. In the former case, during the British Raj, it would have been unthinkable for a white to marry an Indian subcontinental. A Nazi Nuremberg law of 1935 forbade marriage of a German to a Jew, to Romany or Roma ("gypsy"), or to others of non-European origin. Nazi classifications made one a Jew if one had *more* than one Jewish grandparent, but one was a gypsy if only of one-eighth Romany ancestry, or just one great-grandparent or two of sixteen great-great grandparents (Fonseca, 1995, 259). There could be no coherent intellectual defense of such fractions.

Many bigots will readily project one target of their prejudice onto another. Thus, when Americans were repressing Filipino nationalists (1899–1903), it seems that northerners were more likely to see Filipinos as native Americans—as did Theodore Roosevelt, whereas southerners were more inclined to call any and all Filipinos "niggers" (Bain, 1986, 84, 88).

If excepting marriage of man to a woman of otherwise similar social characteristics, the Bogardus measures of distancing suggest that the assumptions of differences usually go with a will of members of the stronger group to be separated from those of the dominated group and often, when they could constitute a threat, even to separate members of the dominated groups from each other, which is a classic form of divide and rule.

In traditional Japan, two groups of outcastes were forced to reside in confined spaces, the *hinin* and the *Eta*. The *hinin* (means "nonpeople") were an outcaste who were something like Europe's Romany (gypsies) in being regarded as inferior because they were itinerants (but were limited by how far they could move, subject to execution if caught outside of their designated territory a fourth time) and because they made a living by some morally marginal ways, such as prostitution, gambling, beggary, or the like. They were sometimes ranked just above the *Eta* near the bottom of the social scale, but sometimes functioned like the *Eta* in managing or executing state prisoners.

The *Eta* (Chinese characters mean "full of filth") were by legends supposedly of some stock other than the majority Japanese, and they were often regarded as not only biogenetically inferior but perhaps as not fully human at all. Majority Japanese used to fear touching them, having them immediately touch one's food, letting them enter their front door on business, or especially marrying them (in recent years this marriage taboo has atrophied). Historically, this group did "unclean" kinds of jobs that majority Japanese would not do: butchering animals, making leather goods, toting garbage or night soil, executing public prisoners, and the like. Yet especially before the Tokugawa rule after 1600, which deepened the outcaste persecution of the *Eta*, they were sometimes valued for such labor as handling furs or leather making, and leading lords *(daimyo)* in the interior or western Japan often permitted them to live in ghettos on their land, sparing them the usual taxes. Whereas, as noted, the Tokugawas made their status increasingly like India's untouchables, the Meiji restoration attempted to reverse course, officially ending discrimination against them in 1871, perhaps in part because of a wish to get them on the tax rolls or use them in the armed forces.

The terms *hinin* and *Eta* were banned, replaced by such terms as *toku-burakumin* ("special communities") or *Buraku*. Lower officials sometimes persisted in discrimination, as when as late as 1926 writing "toku" or drawing a red circle before a known Buraku, whose chances for promotion were harmed. But in the half century following 1871, many Buraku associated with left-wing parties such as the Communists or Socialists, and they became increasingly militant in demanding equal rights and an end to public or private slurs in the mass media, such as allegations of drunkenness on cheap brandy or petty theft of such things as firewood. Although most favored the Jodo shin sect of Buddhism, they got little help from religious organizations. By 1961, with the left parties and labor unions, they made a mass march from Kyushu Island to Tokyo, and they increasingly demanded special programs to assist them, because many continued enduring effects of discrimination. In a recent invited lecture trip to Japan, at an informal lunch at a public restaurant, I was told by a Japanese host that one did not talk of the subject in polite circles.

In the past, *Eta* women were recognizable by leather patches on their kimonos, and men were known by distinctive sandals or imposed hairstyles (the last also true of *hinin*). But although some claim to recognize them by their less formal speech or dress, the Buraku are physically indistinguishable from the majority Japanese, and they no longer can be known by distinctive occupations. About half the former *Eta* entered the higher status occupation of farming, although unlike majority Japanese farmers in being more often part time and renters rather than owners of the land (De Vos and Wagtsuma, 1966). Buraku were once distinctive in eating the meat of livestock, including some internal organs, but now most Japanese do so. Not unexpectedly, Buraku today are no longer confined to residential ghettos, no longer required to wear their hair differently or if women to have leather patches on kimonos, but those who do not move can yet be recognized by their present residence or prior residence, both of which are on Japanese identity cards. Hence to fully conceal their status, important in getting good jobs or at more risk even marriages with majority Japanese, they must move at least twice (DeVos, 1973, 318–20).

Unless use of their labor is an urgent need, the dominant would often block the unwanted at the frontiers, as in a long pattern of immigration restrictions dating from the late nineteenth century in the United States.

Or a disliked group may be encouraged to emigrate, sometimes by violence. Although strangely omitting to mention Spain and Portugal, Nora Levin writes, "Between the thirteenth and sixteenth centuries, Jews were expelled from England, France, Italy, Bohemia and the Germanic states" (Levin, 1968, 10). Her study of the Holocaust makes clear that the Nazis were using political and economic deprivation as well as street thug SA and SS beatings as leverage to encourage Jewish emigration from Germany and from its conquests during the years 1933 to 1938, only thereafter turning to plans to concentrate and kill them instead (Levin, 1968, esp. 78–85). Levin makes clear, however, that major murders of Jews in Poland, largely by the SS but with complicity by the Wehrmacht officers (if complaining that they preferred to prioritize the war), began from the outset of Hitler's invasion of that nation in 1939. In that year, the SS used mythical resettlement plans as a ruse to confine the Jews residentially, as when the fake "reserve" of Lublin, Poland, was used as a marshaling area, first for possible deportation elsewhere, even Madagascar (blocked by failure to take the Suez Canal), and then for trips to the regional death camps of Belzek, Maidenek, and Sobibor. Although many died at other places such as Dachau, all *systematic* death camps were located within Poland (Levin, 1968, 165).

The Nazis also murdered any special non-Jewish Polish political enemies and virtually all of the Polish intelligentsia. Whereas Hitler wanted to enslave the Poles until no longer needed, the former chicken farmer and now Gestapo chief Heinrich Himmler would have preferred to get on with the genocide of all Poles at once. In passing, from 1939 the Nazis began to execute even "Aryan" Germans if chronically ill, physically disabled, or mentally deficient. Contrary to the official claim that they stopped because of objections by clergy, they continued to do so to the end of the war (Bauer, 1982, 208). Henry Adams, writing in the previous century, would not have been amazed at much of this: "Politics, as a practice, whatever its professions, has always been the systematic organization of hatreds" (Adams, 1974, 7).

Assertions of biogenetic inequalities of class or race are waning, and assertions of inborn inequalities of individuals are often held highly suspect. Yet recent so-called ethnic cleansing episodes in disintegrating Yugoslavia remind us that such barbarism is not over. Even the postcommunist Czech Republic in 1993 enacted clever ways to ship recent Romany ("gypsy") immigrants back to Slovakia (Fonseca, 1995, 236). I taught in Slovakia in 1993–1994, where I learned enough Slovensky to hear one vendor at the main Bratislava farm produce market scream at a Romany woman, "Go back to India!" The Romanies, who had been in that part of Europe for some 500 years, did not yet belong there.

The dominated must be kept from, or removed from jobs that are wanted by the dominant ethnics, especially if these are at all politically sensitive.

Already by April 4, 1933, Jews had been purged from civil service jobs in Germany. The apartheid regime in South Africa had an elaborate system of job eligibilities by racial groups. In July 1990, Slobodan Milosevic, the Serbian prime minister of the rump of what had been Yugoslavia, fired Kosovar Albanians from civil service posts, including the local police.

Sometimes excepting household servants, the dominated must also be separated in their residences. Czars, to preserve serfdom, did not permit peasant migrations. The dominated may even be excluded from passing through the neighborhoods of the dominant types, as yet experienced even within a liberal society by "gated communities." When not enslaved, a severely dominated group may be allowed to reside only in certain regions, as when Jews in czarist Russia could not reside "beyond the pale," with the permitted area first defined in 1791 but somewhat expanded later with more czarist territorial conquests. A group may be confined to specific neighborhoods of cities, as illustrated by many imposed ethnic ghettos of history. If the Jews in northern Europe were increasingly pushed into East Europe, the Counter Reformation first strongly ghettoized the Jews of Italy and other Catholic nations, believing they were likely allies of the Protestants, if only because often engaged in trade. By 1939 Heydrich began to force all smaller Jewish communities of Poland into urban ghettos plagued with severe crowding, desperate hunger, and typhus. The Nazis selected Jewish Councils over them, requiring their complicity in making lists of residents, in self-policing, or even in designating who would die first. What at first seemed like a grant of autonomy emerged as just another instrument of their close control and then genocidal destruction. Thus spoke Heydrich: "The concentration of Jews in the cities for general reasons of security will probably bring about orders to forbid Jews to enter certain wards of the city altogether, and to forbid them, for reasons of economic necessity, for instance, to leave the ghetto, to go out after a designated hour, etc." (Levin, 1968, 171).

Such residential separation thus often entails a concentration, and hence often vulnerability not only to routine modalities of control but even destruction.

Often a dominated group was forbidden to own any land. Even in recent years, in Fiji the dominant ethnic Fijians prohibited Hindu Indians from owning any land, requiring them to just lease it from Fijians (Horowitz, 1985, 12). If the dominated have land, it may be expropriated (I use the characteristically Marxist term, which differs from nationalization in not compensating prior owners) by the dominant ethnicity, usually by invalidating the local culture's sense of property: thus European "first discovery" of the land supposedly gave a title to the monarch of the European sponsoring state, ignoring any prior discovery and use by the indigenes. Or the invaders may loudly claim a right of conquest, conveniently forgetting even the (inadequate?) limits of "just war theory" that had been elaborated in Europe since Cicero and Augustine. That required at minimum that a war be declared by a legitimate authority (a state, not a guerrilla band or a self-help settlers gang), be conducted for a just end (such as recovering stolen property!), and be waged by just means (expressly excluding massacres of women and children).

Europeans characteristically did not recognize any collectively owned property by the indigenes, even if they had some space for the concept within their own realms, such as any public parks. As John Bodley notes, for many indigenous peoples, "The concept of *ownership* on other than the group or tribal level was quite irrelevant, because land was to be *used* by individuals and not owned in the usual sense" (Bodley, 1982, 84). He also notes that they often rotated use of large areas of land, and the temporarily resting land was not unclaimed "wasteland" as European cultures liked to assume. For Europeans, property was not owned by anyone if untilled by plows (West African hoes did not count), or was unfenced (the herds of cattle or horses of the Sioux, Nez Percé, or Palouse did not qualify) and not registered in European courts. In a famous 1889 ruling, an Australian court claimed that all land of Australia was *terrum nullius* ("no one's land") from the 1788 British annexation. In the United States, after vast tracts of collectively held tribal lands were expropriated by the whites, from about 1887 federal authorities often imposed the alienation of residual tribal property to individual tribe members, who often resold it to nontribal inholders (Bodley, 1982, 89). Note that the natives cannot win: natives have no right to the land because they are so *different* (no Europeans thus lose land), yet natives are expected to be *similar* enough to the European thieves that they should appreciate the invalidity of their own tribal property claims.

Once stripped of any right to live where they had lived, once debarred from land ownership, the natives get pressed into a narrowed space: For many hunter-gatherers it may mean increasingly remote patches of wilderness where there is little to hunt or gather.

For more urban peoples, it may be different: Carefully confined to ghettos, and further identified with red J's stamped in their passports and yellow stars of David on their clothing, Europe's Jews were by the Nazis eventually further confined—to forced march columns, to gassing vans, to cattle cars, to concentration camps, to killing pits or walls, or from December 7, 1941, to technologically ever-improved gas chambers.

Even as recently as 1993 in Romania's Transylvania, after a fatal stabbing incident, 175 Gypsies were driven from their homes of some seventy-five years, which were then burned by a mob. Other such settlements had been torched elsewhere in Romania from the start of decommunization in 1991 (Fonseca, 1995, 140–42). Extending in some regions such as backland Brazil into very recent years, there is a long history of brutal murder of indigenous peoples, with their leaders first marked for death squad kills (Bodley, 1982, 26–59).

As earlier noted, the "logic" of segregation usually bolsters or at least exaggerates differences. Their slaves aside, bigots do not want the other to reproduce. There is obvious significance in mutilations of genitalia or breasts of victims in communal violence.

Ultimately nothing could make the other group more different than to be nonliving, to be prematurely dead. Here often denial of the very humanity of victims has been commonplace. Yet if the killers *speak* only of differences, they are more than aware of their victims' essential *similarity* to themselves in wanting control over the same land, housing, jobs, women, and so forth. That may fuel such genocidal rages as recently witnessed in Rwanda or in the Bosnian war.

Serbs of Croatia and Bosnia had constituted most of the half-million victims of genocide due to Croatia's fascist Ustasha during World War II, often aided by some Bosnian Muslims. More recently themselves the executioners, Bosnian Serbs rounded up 1,500 Muslim men from the defeated Srbrenica enclave, then locked them in a warehouse that they then attacked with machine gun bullets and hand grenades. In the morning they found some survivors, who were forced to sing Serb national songs before they, too, were slaughtered.

At an extreme, even in death the dominated may be carefully separated from the dominant, as in limitations to certain burial grounds or sortition of the ashes of the dead. In Japan those outcastes once called *Eta* were buried in separate cemeteries. Zealous of their consecrated grounds, dominant religious authorities have even disinterred already buried heretics. Thus the English reformer John Wycliffe, who anticipated much in Martin Luther, had been protected by his king before dying of a stroke in 1384. But by a decree of the Council of Constance (1415), his body was ordered exhumed and the remains thrown in a river. With a lag, that was done in 1428. Or again, the Restoration Anglican high churchman regarded the Independent (nonseparatist Congregationalist) Oliver Cromwell, the Puritan leader, as a heretic. As if in just punishment for his own savagery in killing King Charles I or the Catholics at Drogheda, the authorities similarly worried his remains. Cromwell's body was dug up and publicly hanged (Newman, 1978, 132). My source does not say what they did with Cromwell's remains.

Note well that the so-called logic of segregation, bent on sharpening lines of difference, not only largely refuses fair rewards for assimilators (as many African American critics would say against the feasibility of the ideas of Booker T. Washington, addressed in chapter 4) but can even punish those who attempt it. Indeed, the dominant ethnics may by verbal condemnation or even punishment at law discourage those of the dominated group who may wish to speak like, dress like, and otherwise act like the dominant group. One may be *punished* for attempting to assimilate oneself, especially if attempting to pass as a member of the dominant ethnic group.

In the past, prostitutes were often required to wear gaudy dresses to announce to all their disgrace. Lepers could be required to tote warning bells and could be ordered from the paths of the healthy.

Under the Nazis, as already noted, Jews were required by 1938 to have a large red J stamped in their passports, which made it easy later to have them wear the more infamous yellow stars of David on their clothing. Both indicators made it easy to sort them for death.

If one were oriented toward the same sex, the Nazis looked the other way if one were lesbian, because one could yet bear children for war, but if one were male, if caught in illicit sex one was imprisoned and usually forced to work. Hitler waited for some "cure" to make gays straight and usable as soldiers, perhaps, as argued by a recent book, because he himself was probably gay, not known to have ever made love to a woman (Machtan, 2001). An earlier study reported some testimony that Hitler yet liked to have women urinate, or worse, on his face (Langer, 1972). Unlike Hitler, his SS chief Heinrich Himmler would have preferred to gas all homosexuals, and some were eventually killed. While awaiting their fate, gays wore the numeral (125) of the Prussian statute banning homosexual relations or else an inverted pink triangle, which became a sure death sentence if put over a yellow patch, signifying that one was also a Jew (cf. Johannson and Perry, 1990).

Before going on to say that the Holocaust was for its victims a reproduction of the mythos of hell on earth, Karen Armstrong notes that it was also expressive of logos, being rationally modern in its process:

The Holocaust became the icon of evil for modern times. It was a byproduct of modernity, which from the very beginning, had often involved acts of ethnic cleansing. The Nazis used many of the tools and achievements of the industrial age to deadly effect. The death camps were a fearful parody of the factory, right down to the chimney itself. They made use of the railways, the advanced chemical industry, and efficient bureaucracy and management. The Holocaust was an example of scientific and rational planning, in which everything is subordinated to a single, limited, and clearly defined objective. (Armstrong, 2000, 300)

Whereas being Romany was often a capital crime in much of West Europe from the fifteenth into the early nineteenth century, in the France of Louis XIV they were designated by brands or shaved heads; a gypsy woman's right ear was cropped in Bohemia or her left in Moravia (Fonseca, 1995, 229). The Nazis made the Romany wear distinctive black triangles (for antisocial) or green triangles (for criminal) to mark them for annihilation schedules (Fonseca, 1995, 266). Of some 700,000 Romany in Europe, perhaps 200,000 to 250,000 were slaughtered by the Nazis or their allies (Bauer, 1982, 202, 204).

In May 2000 the Taliban required wearing of some yellow cloth on Hindus in Kabul, Afghanistan, which along with the further requirement that non-Muslims display yellow cloths on their rooftops, must have seemed ominous to many who bore them prior to the military defeat of the Taliban later in 2001. The largely Pashtu tribal Taliban segregation was also imposed on women, especially if married. The Taliban liked the Pashtu tribal saying,

"There are only two places for Afghan women—in her husband's house or in the graveyard." Their enforcers, wielding clubs, made sure that women in public were not only accompanied by either other women or adult male relatives but also dressed in the total coverings called *burqas*, which made it difficult for women to walk or see where they were going. Women were excluded from jobs outside the home (except for obstetrics nurses, because male doctors were not permitted to examine pregnant women except from behind a screen) and debarred from any formal schooling.

A dominated group such as the Jews or the Romany in Europe's history, as noted, were often forbidden to own land. Nor could they serve in the military or other public office, thus pressing them into a narrowed set of careers such as petty commerce, tinkering, entertaining, or the like.

Sometimes the dominant may in a sense punish themselves for their own bigotry. Often the separating extends to encouragements or even mandates of emigration. When Spanish authorities from 1492 expelled the unconverted Jews from Spain, and then from Portugal when the kingdoms were united (1580–1640), they surely hurt their own commercial prospects, just as they enriched those of some places of refuge such as Amsterdam. Plausibly claimed by Leo Strauss and Tom Pangle to be the first liberal political philosopher, Benedict Spinoza was a descendant of Portuguese Jewish exiles. Ousters of the Indian subcontinentals from Idi Amin's Uganda or from Burma must have had similar commercially adverse effects. The Jim Crow laws of states of the American South seemed to do much to keep the region mired in backwardness into the 1960s when military and space race spending finally modernized their economies. The Afrikaaner apartheid policy cost a further price in international economic boycott, as experienced earlier by the white ruling elite of Rhodesia.

Why would many of the dominated ethnic groups apparently accept the segregationist policies imposed on them by the dominant ethnicity? Sometimes, one could argue, it is but a boundedly rational strategic choice when agents cannot pursue more politically active strategies that could change the powers or wills of superior authorities. I have elsewhere called these strategies influencing, recruiting, or restructuring, which respectively make variables of the wills, persons, or powers of superiors (cf. Cook, 2000, esp. 3–21). The strategy of enduring involves submissive adaptation of agents' own wills to the uncontrolled wills of the authorities, thus constituting the flip side of the influence strategy that rather adapts authorities' wills to one's own purposes. One chooses some variant of enduring when one lacks much capability of one's own, cannot form at least a defensive coalition, cannot adopt even the mildest form of an active strategy (e.g., just a humble plea for justice) without worse things happening. Further, enduring looks like the best bet when one can neither exit from the scene of repression nor evade it by concealing one's identity or one's acts.

It may seem perverse to call enduring a "political strategy" at all, because it sounds rather like a white flag of preemptive capitulation. Yet the choice is expected to affect at least minimally the wills of authorities: by enduring, agents hope that the powerful may at least not become more adverse. If there is no hope of being able to make their decisions and policies better, at least by this strategy official decisions may not become yet worse. Often agents may choose enduring not so much to protect themselves as to protect others, fearful that any other choices could have disastrous consequences for family members, for example. Under Legalist rule in Chinese history, for example, *any* illegal act by *any* family member could bring capital punishment to an entire extended family. Stalin in the Great Purge show trials got Bukharin and other innocent defendants to publicly condemn themselves in part by threats against their family members. Up to the 1960s in the American South, many African Americans abstained from any more active strategic behavior because of the credible threat of lynching.

Clearly, enduring can be an instrumentally rational strategy for people in certain circumstances who want to do the best they can with what little they have got. Already low on resources, there may be loss of even more if active strategies are followed. Those at the margin of existence, those finding themselves or their loved ones in extreme jeopardy in the way of physiological needs or safety, are not likely to take chances. Those with little to lose but their chains may pick the chains rather than lose that little. Major students of revolution agree that it is never the poorest of the poor who lead or even actively support a revolutionary effort. For those with least resources, expected values of all strategies other than enduring look as bad or usually worse. One expects to find more choice of enduring among those near the bottoms of social stratification hierarchies. Thus one expects enduring from many undocumented aliens, for to protest many abuses of their condition, such as unsafe labor conditions, may threaten deportation, typically viewed as a worse outcome.

Exchange transactions are rarely balanced when they involve those of unequal power. If enduring seems to permit unilateral shifts of resources from the dominated to the dominant (exploitation), certain postures of enduring seek to curb such extreme asymmetry, looking for at least a negative kind of return. Those who find themselves with rather modest power and who see little hope of increasing their resources through coordination with domestic or foreign allies are most likely to adopt some strategy of the weak, with variants of enduring often signaling the degree of weakness. Often some of the more capitulatory forms of this strategy are actively encouraged in the subordinate groups by dominant social groups. The other strategic fields are more likely to threaten the dominant.

Distinctive enough from my other strategic fields, enduring has variant forms, here ordered roughly from those more favored to those less favored by the dominant:

(1) *Identification.* Borrowing a term from psychoanalysis, one posture may

be a victim's identification with the victimizer. This usually involves a denial that one is victimized at all, an ego defense mechanism to dispel anxiety, guilt, and so on, that would otherwise arise. If the identifiers instead see they are being mistreated, they may alternatively think the authorities are sincerely trying to correct the problem, or would do so if aware ("If the king only knew!"). Such cheering illusions may be internalized rather than being merely a response to immediate incentives. Some view ideologies of ruling groups as if directly imposed on all others in society. Michel Foucault made that more complicated with his concept of a "disciplinary society" whereby all kinds of mediating layers of experts also get into the act (Foucault, 1980). But there is another tradition, stated in the speech of Dostoevski's Grand Inquisitor, that holds that the many also are in complicity with their own subjection. That turn of argument has been elaborated in Paul Veyne's *Bread and Circuses*, which argues that the dominated may be more than merely receptive to ideologies of domination (Elster, 1993, 35–69).

In the identification mode of enduring, one would expect high deference toward the strong, possible scapegoating of the weak, with refusal to accept the reality of their own exploitation when such exists. Here one verbally or actively supports the strong, without any expectation of being given in return preferment by them. If there were any expectation of gain by such applause, it would pass over to what I call the influence strategy. Unlike the next variant, identification paradoxically tends to accept unbridgeable *difference* of the dominant and dominated.

(2) *Assimilation.* Discussion of another variant of enduring must upstage a bit the longer discussion of assimilative strategy among the dominated group offered in chapter 4. Here those practicing enduring may once again avoid any challenge to the dominant, but now show some dissatisfaction with their own status. Perhaps yet supporting the strong, they expend less energy on any applause than in trying to make themselves more like the strong: Without attempting to pass as other than they are (which would be a form of evasion), they try to correct or modify themselves to at least appear to be like the strong. Examples would be strenuous attempts at change of personal appearance (grooming, dress, etc.) to look like those more advantaged, sometimes extending to such extremes as cosmetic surgery (Asian Americans used to have alterations in the almond shape of their eyes), or hair straighteners and skin whiteners (as once used by African Americans).

Some assimilation is often accepted by the dominant, but historically the dominant may instead punish imitation of themselves. In any event, assimilation does not become true incorporation in the more advantaged group unless members of this group fully accept the assimilator as no longer "other." Alternatively, sometimes the very success of assimilation may turn practitioners from it, fearing loss of their group identity. It is interesting when a group has come to recognize that price of its assimilation and shifts to efforts to preserve what distinctiveness remains to its members. Assimilation often means a purely personal view of the problem and its resolution. But the practice of assimilation by many often may eventually reawaken a sense of group identity precisely because of the shock of recognizing that it is eluding them without bringing them real acceptance as equals by the ethnically dominant.

Once again, one crosses over from enduring to influencing if one had assimilated with an eye to controlling the wills of authorities not just in the negative sense (not getting worse) but with the positive expectation of doing better.

(3) *Nondeferential resignation.* Neither applauding nor aping those in superior position, others may practice forms of rather fatalistic acceptance. Involving some perhaps conscious discontent with their lot, this mode yet remains politically quiescent. Adjusting aspirations to beliefs about what is feasible can often bring more satisfaction than to persist in illusory beliefs and leave desires untrimmed or even growing (Elster, 1993, 12 n. 23). One subform, which if elaborated could upstage a section of my chapter 2, involves isolation, often meaning physical withdrawal to avoid much contact with the dominant, like living in rustic retreats or else in an urban ghetto, often with the encouragement by the dominant. Even if not physically isolating themselves, those practicing nondeferential resignation may often strive to live unobtrusively, self-consciously avoiding any behavior that would call risky attention to themselves or their loved ones. Yet another way to be in the world but not of it is a turn to an inner world of fantasy, of wish-fulfilling dreams, of magic, or various modes of religious consolation. Most of the world's great religions originally promised hope for those in otherwise helpless conditions, even if later developments often rephrased the theologies to suit those who were better circumstanced. But in either case the religion may teach that this-worldly inequalities of condition are in the nature of things, even if compensated in some afterlife. Yet those near the bottom of the stratification system can sometimes shift to the apocalyptic mode of insisting that God demands rectification of injustices here and now (see Hill, 1972; Kautsky, 1959; Williams, 1962). But that ceases to be enduring and may even attempt more ambitious strategic choices (usually with failure, because most of such movements in history become wholly repressed).

(4) *Sullen submission watching for another opportunity.* Political quietude is not always fatalistic. Silence is not always consent. There is a kind of enduring that is not inclined to applaud, ape, or indefinitely suffer a condition of powerlessness. The sullenly submissive may know an oppression is politically caused and at least potentially politically remediable. Perhaps most common in either those who once were powerful and have lost that power or in those who have gained in resources to the extent of looking for a chance to mobilize them effectively, this mode of enduring offers least comfort to those currently in power. Often the apparent passivity of peasants, for example, is illusory. As Manfred Halpern has written, "The term 'fatalism' . . . has often been used to describe what is in fact the peasant's shrewdness when he bends with a wind

he cannot resist" (Halpern, 1963, 60). But sometimes that wind may change. Under areas of Russia occupied in 1941 by Nazi armies in World War II, Russians wearing square patches marked "Ost," for "Ostarbeiter" (Eastern Laborer) did forced labor for the Germans (Levin, 1968, 286). But one can well imagine their dream of Nazi military defeats, which began the next year.

Although I do not pretend to have exhausted the possible variants of enduring, I have illustrated several of the more prominent modes (for other discussions, cf. Parkin, 1971, 62, 76–77, 81–81 ff.; Tumin, 1976). Not every objective deprivation will lead to political protest: one must perceive the deprivation, grasp its relevance to a group, see it as illegitimate, feel rage at it, and see the possibility of demanding and getting its removal (Dahl, 1971, 95). Note that even those who make a cost-benefit calculation that could favor political noncompliance may yet fail to do so if a judgment on a specific matter is offset by an even larger accounting: the value of preserving the overall political system, which perhaps could carry also a less calculated charge of diffuse legitimacy (cf. Eckstein and Gurr, 1975, 71–72). Obviously those practicing enduring, for whatever the reason, may never cross over into the realm of disobedience. But enduring can sometimes be not a choice of despair but merely a temporary expedient for advancing the usually more demanding strategies of exiting (in chapter 2) or evading (a section of chapter 4), which often differ from enduring in leaning into disobedience of standing norms.

The costs to themselves of their strategy of segregationism quite obviously depends on whether the strategic reaction of the dominated group takes such relatively passive forms as reviewed here or turns instead to more active forms.

The prejudices of dominant ethnics practicing segregation often means a waste in human labor potential. In the extreme forms, this may appear at the scaffold or in massive prison warehousing (only 5 percent of the world's people, the United States holds about 20 percent of the world's prison inmates, and about 50 percent of these, largely incarcerated for drug dealing, are African American, Hispanics, or Native Americans). In Israel, residential segregations cost even the Jews a regular labor supply, because during political disturbances they often close the border to some 135,000 Palestinian day workers who normally cross over from the Palestinian territories (cf. Minns and Hijab, 1990). Occupational exclusions mean forgoing optimal utilization of talent. The Taliban exclusions of women must have been disastrous for the already parlous Afghan economy.

Another cost of a segregationist strategy even for the dominant group is that many among them are cut off from political affiliations, friendships, and the like. The antebellum South would hang whites who disseminated abolitionist tracts in the South. The Nazis, as noted, banned marriages or sexual relations of so-called Aryans with Jews or Romanies. The Rwanda Hutu perpetrators of genocide also killed a few thousand Hutus who tried to protect Tutsis.

When segregation not only differentiates weaker groups from the strongest but also from each other, it does facilitate divide and rule. However, it also tends to undermine the stronger group's inconsistent claim to similarity with all in claiming the existence of a common interest or their own ability to represent it in their leadership of the society.

Another absurdity is that if every difference is treated as enemy, even the dominant group would ultimately divide itself (Norton, 1988, 55–57). That sometimes really happens, and even the policy of division may be at issue among them, as in the late history of apartheid South Africa, which can best be understood as an ultimately failed project of divide and rule through "re-tribalization" of all nonwhite ethnicities, without doing the same for the white ones (Adam, 1971).

But the major counterproductivity in segregation can become encouragement of a distinctive kind of separation policy by the dominated, as in a minority group's nationalist militancy. Some may tire of the repression, as seems evident for some Israeli Jews regarding the relatively mild segregation of Israeli Arabs from 1948, or the more severe forms sometimes directed to the Gaza and West Bank Arabs from 1967. Frustrated Palestinians interested in improving the kill ratio of Jewish to Arab deaths turned to suicide bombings. This seemed triply vile when adults who did not themselves volunteer persuaded even children to become bomb delivery vehicles against civilian targets such as restaurants or buses. In reaction to this, Ariel Sharon ordered destruction of Yasser Arafat's helicopters so he could not go from the West Bank to Gaza, while further using Israeli tank forces to first isolate the West Bank city of Ramallah and then Arafat's headquarters compound within Ramallah. Finally, he was confined to but a few rooms. Under Sharon's direction, in response to each violent act against Israelis, they would demand that his police forces arrest the terrorists, but at the same time use helicopter rockets to blow away the police compounds that would have the communication links, intelligence files, lockups, and so on, necessary to do that. When nothing seemed to work, Sharon began take-backs of some Palestinian territory after each fresh suicide bombing. Some Israeli Jewish army officers (the "refuseniks") said that they would no longer participate in the military actions on the West Bank.

Although a dominated group's more militant response can take the form of simple ethnic tumult, as in the *intifada*, in other cases it may stimulate separatism, often with violent civil warring and sometimes by successful secessions as well.

What kind of fears cause people of one ethnic group to impose segregation or even genocide on another ethnic group? Bigots have loved to emphasize how their targets are very different from people like themselves, but their dark secret is that they really know they are very similar, wanting the same security, economic life chances, and status they want for themselves. Yet sometimes abnormal psychology intervenes: Hitler was a compulsive hand-washer, and his rhetoric associated aliens with invasions of microbes (Fest, 1974, in

Reilly, 1992, 245). Richard Koenigsberg argues that Hitler lived in a fantasy world from his boyhood: Although he could not protect his mother from sexual degradation or corruption by the father (his Austrian father, Alois, but also Jewish doctors) and her early death to cancer, he could save maternal Germany from the same (unworthy Austro-Hungarian rulers, the Jews). Hitler's rhetoric more than suggests these parallels: syphilitic microbes or cancer/invaded body/weakness or death of the individual organism/ruthless actions to prevent, such as isolation of the sick: Jews or Bolshevik incitement of class conflict/invasion of the body politic of Germany/weakness or death of the larger organism/ruthless cures such as elimination of Jews and communists within and warring on similar or other enemies without (cf. Koenigsberg, 1975, esp. 5–29).

There can be an even darker, dirty little secret that the most virulent and violent bigots may hide even from themselves: They secretly suspect that they themselves are inferior, and hence they could not successfully compete. They thus need to disparage, handicap, imprison, exile, or even kill rivals for what is wanted. Adolf Hitler, beyond his possible fear that he himself was partly Jewish (one grandmother became pregnant by an unknown father when working as a domestic in the home of a Viennese Rothschild), seems to have also worried about exposure of his likely gay sexual orientation, which he masked by displays of machismo. Also, he early had become unhinged by twice being rejected from a Viennese school of art and design. In a revealing 1931 interview with Richard Breiting, he conceded, "I really wanted to be an architect. The Vienna Jews knew how to stop that" (Calic, 1971, 67).[1] This is said not in any sympathy for such a monster as Hitler, but only to understand how a monster could have become formed. As the artist Goya once put it, "The sleep of reason produces monsters." Poorly understood nightmares in the minds of some can make nightmares in the real world for others.

The separatism of a dominant ethnic group, or segregation, can sometimes be a mere strategy for control with maintenance of inequality, especially when the target group is quite large and its labor is wanted by the dominant ethnics (e.g., white-ruled South Africa's apartheid). But in other cases it can culminate in genocide, especially when the attacked group offers few skills thought needed by the dominant (they are sometimes wrong) and when it is too small to resist effectively (which is usually true, even if the executioners may circulate propaganda citing them as a great threat to dominant ethnics). Civilization is restraint, but it is not doing very well. The last century was the most genocidal of all of human history. It is apparent that we must learn to identify in advance the minorities at risk and ask what can be done to protect them (Gurr, 1993, 2000; Heidenrich, 2001).

NOTE

1. I owe this citation to my student, Marwan Aljarwan, "Origins of Anti-Semitic Policy in Hitler's Germany."

CHAPTER 2

Separations as Separatisms: Strategies of the Weaker Ethnic Group

> How far can love for my oppressed race accord with love for the oppressing country? And when these loyalties diverge, where shall my soul find rest?
>
> —W. E. B. Du Bois, *Autobiography* (1968)

W. E. B. Du Bois had a lifelong problem with his political identity. He had hoped to assimilate as an American professor of sociology in white-dominated, quality academic institutions. But as an African American he was to experience early segregation and later prejudice, frustrating his academic career. Ultimately to "find rest" he chose not only to become a communist but to emigrate to Africa, where he died in 1965.

Could an African American have accepted segregation? Only in part, as when the founder of the Black Muslims, Elijah Muhammed, agreed with right-wing white segregationists in wanting no racial mixing, as well as in mutual opposition to Israel. However, Muhammed had a vision of the constituting of a black nationalist enclave somewhere in American territory, which would have been another sort of separatism of a weaker ethnic group.

This last bridges the way from discussion of separatism as segregation to separation as *separatism*, whereby the weaker ethnicity itself may accent its differences from the dominant ethnicity and even initiate the distancing in varying ways. But they do not further accent differences among themselves, which could cause the kind of fragmentation and political weakness that Gestapo chief Heydrich advocated for East Europeans, as illustrated at the beginning of chapter 1. Separatism, which invariably assumes genuine solicitude for the weaker group, is also distinctive from segregation in never accepting claims that the group is biologically inferior, and rarely admitting (if more often believing) it could be culturally inferior.

Hereafter assuming the state is yet firmly dominated by a stronger ethnicity, separation as a strategy of the weaker ethnic group can come in four principal forms of distancing behaviors: (1) individual migration from the state, (2) collective migration from the state, (3) collective migration to a borderlands region of the state, or (4) gaining independence for some usually borderland region, by pursuit of a secessionist movement. I begin by addressing the first three variants, then shift to secessionism.

I. SEPARATISMS AS SITUATIONALLY MOTIVATED EXITINGS

As a preface to discussions of the first three forms of migration, I comment broadly about what I have called "exiting" as a political strategy (in Cook, 1983; Cook, 1991, 117). By the strategy of exiting I primarily refer to physical removal of oneself from the reach of unfriendly authorities. This is roughly the opposite of the recruitment strategy of moving self and friends into their positions. The exiting strategy is common even among nonhuman forms of life, whenever motility permits physical removal from predators or even from threatening members of the same species. But among other differences, humans often have more definite territorial boundaries and more variegated situations behind them.

Albert O. Hirschman has used a partly convergent concept. But unlike Hirschman, I would not regard as exiting mere abstentions from membership or participation in the political process (e.g., nonvoting). If not wholly *apolitical* in motive, abstentions could often serve what I call the influence strategy of attempting indirect or direct persuasion of political authorities (especially if through a publicized electoral boycott). Similarly, a walkout from a political party convention or a resignation from a government will not here be called exiting. Nor would I follow Hirschman in extending the term to upward mobility from one's class of origin (cf. Hirschman, 1970, esp. 43 ff.).

I will not belabor the extreme exit of suicide, although such a desperate form of exit from an impossible situation has been practiced by Zealots on Masada, by Mark Antony and Cleopatra, by Seneca and other historical figures. Jean-Paul Sartre argued that the proof of our freedom is that death, perhaps self-inflicted, is always an open option. But suicide is not that open when potential suicides must think of obligations toward family or friends. Perhaps a politically motivated suicide, one aimed to make a statement, could be expected to bring severe recriminations against kith or kin. Nor will I dwell on the "escapism" of madness or fantasizing, unsure that the former is a choice at all, and construing the latter as really but one variant of a more passive set of strategies I have called "enduring," as reviewed in chapter 1.

As Hirschman recognized, one sort of exiting is withdrawing from economic involvement with a firm. On a larger scale, that can be practiced by a firm in relation to any level of territorial political unit, including the nation-state. But this is a movement of business operations more than the persons of top corporate leadership. As Robert Gilpin phrases it, "The multinational corporations are increasingly indifferent to national boundaries in making decisions with respect to markets, production, and sources of supply" (Gilpin, 1975, 221). Some U.S. corporations are even relocating their headquarters for purposes of more political influence or shaving something off taxes, as in many relocations of incorporations to Bermuda, causing a move in Congress to make that illegal.

For purposes of this discussion, my definition of exiting primarily refers only to migrations and secessions. Yet even then certain kinds of migration may be forced rather than freely chosen, and compliance would thus be better placed in the political strategic field I have called "enduring" (usually the sullen submission variant). History shows many cases of forced deportations of whole population groups, such as the virtually forced ousters of Vietnamese from Pol Pot's Kampuchea (Cambodia) and of the Chinese from South Vietnam in the 1970s. There is an admittedly ragged line between deportation and voluntary emigration. Terrorizing a group may almost compel exit, as in the "ethnic cleansings" of Croatians against Serbs and Muslims, and then Serbs against Bosnians and Kosovars in the early 1990s. In American history, the descendants of slaveowner whites who had fought to block emigration of fugitive slaves before the Civil War would in its sequel often encourage emigration from their region of freed blacks, and some local authorities even used welfare funds to buy southern blacks one-way bus tickets to Chicago (Gilliam, 1975, 37–39). In other cases individuals may be forcibly deported (Alexander Solzhenitsyn was pushed onto a plane departing from the USSR in 1974, not to return until 1994) or put under such inordinate pressures that they must leave. Even apoliticals may not be wanted, as Anne Norton writes: "The poor are often encouraged to emigrate by the nations in which they reside, while they are unwillingly received by those to which they immigrate" (Norton, 1988, 74). Although elites in many political systems have actively encouraged exit of what they regarded as "undesirables" (really just another form of segregation), I regard as exiting only those migrations that have *some* element of free choice in them.

Such voluntary migrations may be either within a certain unit such as the nation-state or between units as in present international migration. Most migration at most times may be largely economic in motivation, flowing from regions of lower economic opportunities toward regions of better life chances. Although one may question the suggestion that people are like superheated molecules within a boiler, Henry Shryrock writes, "People tend to move from areas of high fertility and low economic opportunity to those of low fertility and high economic opportunity. Migration is thus a safety valve for relative population pressure" (Shryrock, 1964, 1). As noted, I address only migrations that have at least some mixture of political motive, if only because their low opportunities at the place of origin rather directly arise from economic policy. Many among the one in nine East Germans who migrated West before the Berlin Wall, or among the one in six Cubans leaving communist Cuba, were surely political rather than merely economic migrants, but it is impossible to say just how many, especially when human motives are often mixed.

Having defined exiting primarily as choice of politically motivated migration from a territorial political jurisdiction, I may add that the strategy may be *feasible* only under two important conditions.

First, agents are able to leave, having the necessary resources to do so, even if sometimes debarred from migration by local authorities (in which case exiting is normally accompanied by the strategy of "evasion," or concealment of who you are or what you are doing, if either is punished). The Berlin Wall stands for the main obstacles to emigration from communism from 1962 to 1989.

Second, agents can envision improved life chances in some other territorial political jurisdiction, whether in some differently policed city or poorly policed borderland area or else abroad. That is, a migration *from* normally supposes a place to migrate *to*, if at worst only into detention should the authorities at the place of destination not favor entry.

Places to migrate to may be especially difficult for international migrants, because either economic or political criteria may stop their entry. Relatively unskilled laborers in the more advanced nations may oppose high inflows of cheaper labor that could appear to block them from jobs or higher pay (cf. Portes and Bach, 1985). Or sometimes an inflow of large numbers of migrants could be domestically opposed by those fearing it would tip a political balance against them, especially when ethnicity is salient in political cleavages. The U.S. adoption of national origins quotas in the 1920s blocked entry of many Jewish refugees from Hitler in the 1930s and early 1940s.

Let us first look at within-nation migration. As true of international migration, this strategic choice supposes a capacity to move as well as more politically attractive jurisdictions toward which one can move. The former has often been blocked by authorities as part of a strategy of control, as typified by obstacles to movements of medieval serfs or to movement of modern ex-convicts released on parole. Yet even for serfs there were often attractive destinations for illegal moves, as indicated by the German saying, *Stadtluft macht frei* ("City air makes one free").

If medieval principalities often permitted special privileges for cities that had bought or fought for that right, in recent history many federal systems permit considerable autonomy to subsystems, with the usual consequence of some policy diversity among them. This is illustrated by the American states or Canadian provinces as well as the local government units within each. Both the United States and Canada have histories whereby some found more freedom by migration to relatively unpoliced frontier areas, not yet organized as states or provinces. In the case of the United States, many African Americans migrated to northern states not only for economic opportunities but sometimes also in quest of greater political rights. Or many gays used to migrate to certain urban areas (San Francisco or Austin were well known) to secure relative freedom from legal restraints on theirlifestyles—antihomosexual ordinances were either left unenforced or were repealed. Although other such cases could be cited, it is apparent that many modern nations have uniform application of policy within their territories, which destroys any advantage of within-nation migration and makes only international migration a workable use of exiting.

Before the U.S. Civil War, nationwide enforcement of the Fugitive Slave Law required runaway slaves to keep on moving via the underground railroad through the northern states into Canada. Even in recent history, something like an underground railroad of international reach has been used to save pregnant but unmarried women from certain Arab nations from the practice of "honor killings" by male relatives, getting the women to West European or other refuges. There is a long history of recourse to international migration by persecuted religious heretics, perhaps most recently illustrated by the flight of Bahais from Islamic revolutionary Iran. But international exiting may be most important now for fleeing political heretics. They seek out another nation in hopes of asylum, or at least in confidence that they will not be extradited to the nation that would punish them for their flight as well as for their heresy.

Recall that this strategy supposes either open doors for exit or else a complementary strategy of evasion, as in use of disguises or false documents to slip out of a country. Most regimes may be eager to rid themselves of political undesirables. Sometimes it can be a miscalculation, as argued by Lyford Edwards: "In itself, emigration is a preventive of revolution. Oliver Cromwell desired to get away from England and to settle in Massachusetts. He was stopped at the dock by officers of Charles I. Had he been allowed to leave the country, it is conceivable that Charles I might have died of old age" (Edwards, 1927, 33). Blocked emigration most often arises when the would-be emigrants are wanted for labor, as classically true of slaves. In the early manufacturing era, England forbade emigration of skilled factory laborers who could leak vital technological secrets to other nations. Apart from Yugoslavia, most formerly communist nations frustrated emigration of needed laborers, especially those who held advanced education at state expense. The former Soviet Union especially opposed exit of those who could hold military secrets, as well as having unevenly closed the door to exit of numerous Soviet Jews (not only to avoid offending Arab states should they go to Israel but even more to head off an avalanche of like claims by other nationality groups). Another common blockage of emigration concerns draft-eligible youths.

Exceptions aside, most national authorities are as eager to encourage emigration of "undesirables" as they are to discourage entry of the same. When many nations define undesirables in a similar way, it means that many find international migration effectively closed to them. The United States, for example, has at times in its immigration laws tended to block entry of the poor, illiterates, those lacking in a nationally needed job skill, those of certain mental or physical disabilities, certain ethnic or nationality groups, those with prison records, prostitutes, polygamists, gays, anarchists, Nazis or communists (Fuchs, 1968, 2). Although lacking any restriction on female immigrants, such a list otherwise mirrors many of the disadvantaging attributes that define stratification dimensions of American society. Other nations have been similarly restrictive. As I write, some citizens of western European states are anxious about how an expanded European Union exposes them to an influx of Romany ("gypsies") or other distinctive peoples from eastern Europe. Right-wing populist parties, tapping into xenophobia, made startling gains in Italy, Portugal, France, the Netherlands, and Denmark, usually demanding not only an end to most economic immigration but also to alleged abuses of political asylum. Hence at any time one may expect tens of millions of homeless refugees as well as at least hundreds of millions of people who would like to migrate *from* but can find no suitable place to migrate *to*.

In normal times of a long-stable regime, it is not surprising that often those who would most like to emigrate are those who accumulate disadvantaging attributes, those lower rather than higher in the stratification system. Elaborating, a "disadvantaging" attribute could be defined as a membership category that predicts more unemployment, underemployment, or receipt of less than equal pay for equal work. Also, it often predicts a wish of many holding the attribute that they could correct or conceal it to promote their economic life chances. Also, the presence of the attribute tends to thin out as the importance of private and public offices rises, being hence rare on lists of chief executives of corporations or of principal national leaders.

Yet the pattern need not be frozen forever. The essence of social revolution is rapid, partial restratification of society, such that some of those who had been high become low and vice versa. Hence it has been observed that progressive radicalization of a revolution is usually registered in the initial exit of higher class counterrevolutionaries, then middle-class moderates, and finally disillusioned members of the lower classes, whereas a post-Thermidorean reaction may mean a reversed sequence of migrants returning (Brinton, 1958; Edwards, 1927, 127 ff.). If evident in the French or Russian revolutions, the pattern seems clear in more recent revolutions of Cuba, Southeast Asia, or Iran. Later waves of migrants from Cuba were also less white.

Political emigration often bears the opportunity cost of foreclosing for the present the possibility of pursuing strategies to change authoritative policies. As Albert O. Hirschman has put it, "presence of the exit alternative can . . . tend to *atrophy the development or the art of voice.*" By voice he means a catchall category for "any attempt at all to change, rather than escape from, an objectionable state of affairs" (Hirschman, 1970, 30, 43). Obviously that would include what I prefer to differentiate as distinctive action strategies of influencing, recruiting, or structuring (again in Cook, 1983, 1991; but see especially Cook, 2000, esp. 3–21). In a later book, Hirschman agreed with A. H. Birch's rejoinder that on the contrary sometimes the available option of emigration is needed to embolden those who would criticize a regime (Hirschman, 1981, 238). An example would be Lenin's exile to Switzerland so he could stay out of czarist prisons and publish a radical political newspaper, printed on onionskin paper so its copies could be smuggled back to Russia under clothing. Perhaps one could add that often a credible threat to emigrate can give bargaining leverage in the play of the influence strategy, provided that national authorities either would prefer to retain talents without forcibly blocking exit, or if they fear the propaganda boon to rivals should there be a mass exit from their nation. Yet Hirschman's original observation may be valid within many specific country cases.

It is quite another matter when actual emigration becomes not capitulation but merely a way station to better make use of the more active strategies of politics. From a protected location abroad, perhaps agents will be more successful in the influence strategy—creating, delivering, and reinforcing messages directed not only at their homeland but also at potential outside allies. Although Machiavelli wisely warned against trusting the claims of exiles, often a host nation may be made an instrument to oppose the regime in the homeland. This can lead to disasters, such as the 1961 U.S. sponsorship of the Bay of Pigs invasion of Cuba. In 2002 prominent Iraqi exiles lobbied Washington, D.C., for a like attempt against the Saddam Hussein regime in Iraq. Often exile organizations tend to fragmentation, internecine quarrels, and impotence, but in other cases they may go on to apply the recruitment or structures (shifts in powers among institutional units) strategies toward their homeland, subverting the oppressive regime (Garibaldi, Lenin, Castro, and Khomeini, among others, have led such returns). In sum, far from being a terminal strategy, exiting can often be merely instrumental: If so, flight is but a preparatory step to an effective fight.

Although he missed the strategic field of "evasion," which I address in chapter 4, the philosopher John Dewey understood the strategic fields of enduring and exiting, as well as more active strategies to change authoritative decisions: "If a man finds himself in a situation which is practically annoying and troublesome, he has just two courses open to him. He can make a change in himself either by running away from trouble or by steeling himself to Stoic endurance; or he can set to work to do something so as to change the conditions of which unsatisfactoriness is a quality. When the latter course is impossible, nothing remains but the former" (Dewey, 1929, 232–33). Let us turn to a few individual examples.

II. SEPARATING AS INDIVIDUAL EMIGRATIONS: DESPAIRING BLACK NATIONALISTS OF THE UNITED STATES

Although one could also address the broadly assimilationist Frederick Douglass, who took an interest in Ulysses Grant's failed project of sponsored emigration of some freed slaves to Santo Domingo, I discuss the cases of Martin Delany, Marcus Garvey, W. E. B. Du Bois, and Stokely Carmichael to illustrate strategies of both collective and individual emigration.

Martin Delany (1812–85) was the outstanding black emigrationist of the nineteenth century. He was born to a slave father and free mother, obtained education, and ultimately became a physician and a major in the Union Army just before the end of the Civil War. Unlike Frederick Douglass, Delany had become an abolitionist opposed to black alliances with whites. Although Douglass had early regarded emigrationists as really running away from the problem of abolishing slavery, and while Douglass himself became a militant integrationist in strategy, Delany believed that former slaves would want to migrate back to Africa. In 1859 he had visited Liberia, and he also explored parts of Nigeria with the vision of Yorubaland as another point of debarkation. Delany had also toyed with the idea of black emigration to elsewhere in the New World, such as to the Caribbean or Brazil, but he would increasingly accent a pan-Africanist vision. He was one of the first to claim great creativity in black African history, asserting that the ancient Egyptians were blacks and imparted their wisdom to Arabs, Jews, and Europeans. He always dreamed of a second trip back to Africa, even hoping he would be made the U.S. ambassador to Liberia, but it was not to be. He died in Wilberforce, Ohio (Griffith, 1975).

Marcus Garvey (1887–1940) was to be the foremost emigrationist of the early twentieth century. He was born in Jamaica in the West Indies, where he also was to have a major base in Trinidad. But as a flamboyant speaker and publicist (*The Negro World*), he gained broad followings in lower class black populations throughout not only that region but also in the United States and Africa. He formed the Universal Negro Improvement Association (UNIA), which urged a range of labor rights improvements and other progressive reforms. Garvey hoped to move its headquarters to Liberia, but by 1934 its president banned any presence of Garveyites there. Although Garvey had espoused land reform in the Caribbean, he was no socialist and he was eventually sharply attacked by Marxists of various persuasions. Yet his militancy got him banned from many places, and when he had come to the United States, the young J. Edgar Hoover held him suspect because he had spoken favorably of Lenin's distinctive revolutionary effort. The financial affairs of the Garvey organization were chaotic, and it was linked to bankruptcies of two steamship lines. In 1923 Garvey himself was convicted of mail fraud against stockholders of the Black Star Line Corporation. Unsuccessful in appeals, in 1925 he entered the Atlanta Penitentiary. However, in 1927 his sentence was commuted to deportation. As his movement began to wane, Garvey made his way to London, where he would eventually die. He often spoke at the "Speaker's Corner" in London's Hyde Park, where Marxists heckled him. He had earlier denounced European colonialism in Africa, and he loved two slogans that were not original with him, "Africa for the Africans" and "Back to Africa." He dreamed of an independent Africa constituting "a big, Black republic," a homeland for the black diaspora. Yet he curbed his denunciation of British imperialism in his last years, favoring at least temporary unity to stop fascism (cf. Cronon, 1973; Hill and Bair, 1987; Lewis and Warner-Lewis, 1994).

Unlike Frederick Douglass or Booker T. Washington, William Edward Bernhardt Du Bois (1868–1965) was not born into slavery but rather to a long free, African American family residing in the western Massachusetts town of Great Barrington. The population of some five thousand held only twenty-five to fifty blacks. Many of these were partially white ancestry as true of Du Bois (his paternal aunt passed as white and had white children). If anything, the residents of the small city's Irish slum were more the object of prejudice than were the community's blacks.

Du Bois's mother had descended from a patrilineal ancestor named Bernhardt, freed from the Dutch owner of the same name as a reward for military service with the patriots during the struggle for independence. Du Bois's father, who gave him his French last name, had ancestral ties with Haiti. But his father abandoned the family, to the lasting sorrow of W. E. B. Du Bois's mother. Soon after, for unexplained reasons, she left the Episcopalianism that had been followed by both sides of the family to become a Congregationalist.

Congregationalists had been prominent in organizing African American colleges in the Reconstruction South. Locally, white Congregationalist ministers led the effort to raise a scholarship for W. E. B. to attend college. Although he had wanted to start at Harvard, he could not afford it and instead took a bachelor's degree at Fisk in Tennessee. Begun in a Civil War–era military installation, Fisk was then a small, predominantly black college with mostly white faculty. Before graduating with only five in his class, Du Bois began to identify strongly with the black community. This deepened in two summers of elementary school teaching of black pupils in remote places of the Tennessee hill country.

Once he graduated from Fisk, Harvard University admitted Du Bois for advanced studies on the condition that he begin at junior standing. Although that seems outrageous, even Du Bois conceded that some new southern black colleges were scarcely more than high schools. He found Harvard stimulating, especially in the teaching of philosophers William James and George Santayana. In his *Autobiography*, Du Bois says, "I was repeatedly a guest in the home of William James; he was my friend and guide to clear thinking" (Du Bois, 1968, 143). He knew Josiah Royce, who theorized about linkages among loyalties, and he was acquainted with fellow student Herbert Croly, the later intellectual leader of the Roosevelt wing of the Progressives. Du Bois's distinguished friends would later include Hull House founder Jane Addams, the famous lawyer for the underdog Clarence Darrow, and the black athlete-actor-singer Paul Robeson.

Like everyone around him, Du Bois started off as a Republican in Massachusetts, where he observed town meetings in action. He admits that in 1888 one of his heroes was Otto von Bismarck, and the Populist movement of the early 1890s barely touched him. Yet he early grew into African American consciousness. He wryly notes that a white woman at a Harvard reception persistently wanted to believe that Du Bois *must* be a waiter. He had already developed skills in journalism and public speaking when at Fisk, and he distinguished himself at Harvard in both. He gradually shifted his interests from philosophy to history and politics, and he would have been a sociologist if such a department had existed during his student days.

Once he had finished a master's thesis, Du Bois succeeded in obtaining a Slater Fellowship for study in Europe, which required his persistent pestering of President and then ex-President Rutherford Hayes, who had expressed doubts that any blacks could qualify. Du Bois, who would later make many trips to Europe, traveled widely during his study abroad. He acknowledged that he became so much a Francophile that he would have settled in Paris but for his commitment to the liberation of blacks in America. The French prided themselves on their assimilationist posture toward the Africans of their colonies. But Du Bois's place of study was to be the University of Berlin, which refused (ironically, like Harvard vis-à-vis Fisk earlier) to credit Harvard work, and Du Bois eventually had to take his Ph.D. from Harvard. At Berlin, he heard lectures by the centrist sociologist Max Weber and the rightist historian Heinrich Treitschke.

Back in the United States, he took his first job at the African American Methodist college, Wilberforce. In 1896 he married a woman from Cedar Rapids, Iowa, whose father was an African American hotel cook and mother, a German housewife. Although the couple's son died in infancy, they had a daughter who survived. Their marriage lasted over a half century. After she died, Du Bois married Shirley Graham, who was forty years younger than himself, and by her he had another son who lived.

Weary after only two years of the administrative politics of Wilberforce, he shifted to a soft-money research job with the demeaning and novel title "Assistant Instructor" at Ben Franklin's offspring, the University of Pennsylvania. For a year and a half he did a sociological study of the ghetto blacks of Philadelphia, culminating in his *The Philadelphia Negro* (1898). In his judgment blocked by racial bigotry from a deserved professorship at Pennsylvania, he then relocated to the less prestigious Atlanta University, where he taught for thirteen years.

One wonders if part of the discrimination against him was his awakening political militancy. If he had begun as a Republican, his politics shifted left-ward by turns into Progressivism, social democracy, and ultimately commu-nism. His life was filled with political activity, including his leading role in the Niagara movement. It first met in Buffalo in 1905 and was formally organized in Washington, D.C., in 1906 (the year in which its members made their second conference a barefoot pilgrimage at the grave site of John Brown). Nearly all Niagara members later joined the National Association for the Advancement of Colored People (NAACP). The Niagara movement and the newspaper, *The Crisis*, founded and edited by Du Bois, sought both full po-litical rights and enlarged economic opportunities for African Americans, standing to the left of Booker T. Washington, even if remaining in a distinc-tively integrationist orientation.

By contrast, Booker T. Washington tended to avoid politics, though he did write one letter urging that Louisiana not use race but literacy to restrict suffrage. Du Bois asserted that Booker T. Washington had sold out to his white philanthropists, who wanted blacks to be kept in a subordinate place where they would be useful checks against excessive demands from white labor. Against Booker T. Washington's movement, even if for the moment only a "Talented Tenth" of blacks could attain higher education and higher status roles in society, Du Bois held that they would be invaluable in pro-moting the liberation of African Americans. Hinting without any offered evi-dence that Booker T. Washington's *Up from Slavery* may have been ghost written, Du Bois complained that a "Tuskegee Machine" had been given de facto authority over not only the flow of white philanthropists' money but also recruitment of blacks into university and other posts. He also complained that in saying that blacks were yet quite backward, Booker T. Washington had been almost apologetic for white denials of black voting and other civil rights through "Jim Crow" laws.

The NAACP would from its start in 1910 to the present emphasize militant litigation on behalf of equality of civil rights for African Americans, winning a long series of victories culminating in the most notable *Brown vs. Board of Education* decision in 1954. Prior to World War I, Du Bois had written off the Taft Republicans and had made an appeal to the Bull Moose Progressives to back civil rights for blacks, but Theodore Roosevelt spurned him. After securing from Woodrow Wilson a vague expression of support, Du Bois tilted toward him, only to feel betrayed by Wilson later. A major defeat was Wilson's creation of segregated military units to fight World War I (nonwhites had to tear a corner off their registration certificates).

When yet inclined to voluntary assimilation and integration as the strategy for his race, Du Bois disdained Marcus Garvey and his emigrationism, once it became prominent at the outset of the 1920s. But Du Bois was moved by a mix of motives in his increased turn toward separation as separatism. One was his frustration in seeking personal assimilation, such as his denial of the University of Pennsylvania professorship, plausibly due to the informal segregation policy of whites. The other was the rise of Jim Crow laws and the mentioned military segregation, both being legal expressions of the segregationist strategy of white politicians. What is the point of trying to assimilate if the other race never accepts you as fully similar to themselves, hence refuses to accord equality of rights and opportunities? Segregation would continue in the military until ordered to be ended by Harry Truman. Segregation would continue in some forms in many southern states until Du Bois's death in 1965. Martin Luther King was attempting to desegregate Memphis public service jobs when assassinated in 1963.

Just after World War I, in 1919 Du Bois with a Senegalese cooperator organized the Pan-African Congress, meetings of which he would attend in future years. From 1934 through 1944, Du Bois was chair of sociology at Atlanta University, only to find himself on very short notice involuntarily retired, due to his politics. Du Bois had come to regard himself as a democratic socialist even before World War I, and he kept migrating leftward thereafter. In the 1944–1948 period he had returned to work at the head office of NAACP, but he became embroiled in conflict with its secretary, Walter White, and Du Bois was forced to resign. One bone of contention was White's support of Truman in 1948, when Du Bois backed Progressive Henry Wallace.

Du Bois then turned to involvement in New York leftist organizations, including the Peace Information Center, which in the post–World War II years became viewed as a communist front organization. Du Bois found his passport revoked by the Cold War State Department from 1951 to 1958, until the Supreme Court ruled that Congress had given no such authority. Although the ostensible reason of the State Department was that Du Bois refused to sign a statement that he was not a Communist Party member (he was *then* not, but he refused to sign out of principle), the real reason was that he would have spoken out abroad against American segregation. But in 1959 Du Bois did join the American Communist Party, and in that year the Soviets awarded him the Lenin Peace Prize.

Although involved since the 1920s in the Pan-African Congress movement, during the 1950s Du Bois became even more interested in pan-Africanism, especially encouraging academic study of Africa, for he complained of "the exploitation and almost universal underestimation of Africans" (Du Bois, 1968, 34). By 1961, as a final expression of his separatist leanings, he even moved to Ghana, residing there until his death in 1965.

In his economic views, Du Bois had noted that Harvard was becoming reactionary when he had entered as a student, emphasizing only a shift from protectionist to free trade capitalist economics and dismissing too lightly the works of Henry George as well as Karl Marx. For a time Du Bois had embraced reform capitalist economics of the Progressive variety. But Du Bois eventually was to acknowledge that "people's capitalism" was an illusion, and his *Autobiography*, which appeared in foreign languages in 1964, the year before his death, says, "I believe in communism" (Du Bois, 1968, 57). He believed that central planning was succeeding in getting growth while at the same time offering more equitable distribution. Although the Soviet Union's experiment could fail, he held, the very effort was progress (Du Bois, 1968, 30). Read now, he was quite uncritical of communist rule, even stating approvals of the USSR repression of Hungary in 1956 and the Chinese repression of the Tibetan rising in 1959.

He expressed resentment of the capitalist ruling class, especially its conspicuous consumption. He speaks of well-dressed Fifth Avenue women as essentially just "prostitutes," far beneath the example of communist Chinese women, wearing pants so they could do some useful labor. Also, capitalist inequality had ugly consequences in domestic security policy, including, he claims, the lynching of 1,700 black Americans in the United States in less than a decade, 1885 to 1894 (Du Bois, 1968, 122). He believed theories of imperial exploitation of cheap labor and raw materials, all at the cost of small wars in the colonial areas and great wars among rival imperial powers. He became active in the peace movements, denouncing the arms race and the Vietnam War.

Du Bois, who had always previously expressed appreciation for African American spirituals and other church-related music, came to regard all religion as superstition. He even says that the separation of religion from all education was "the greatest gift of the Russian revolution to the modern world" (Du Bois, 1968, 43). In short, an embittered Du Bois ended up by rejecting some main currents of American political thought, its constitutionalism that had failed to outlaw Jim Crow laws, its allegedly destructive capitalism, and not only its pronounced Christianity but any religion at all.

A generation younger, Stokely Carmichael (1941–1998) would follow a similar itinerary, moving from a politically assimilationist standpoint to separatism, culminating with his similar emigration to Africa. Carmichael came to the United States from Trinidad in 1952, eventually becoming enrolled at predominantly black Howard University. He then joined the Congress of Racial Equality (CORE), but it was not militant enough for his taste. Although it had been a spin-off from Martin Luther King's Southern Christian Leadership Conference, the Student Non-Violent Coordinating Committee (SNCC) attracted him next, because it vigorously pursued voter registration of blacks in the American South, even in the teeth of beatings and also some killings of voter registration workers. By 1966 Carmichael was president of SNCC, and his fiery oratory was especially displayed in his speech, "Black Power." SNCC had included white members and also enlisted nonmember supporters in such activities as fund-raising to assist southern voter registration of blacks, which involved even this author in New Jersey. But Carmichael had announced, "before we can enter the open society, we must first close ranks," and whites were invited to leave SNCC. Becoming even more militant, in 1967 Carmichael joined the separatist Black Panther Party, even becoming its prime minister in 1968. It called for community control in black neighborhoods and more vaguely looked to a black-ruled region somewhere in the American South. But the Black Panthers would increasingly become involved in rather pointless shootouts with the police, taking many Black Panther leaders away to prison. In 1973 Carmichael chose, like Du Bois who had died there eight years before, to emigrate to Ghana, although he soon relocated to Guinea. Having chosen an African home, he also chose an African wife, the South African singer Miriam Makeba. He even adopted a more African name, Kwame Touré, apparently after Kwame Nkrumah (independence leader in Ghana) and Sekou Touré (then leader of Guinea). This was in striking contrast to the assimilationist Booker T. Washington, who had chosen for his last name that of the father of his country. Like Du Bois, Carmichael would die in Africa, which Booker T. Washington would never visit (cf. Grossman, 1993, 197–98).

Separation by emigration can sometimes be hard on one's career. Du Bois and Carmichael almost dropped from at least the American public view once they had emigrated to Africa.

III. SEPARATING AS COLLECTIVE MIGRATIONS TO BORDERLANDS

Other exits may follow a collective mode, and one variant is migration of a people into some inaccessible borderland, often a mountainous, swampy, or thicket region little penetrated by the authorities of an empire or nation-state. Thus, although the Hmong people may have originally migrated from somewhere in the vicinity of northern India, when they eventually settled in such states as China or Laos, they often sought further security by migration to mountain regions where they were largely left alone. However, many Hmong were recruited as allies by the United States in the Vietnam War, and after the American exit many were to become American immigrants in a variety of local concentrations.

In passing, recall that sometimes a dominant ethnic group would when segregating impose some differentiating item of clothing, brand, or the like, to designate the dominated group. But when an ethnic minority itself initiates some collective strategy, the minority itself may want to mark its membership. Thus writes Stuart Kaufman: "Group identity is indeed for most people ascriptive—that is, assigned at birth—and is often marked on the body, either naturally as racial characteristics or carved on by circumcision, tattoo, or other artificial process" (Kaufman, 2001, 23). Usually such borderlands peoples are at least distinguishable by their clothing. The Hmong, for example, have very distinctive needlework designs.

IV. SEPARATING AS COLLECTIVE EMIGRATIONS

Although less true of cases of individual emigration, in collective emigrations, as with secessionist struggles, the weaker minority will, like the stronger minority regarding it, construct a self-image that accents difference. But whereas the dominant ethnic segregationists may have viewed the weaker group in terms of almost everything bad, here the weaker group sees itself just as good as, if not better than, the stronger group.

As known from the famous example of Moses leading the Jews out of Egyptian bondage to the promised land, a weaker ethnic group may simply pick up and leave the relevant political community, often experiencing great costs or hardships on the way. The Puritans who settled in New England in the early seventeenth century took a parallel view of themselves, if not quite wholly escaping British political authority.

Although I have already briefly reviewed the advocacy of collective emigration to Africa by Daniel Delany and Marcus Garvey, I will add mention of Mississippi's Choctaw emigration. The Choctaws were one of the five so-called civilized tribes of the South (the others were Cherokees, Chickasaws, Creeks, and Seminoles). Like other Native Americans, these tribes had been steeply reduced in numbers by European diseases to which they lacked hereditary immunity. Their lands were further reduced by force or fraud as white settlers increased in numbers. No longer able to make a living by hunting and gathering, most took up agriculture, and they assimilated voluntarily in other ways (especially the Cherokees). But they were confronted by white-controlled state authority with even more restrictions on them. The Mississippi state government in 1830 enacted a law aimed at the Chickasaws and Choctaws imposing a year's imprisonment and a thousand dollar fine if any among them were to use the title of "chief," obviously trying to strip them of any leadership. The existing chief of the Choctaws assembled his people to announce this and other restrictive laws. The tribe then unanimously chose to emigrate from Mississippi to freer territory. They traveled up to Memphis, Tennessee, in order to take a ferry over into the Arkansas country, financially aided by the U.S. government, which had otherwise refused to intercede against such repressive legislation. The French social philosopher Alexis de Tocqueville happened upon their crossing of the Mississippi, and he left us this poignant word portrait of the event in 1831:

It was then the middle of winter, and the cold was unusually severe; the snow had frozen hard upon the ground, and the river was drifting huge masses of ice. The Indians had their families with them, and they brought in their train the wounded and the sick, with children newly born and old men upon the verge of death. They possessed neither tents nor wagons, but only their arms and some provisions. I saw them embark to pass the mighty river, and never will that solemn spectacle fade from my remembrance. No cry, no sob, was heard among the assembled crowd; all were silent. Their calamities were of ancient date, and they knew them to be irremediable. The Indians had all stepped into the bark that was to carry them across, but their dogs remained upon the bank. As soon as these animals perceived that their masters were finally leaving the shore, they set up a dismal howl and, plunging all together into the icy waters of the Mississippi, swam after the boat. (Tocqueville, 1945, Vol. 1, 352–53; see also 364 n. 21)

One guesses that the U.S. government forbade transport of any animals. Although left unsaid, the dogs must have perished. As for the Choctaws, they were not to remain very long in the Arkansas region but were pushed onto the Oklahoma reservation, and even that was whittled back as white farmers coveted its lands and tribal communal land holding was ended (cf. Perdue, 1980/1993).

Although the Choctaws got only more disappointments for their trouble, one might make a list of preconditions for a collective emigration: Unless their own leaders coerce them, it usually supposes the free consent of the followers to follow. It supposes either that the authorities would not coercively prevent their exit or else that they can either evade or successfully fight them. It supposes that they either have the financial and logistical capacity to exit, or that some other group provides these things to them. Like individual emigration, it supposes someplace to migrate *to*, where the conditions would be more attractive, and for many this is not available.

V. SEPARATING AS REGIONAL AUTONOMY OR SECESSION

Perhaps "sectionalism" is the best blanket term for two distinctive kinds of aspiration in a subordinated ethnic group: autonomy and secession. For the most, I reserve autonomy to chapters 5 and 6, because it is a moderate kind of demand that essentially aims at accommodation of two ethnic groups. But I here merely show how autonomy is different from secession.

Autonomy derives from Greek roots *autos* ("self") and *nomos* ("law"), obviously implying that those seeking it want more home rule for their region. But if an ethnic minority seeks only "autonomy," as true of most of the Catalan minority of Spain, they do want more local control but do not want to leave the present political community (cf. McRoberts, 2001). Similarly, the Dalai Lama, the principal leader of the Tibetans, has insisted from his exile in India that his movement aims only at autonomy, not secession, and he has assured the Chinese government that he opposes all recourse to violence. But the authorities of the People's Republic of China do not think him sincere. Sometimes a group that claims to aim only at more autonomy may really aim at ultimate secession, which is full independence. Or even if not necessarily intending that among many at the leadership level, it eventually evolves that way, as arguably true of the Slovak Republic separation from the Czech Republic in 1993.

But sometimes an announced program of secession may really have the more modest aim of securing more autonomy; that is, the secessionist gesture is just a sophisticated strategy by which an ethnic minority hopes to get a more generous accommodation as discussed in chapter 6. Alternatively, announced secessionists may simply tire of a long armed struggle and lower their sights to more autonomy only, which seems true of the Karens of Burma, who know they need economic assistance from Burma but would like the accommodation of a federal constitution (Bartkus, 1999, 46–78).

Both autonomist and separatist movements are politically important. Since the 1940s, over eighty peoples have sought either more autonomy or independence from the state in which they live (Gurr and Harff, 1994, 18–19).

When a group aims at "secession," they quite literally want to move themselves and the regional territory they inhabit out of the political community, either to become absorbed by another state, normally of ethnic similars, or else to become an independent political community on their own.

Samuel Huntington has suggested that secession is the political equivalent of divorce ("Foreword" in Nordlinger, 1972). But to extend that metaphor, many who attempt secession would argue they had really been trapped in a very bad marriage, often one that was initially forced and hence invalid in any case.

As in some collective emigrations, secessionist efforts often involve a shift from merely self-interested motivation to concern for a group's collective good. As I have shown elsewhere (Cook, 2002, 65–76), most autonomist or separatist movements arise from ethnic groups that are both economically and politically disadvantaged. When writing that, I was unaware of a convergent account previously offered by Donald Horowitz. He concluded that secessions are only rarely pursued by educationally "advanced" groups or by "advanced" regions, but are most often favored by "backward" groups of "backward" regions. As he explains it, a common grievance is that within the larger state they cannot attain civil service posts, military officer slots, or business positions in proportion to their numbers: "Backward groups in backward regions can escape disagreeable competition by withdrawing from an undivided state" (Horowitz, 1985, esp. 229–97, citation 256).

However, in the recent breakups of the Soviet Union and Yugoslavia, the most *economically* advantaged republics (the Baltic republics, the Slovenes and Croatians) led the way. In the Soviet Union the most *politically* privileged republic, Russia, was among the leaders, whereas the economically lagging republics of central Asia opposed the breakup of the Soviet Union, because they had been net gainers in taxation and expenditure (Bartkus, 1999, 41–43).

The breakup of the Soviet Union came in two waves: In the first wave, the Baltic states, which had been net losers in fiscal exchange with USSR, first withdrew: Lithuania in 1990 was to lead the other two Baltic states, Latvia and Estonia, out of the Soviet Union. That was accepted by presidents Boris Yeltsin of the Russian republic and Mikhail Gorbachev of the Soviet Union by September 1991. In the second wave, after a failed army-KGB coup attempt, leaders of the Russian, Byelorussian, and Ukrainian republics led the remaining twelve Russian republics out of the Soviet Union, which then ceased to exist (cf. Taras and Ganguly, 2002, 132).

In Yugoslavia the *politically* privileged republic, Serbia, resisted the breakup, successively but futilely using force against the Slovenians, Croatians, Bosnian Muslims, and Albanian ethnics in Serbia's Kosovo province.

Classic "just war" theory dates back to Augustine and even Cicero, and it assessed the justice of the initiating authority, the aims, and the means used. It did not accept secessionists as a "just authority" in the making of war. International law, influenced by such Roman Catholic natural law theories, has typically weighed in favor of existing states and against those who would break them apart. Even Secretaries General of the United Nations have recurrently announced their presumption against secession from any existing member state. At least short of genocide, the principle of "nonintervention in the internal affairs of another state" is given precedence over "self-determination of peoples." Finally, although eventually accepting the dismantling of land and sea empires in the twentieth century, the "world community" (read: opinion of principal foreign policymakers, especially among the great powers) has also been usually biased against the aspirations of new states.

The irony is that once a secession effort has succeeded, the bias against secession neatly turns about. There now is a presumption in just war theory, international law, and in stands of leaders of major states against any future attempt to reincorporate the state as well as against any further secession from the new state, which could be led by a disgruntled local minority. Can this contrast of before and after be intelligibly defended? Perhaps it could by extending to the political order what David Hume suggested as prudential rules regarding private property: presumption in favor of present possession, transference only by consent, and keeping covenants. But Hume was a self-described Tory, and he worked from within very conservative horizons (on the ethics of secession, see Buchanan, 1991; Walzer, 1986).

If inconsistent over time, positions can be wildly inconsistent even in one slice of time: the concept of "self-determination" of peoples dates back at least to an 1865 resolution of the International Workingmen's Association favoring independence for Poland (Connor, 1972, 331). Even that use should have signaled to us the function of the apparently liberal-democratic phrase in political conflict: *Agents tend to endorse the phrase to unify or empower their friends, or else to disunite or disempower their enemies, but they do not want to hear it when it would divide or disempower their friends or else unify or empower their rivals.*

The victors in the war and creators of the League of Nations after World War I favored "self-determination of peoples" for territories controlled by the defeated German, Austro-Hungarian, and Ottoman empires, *but almost nowhere else.* The victors of World War II and founders of the United Nations similarly welcomed immediate "self-determination" for only those peoples ruled by the defeated Germans, Italians, and Japanese. During the Cold War, hypocrisy also reigned, for the United States welcomed self-determination that could (and ultimately did) divide communist states, just as the Soviets took some pleasure over such movements within states allied with the West.

Just as dominant ethnic group segregationism can have some adverse consequences for even members of that group, so ethnic minority separatism can have some ugly consequences for some among their own. In order to separate from the dominant group, they have a tendency to project very sharp lines of difference with that group, and this goes with accenting a related set of similarities supposedly making the subordinate group one. They may not only deny the existence of local differences but openly work to expunge those which cannot be denied. They may turn to an aggressive assimilationism to repress the different such as discussed in chapter 3, as when some leaders of seceded Baltic states or Ukraine have threatened to eliminate use of Russian among them.

After the French Revolution, right-wing political leaders began to discover that nationalistic appeals could also work for them (Hardt and Negri, 2000, 101–5). Nevertheless, this did not preclude some progressive invocations of nationalism by peoples seeking to shake off the shackles of empire. But Hardt and Negri see adverse consequences even for some members of subordinated groups seeking their own liberation from a newly regnant nationalism:

As much as those walls appear progressive in their protective function against external domination . . . , they can easily play an inverse role with respect to the interior they protect. The flip side of the structure that resists foreign powers is itself a dominating power that exerts an equal and opposite internal oppression, repressing internal difference and opposition in the name of national identity, unity, and security. Protection and oppression can be a sword that at times appears necessary despite its destructiveness. (Hardt and Negri, 2000, 106)

They later add, "As soon as the nation begins to form as a sovereign state, its progressive functions all but vanish" (Hardt and Negri, 2000, 109).

There are often action-reaction turns in ethnic minority preferences: Thus a separatist turn of a weaker ethnicity may be in large part reactive against a perceived aggressive assimilationism on the part of the dominant ethnicity, which can mean that cultural survival (status symbolics of language, religion, etc.) is of more immediate concern than economic unfairness. One thinks of the Basque separatists, who persist out of linguistic motives, even though their region is a leading industrial area of Spain, and other Spaniards do not mean to threaten their physical security. But in other cases a regional lag behind the others in economic development may join with cultural survival concerns in explaining a separatist turn, as suggested by Quebec. Even an unplanned assimilation, such as gradual economic development of a heretofore backward region, can awaken cultural anxieties, especially in a linguistic or religious minority growing fearful of lost identity.

A region-based ethnicity may function something like an economic interest group, and its "nationalism" may rise or fall depending on its perceived influence at the center. Thus Hechter suggests that Scottish nationalism has tended to rise when Conservatives dominated Westminster, but at least for a time would wane when the more sympathetic Labour Party did so. But after a lag they could also become disillusioned with Labour for not heeding their special concerns (Hechter, 1999, xxi). Labour prime minister Tony Blair, anticipating the inevitable, moved to permit by referendum devolution of powers to renewed Scot as well as Welsh national parliaments, with the Scots winning a larger devolution.

Uneven development has often encouraged secessionist movements. I have elsewhere recommended the view that a country should be viewed as a kind of coalition, often originally aimed at military security. One may especially see the coalition nature of a political community as it is struggling to emerge or when it is falling apart (Cook, 2002, esp. 35–76). Thus Colley has noted that Great Britain arose as a Protestant coalition against Roman Catholic Spain or France (Colley, 1992, 5). England annexed Wales in 1536. Although sharing a monarch from 1603, Scotland was joined with England into the United Kingdom in 1707. Although in part occupied by people coming from England since the time of the Norman invasions, Ireland was annexed to Great Britain as late as 1801. However, Ireland's predominant Roman Catholicism fit poorly, and British law discriminated against Roman Catholicism until 1826. Once Britain had been weakened by World War I, the Irish became strongly insurgent, and by 1921 most Irish counties but for the region called Northern Ireland or Ulster seceded from Great Britain.

Let us review some secessionist movements around the world, looking in turn at the Americas, West Europe, East Europe, Asia, and Africa:

North and South American Separatisms

In North America, the secession of the South was reversed by military force during the U.S. Civil War (1861–65). More recent separatist movements have existed not only in Quebec but potentially among Cree Indians within that province, should Quebec ever secede (cf. Carment, Stack, and Harvey, 2001). The Inuit in the north central reaches of Canada asked and got a sparsely populated but territorially vast province of high autonomy, Nunavut (cf. Duffy, 1988).

Separatist risings have also occurred among Mayan Indian villagers in Chiapas, Mexico, largely as a reaction to Mexico's joining the North American Free Trade Association: They feared that outsiders would plunder their forestlands. Zapotec natives in Oaxaca state have also been restless. Traveling with my family within Oaxaca, the author has heard even small boys thump their chests and proudly call themselves Zapotecs, while otherwise speaking Spanish with me. Other separatists arose among Mayas of Guatemala, as well as among the Mosquito Indians of Nicaragua.

Leaving aside some Caribbean secessionists, some native peoples in the backlands of Ecuador and Brazil have been restless, sometimes resorting to kidnappings of outsiders to advertise their grievances and collect ransoms, although lacking capabilities to secede. Colombia for a time tolerated de facto secessions of first one, then two rebel areas as a gesture of goodwill as the government unsuccessfully sought a negotiated accommodation.

West European Separatisms

In West Europe, some groups seem primarily concerned only with more autonomy to protect their regional languages, such as the Provençal speakers in southeastern France (Occitanie), the Catalans of Spain (given constitutional guarantees in 1978), or the Welsh (on the Catalans, see McRoberts, 2001). Secessionist separatism in West Europe had peaceably occurred when Norway left Sweden (1905) with grievances about lack of consuls for primarily Norwegian merchant mariners as well as protective tariffs for Swedish manufacturers. Iceland with other grievances peaceably left Nazi-invaded Denmark (1944). In 1848 an attempt of Hungary to exit the Austro-Hungarian empire was forcibly repressed. Today separatist sentiment is found among the Catholic minority of Northern Ireland, many Scots, some Basques of Spain, Lombards of north Italy, and Corsicans of France.

Michael Hechter notes that the "Celtic fringe" of Great Britain, consisting in Scotland, Wales, and Northern Ireland, has tended to aspire to more autonomy or in the case of the Catholics in the latter, even separation. He notes that the original linguistic difference is waning as Gaelic and Welsh are now less used, but the religious difference is great in that Scotland and Wales are Nonconformist in favoring Presbyterianism or Methodism over the Church of England, whereas many in Northern Ireland are Catholic (Hechter, 1999, 318). But these areas are as a "periphery" to the English "center," zones of lagged economic development or even decline. This fuels the persistence of their sense of difference, their hope that they would have more freedom to develop those economic policies that are best for themselves, rather than have imposed what may work best only for England. The uneven development can be regarded as a kind of "internal colonialism," Hechter argues. Often voters in the fringe areas, as noted, will tend to vote more for Labour rather than a nationalist party to counter any Conservative ascendancy in the British Parliament.

Northern Ireland/Ulster

The population of Ireland once contained up to 10 percent Protestants alongside its 90 percent Roman Catholics, but many Protestants left Ireland due to violence in the years 1911 to 1916. Recent estimates hold that only 2.5

to 5 percent of the present-day Irish population is Protestant. It is clear why the some 70 percent Protestant population of Northern Ireland does not want their territory to become part of Ireland.

But one may just as readily understand why the just under 30 percent of Northern Ireland's population, which is Roman Catholic, could be restless. Catholics in Northern Ireland have long made plausible claims of discrimination in jobs, in housing, in representation (gerrymandered districts), and in excessive use of police violence against peaceable Catholic demonstrators (cf. Darby, 1995; Dunn, 1995; McGarry and O'Leary, 1995; Mallie, 2001; Taylor, 1999, 2001; Tonge, 2002). After years of violence, in 1995 the governments of Britain and Ireland reached an accord assuring majority rule in Northern Ireland, but with some voice for the Republic of Ireland in assuring the rights of the Catholics within Northern Ireland. In 1998 a power-sharing accord was worked out for the Irish Republican Army/Sinn Fein and the Protestants there, but implementation has been stalled by failure of the armed factions to turn over their arms, as the agreement requires.

Wales

In 1925, the Plaid Cymru or Party of Wales was established, but it never became a strong secessionist movement, in part because of the near-disappearance of the local Welsh language as most of the locals assimilated to English. From 1536 English monarchs did not outlaw use of Welsh, but the school system was to be in English, causing the language to die out. The Tony Blair Labour government accorded limited autonomy to a Welsh parliament (cf. Berresford, 1968; Davies, 1989; Sandberg, 1981).

Scotland

Although Gaelic also was to retreat in Scotland, there would be more life in the Scottish nationalist movement, headed up by the Scottish National Party, founded 1934. As earlier noted, the British government in an accommodative strategy has sought to placate the Scottish nationalists as well as the less active Welsh nationalists by creating regional parliaments, which are now in place in the named regions. But some Scottish nationalists want to go further, and among them is the well-known actor Sean Connery (cf. Brand, 1978; Finlay, 1994).

Basques

The Basque Land and Liberty movement has conducted a long insurrection against Spanish authority, costing some 800 lives from the early 1960s, resorting to terroristic violence as both local and national public opinion turned away from them, especially after Spain had devolved more central powers to regions (cf. Collins, 1990).

Lombardy

The Lombards or northernmost Italians live in a vigorous industrial area, which by most accounts gives more to the Italian state than it gets back. They resent Italian state subsidies to the economically lagging southern Italy. Chiefly centered in the Milan area, the Northern Alliance has demanded more regional autonomy, which the Italian state has granted. But there is some talk of possible independence.

Corsica

Many Corsicans aspired to independence as early as the eighteenth century, when patriots even asked the philosopher Jean-Jacques Rousseau to write up policy for them, which he did, even imagining his personal presentation there of his ideas like a classic lawgiver. His *Project for Corsica* envisaged a largely agrarian state, which would prevent growth of a large city by migration of the capital. But about that time, Corsica was passed from control of an Italian state to France, and a native Corsican, Napoleon Bonaparte, soon ruled France. Since the 1970s, several separatist groups turned to violence, sometimes against each other. Although the French parties of the right opposed it, a Socialist-Green coalition in late 2001 devolved considerable cultural autonomy, including schooling in the Corsican language, but Green fear of unchecked development held back wanted powers in that sphere.

East European Separatisms

In East Europe, separatism only seemed to exhaust itself in the falling apart of the Soviet Union (1991), Yugoslavia (1992), and with a lag, dissolution of Czecho-slovakia into the Czech Republic and the Slovak Republic (1993). Latvia, Estonia, Moldova, and Ukraine worry about loyalties of large russophone minorities left among them.

Slovakians and Romanians have wondered whether their Magyar (Hungarian) minorities would remain loyal, although it presently seems that these fears were exaggerated. As if in revenge for the Hungarian campaign against Slovensky after 1867, some Slovak politicians after 1993 wanted to stamp out Magyar street or village names, and so on. Slovakia's lag behind Hungary in economic development could cause some of their Magyars to think of the advantages of being Hungarian.

By the 1990s the Yugoslav economy was a disaster, with some 17 percent unemployment and a 400 percent inflation. Even so, the publics of both Slovenia and Croatia, which were the first to exit, wanted only more autonomy, not the independence sought by their leaders (Kaufman, 2001, 178, 201). What is left of Yugoslavia, just Serbia and Montenegro, may yet lose Montenegro, currently in reconsideration of the bond between the last two republics. By 2003 the republics had officially abolished the name Yugoslavia and what may be the world's only true confederation plans to reconsider its weak bond in a few years. Serbia could also lose its province of Kosovo, populated mostly by ethnic Albanians. If NATO intervened there in its 1999 bombing campaign to stop an ethnic cleansing by Serbians, NATO states do not seem to want to further "balkanize" the Balkans. In 2000 the electoral defeat and removal of Slobodon Milosevic, later on trial for war crimes in the Netherlands, at least offers hope that no more violence will happen.

Macedonia's Albanian Ethnic Minority

Macedonia also worries about loyalties of a sizable ethnic Albanian minority, perhaps 20 to 30 percent of the total population, some of whom took up arms in 2001. They seem to have been accommodated, however, with integration of the police, a fair share of power, and creation of an Albanian-language university where they are in high concentration.

Trans-Dniester Russophones

Moldova, whose population largely speaks Romanian, was divided into three factions upon independence from USSR. Many wanted merger with Romania. Others wanted simple independence. But there were also the trans-Dniester russophones, who would fear and fight merger with Romania and even be uncomfortable being dominated by Romanian speakers in independence. They were offended at moves to make Romanian the official language and have it be put into the Latin rather than Cyrillic alphabet. Although *ethnically* only about one-eighth to one-fourth Russian (the largest group are ethnic Ukrainians), the trans-Dniester population for the most part speak Russian, and they differ from most other Moldovans in not also knowing Romanian. The territory in question, however, does not touch Russia but is a long north-south sliver bordered by Ukraine to its east. When many Romanian speakers were contemplating merger with Romania, the russophones in question brandished arms to assert de facto independence from Moldova (cf. Kaufman, 2001, 129–60). In a yet unresolved state, the region is reputed to be rife with smuggling and other criminal activity, including arms sales to terrorists (*New York Times International*, March 5, 2002).

It is rather surprising that the Ukraine was after the Baltic states in leading the favor of secession, because after the Great Russians, the Ukrainians were best represented in top offices of the USSR Communist Party as well as the state structures (cf. Bialer, 1980; also, Laitin, 1998, 74). But they resented the secondary status of the Ukrainian language, even if close to Russian, with mutual intelligibility. Now that they are independent, some Ukrainians worry about possible separatism from their russophone minority, especially those concentrated in the Crimea to the south (where they have been locally diluted by returning Crimean Tatars) or in its northeast, as around Poltava. But there are also many russophones within Kyiv (to the russophones Kiev), where the author lecturing there in 2001 heard both Ukrainian and Russian in the streets or in locally available television programming. State policy has been broadly accommodative to its linguistic minorities, however.

Upon leaving the USSR, Georgia faced a small-scale civil war in 1991–1992 (some 200 died), which ousted the nationalist leader Zviad Gamsakhurdia, who eventually committed suicide when the successor regime of Eduard Shevardnadze cut a deal with Russia. Georgia also faced skirmishing with two secessionist non-Georgian linguistic groups.

South Ossetia

The first was going even before Gamsakhurdia's fall, involving the wish of the linguistically distinct South Ossetians to secede from Georgia in order to join Russia's region of co-ethnics in North Ossetia. But Russia has stated that it would oppose any violation of Georgia's territorial integrity. The Ossetian language is unlike Georgian, being related to Afghanistan's Pashtu. Before agreeing to a cease-fire, the South Ossetians had skirmished with little more than their hunting rifles.

Abkhazia

Another secessionist move in Georgia occurred in the Abkhazia region of its northwest, bordering the Black Sea. Focused about the city of Sukhumi, the Abkhazian capital, it is a sunny vacation area popular with Russians, and it grows grapes for wineries. Ethnic Abkhazians, the longest resident people of Georgia, are a mix of Orthodox Christian and Sunni Muslims. Stalin was a Georgian, and he had suppressed schooling in Abkhazian, and Abkhazians fear its loss. They were already reduced to a minority of the local population, as many ethnic Georgians and other ethnic groups had immigrated to their region. Some violence erupted as early as 1989, even before the collapse of the USSR, and more fighting occurred in 1992–1993, with many brutalities of Georgian troops against the local population. Abkhazians were covertly given military assistance by Boris Yeltsin, president of Russia, which eventually stationed "peacekeepers" there. Abkhazians had been offered under Gamsakhurdia a regional consociational regime offering them 43 percent of legislative seats when they were only 17.3 percent of the region's population. However, the Abkhazians later availed themselves of a kind of de facto secession as yet unresolved with Georgia. They felt threatened and strongly objected in 2002 when the United States sent military advisers meant to bolster the Georgian armed forces effort to oust al-Qaeda and Chechnyan Islamic rebels from another region bordering Chechnya. Abkhazians have stepped up their effort to secure some association with Russia (cf. Hewitt, 1998; Kaufman, 2001, 85–127).

Nagorno-Karabakh

Leaving behind the troubles of Georgia, Azerbaijan faces a de facto secession of the Armenian-populated mountain enclave of Nagorno-Karabakh, which is like the Trans-Dniester region of Moldova in its physical separation from any ethnically similar protector nation. A nonborder region secession is rare among secessionist cases. Most Azerbaijanese are Muslims, whereas the Armenians are largely Orthodox Christian and speak a distinctive language. Armenians previously living elsewhere in Azerbaijan often fled to the region for safety. Although violent incidents had occurred several years earlier, the Armenians of the region took up arms and fought from 1990 to 1994, and the dying reached some 20,000, with about a million persons forced from their homes. As in Yugoslavia, "ethnic cleansings" were common (Spencer, 1998, 22; also, Kaufman, 2001, 49–78). Although the region remains in a cease-fire mode, Nagorno-Karabakh remains in de facto secession.

Tartarstan

Within postcommunist Russia, Turkic-speaking, largely Muslim Tatarstan is a restless republic. The year after the collapse of the Soviet Union, in 1992 its local leaders arranged a referendum on a constitutional provision by which they declared themselves to be "independent" in the sense of international law, although choosing to retain a special association with the Russian Federation. Largely as a reaction to this, it appears, Vladimir Putin in 2000 secured passage of a law by which the Russian Federation president could remove from office any republic official who maintains laws inconsistent with the Russian Federation.

Chechnya

Russia yet faces considerable separatist sentiment in twice-battered Chechnya. During World War II, Stalin was so worried that ethnic minorities could collaborate with the Germans that he moved 3.3 million of them away from the front, often to life conditions of great hardship in colder places than they had known (some had only tents for shelters). One such people were the Chechens, a Sunni Muslim people of the northern Caucasian mountains. Some 400,000 Chechens were from 1944 to 1956 forced to live in Kazakhstan or Kirghizia. Cold, hungry, ridden with typhus from poor sanitation, up to a fourth of them died during the early years away from their homes. Stalin, who would himself die in 1953, even deprived children of schooling in their Chechen language, but he ultimately failed to assimilate them, as was true of the czars before him (Pohl, 1999, 1–2, 5, 79–86, 93–107). But the animosity of the Chechens later fed their separatism. In 1992 they declared their independence, and Boris Yeltsin sent in armed forces (1994–1996). The first phase of intervention killed perhaps 80,000 to 120,00 persons (Spencer, 1998, 22). After a series of bombings in Russia blamed on the Chechens, with more charges that crime syndicates were based there, Vladimir Putin ignored a previous accommodation and reinvaded the region (2001–2002), with unknown numbers of dead. The Chechens have not been pacified as I write, and much of the land has been devastated by the fighting. But intermediaries of the two leaders, Vladimir Putin and Aslan Maskhadov, were informally talking in 2002.

Sakha/Yakutia

There is at least some autonomist sentiment among the Yakut natives of Siberia. The latter are a Turkic language minority of herders and hunters separated from other Turkic peoples by a Mongol invasion. The czarist subjection of their region left many bitter (Okladnikov, 1970). Although Russia's Sakha Republic contains most Yakuts, they are concerned about losing their identity through an unplanned assimilation due to in-migration of Russians (cf. Jordan and Jordan-Bychkova, 1998).

Asian Separatisms

Turkish Cypriots

Only about 16 percent of the population, Turkish Cypriots had been placated from 1960 to 1974 with a consociational or power-sharing constitution, which was threatened in 1963 by Greek opposition, which led to some violence. But even consociationalism suddenly looked like inadequate protection for many Turkish Cypriots. Confronted by a threat by the Greek Cypriot majority to merge Cyprus with Greece, Turkish Cypriots in 1974 welcomed the protective invasion of the island by nearby Turkish forces, soon creating a Turkish Cypriot enclave of 36 percent of the land of Cyprus, far more than proportional to their population. The island has since continued its division without resolution of the conflict, even if the twin governments of Greek-Cypriots in the South and Turkish-Cypriots in the North have long begun cooperation on mutual interests, such as encouragement of tourism. Only Turkey accorded the northern government diplomatic recognition, however. Both groups are interested in joining the European Union, and that organization as well as the United Nations have attempted to mediate an accommodation. The sticking point is that the Greek-Cypriots would like a unitary or at least a federal government, whereas the Turkish-Cypriots speak of a loose confederation, which would be the only true confederation in the world, if that of Serbia and Montenegro fails. By definition, in a confederation any central government is wholly the creature of the states or provinces, as in the United States before 1789 or in Switzerland before 1848 (cf. Borowiec, 2000; Joseph, 1997; Theophylactou, 1995).

The Kurds

The larger, Asian part of Turkey has had a long secessionist movement among the Kurds, who also have been restless in northern Iraq, and smaller numbers live in Iran and Syria as well. The Kurds in Iraq rebelled near the end of the Gulf War, and Saddam Hussein used up to 280 poison gas (mustard gas plus a combination of nerve gases) attacks on them, at one point brutally killing nearly everyone in a village, including noncombatant women and children (Middle East Watch, 1993). Although the Kurds of Iran have also experienced periods of repression, I focus here on the Turkish Kurds.

As the Ottoman Empire disintegrated after being on the losing side in World War I, Mustafa Kemal, also called Ataturk (d. 1938), strove to protect a Turkish heartland, and he had allied with the Kurds to prevent secession of Armenia and to support a population exchange with Greece, shipping out Greek Orthodox religionists and receiving from Greece their Muslim population. But by 1924 he had secularized his regime and abolished the religious office of the Caliphate, which offended some Kurds, who were, like the Turks, mostly Sunni Muslims. With a series of rebellions in the region, Ataturk decided to aggressively assimilate the population, as elaborated in chapter 3 (cf. Barkley and Fuller, 1998). This led to a reactive secessionist movement of the Kurdish Workers Party, which retains some viability even now, notwithstanding capture abroad and imprisonment in Turkey of its principal leader, Abdullah-Ocalan, who now claims Turkey's Kurds will henceforth ask only autonomy.

Bangladesh

Largely speaking Bengali, unlike the languages of West Pakistan, East Pakistanis formed the Awami League to protest national parliamentary dominance by West Pakistan. Bengalis complained that their region lagged in growth because they gave too much and got too little from West Pakistan. Both sides talked as if expecting an accommodation. When the government sought to prevent the convening of the Awami League, and when the Pakistani military suddenly began to gun down Bengali demonstrators, the League moved for independence in 1971. In the ensuing violence, up to 10 million Bengalis may have died, with perhaps 13 million more, especially Hindu Bengalis, forced into exile in neighboring India. These factors, plus a convenient opportunity to divide an enemy regarding Kashmir, led India to send in its army to aid the native Bengali rebels, the Mukti Bahini. This enabled the Bengalis to make good their secession from Pakistan. The new nation of Bangladesh acceded to India's request that they take back the refugees (cf. Chadda, 1997, 84–97). Given the scale of dying as well as continued inability of Bangladesh to create a sound economy, one is reminded of Metta Spencer's view that often the costs of secession are so high in the way of dying, economic disruption, and interpersonal frictions that one may often question its wisdom (Spencer, 1998, esp. 22–24).

Pakistan has since also feared a possible secessionist movement among its Pathan or Pashtu-speaking tribe, who feel a kinship with co-ethnics in southeastern Afghanistan. Many of these resented Pakistan's turn against the Pashtu-dominated Taliban to aid the United States–led invasion of 2001–2002.

The Sikhs of India

Neither Muslim nor Hindu but influenced by both, the Sikh religion dates from its founder Guru Nanak (d. 1538) and became central to a minority of the population of preindependence Punjab. But most had to flee their lands to avoid death at the hands of Muslims in West Punjab in 1947–1948, largely settling into East Punjab, which in the partition became part of India. Although many Sikhs were active within the Congress Party of India, others joined the Akali Dal, which advocated independence as "Sikhistan." While that was not to be, tensions rose on many issues: Hindu immigrations to Punjab at the northern tip of India, the Hindu preference for inheritance laws with more equality for women, characteristic Sikh contempt for Hinduism's high castes (*varnas*), and division of irrigation waters. The green revolution brought prosperity to Sikh wheatlands, but it also boosted their need for irrigation water, which they claimed was unfairly diverted by new canal construction to the neighboring Hindu state, Haryana. Sikhs now wanted independence under the new name, after Khalsa or Sikh brotherhood, "Khalistan." In the 1980s shootings began, and some weapons were stashed in the Sikh's Golden Temple at Amritsar. Indira Gandhi, calling it Operation Bluestar, ordered the temple invaded in 1984. Among the many dead (700 soldiers but perhaps up to 3,000 civilians) was an extremist Sikh leader, Sant Bhindranwale, who had espoused more violence than had been accepted by the Akali Dal. In revenge for the temple invasion, two trusted Sikh members of her bodyguard assassinated Indira Gandhi. Many Sikhs outside of the Punjab, working in jobs such as India's military or as transport workers, were then murdered by angry Hindu mobs. They could readily identify Sikh men by their turbans or common use of the last name Singh. This communal revenge may have killed over 4,000 Sikhs. A 1966 partition had reduced Punjab (too much so, some Sikhs thought, coveting Chandigarh and two other border areas) such that it came to have a Sikh majority of about 60 percent. But Punjab Sikhs themselves are divided on the advisability of secession (Chadda, 1997, 49–60, 123–40).

The Tibetans of China

Once China had recovered from its divisions and military occupations, in 1951 it sought to reassert its prior dominance over Taiwan and Tibet. The American fleet blocked recovery of Taiwan, which remains in de facto secession to this day, with many Taiwanese favoring a risky declaration of independence (cf. Cheong, 2001; Copper, 1990; Lee, 1991). But China did reenter Tibet in 1951. It later also repressed a 1959 rebellion, which led to the exile of the Dalai Lama. China may have killed up to a million Tibetans (Donnet, 1994; Spencer, 1998, 30). As earlier noted, the Dalai Lama has been distrusted by the Chinese government, which argues that although he speaks for autonomy for Tibetans, he really aims at secession. While in the past the Chinese governing officials permitted or encouraged closure of many Buddhist temples, as elsewhere in China the government has encouraged preservation and rehabilitation of some of the larger places as tourist attractions, as I observed when traveling through central China in 1991. Some places destroyed during the Great Proletarian Cultural Revolution are even being rebuilt. China does not permit return of the Dalai Lama to it, but the Potala palace in Lhasa is now valued as a tourist draw. If the prior governor of the province militantly tried to suppress Buddhism among party and government elites, the most recent governor, Go Jinlong, has only noted that atheism is expected of Communist Party members, and it goes without saying that few public posts go to those who are not party members. The government disputes claims that China is attempting to saturate the local population with Han Chinese immigrants, and the governor of the province recently asserted that of the 2.6 million people there, 93 percent are ethnic Tibetans. Tibetan nationalist critics retort that such figures ignore large numbers of undocumented Han immigrants in the cities as well as the large Han dominance in the military presence within the province (*The New York Times International*, Nov. 7, 2001). Nevertheless, China has announced a major push to bring in more investment capital to help the region escape its relative backwardness, announcing a wish to bring Tibet up to the national level of per capita income by the year 2012. But often incidental to such development plans is enticement of more Han Chinese into the region to provide needed technical skills. By one independent account, the Chinese outnumber Tibetans two or three to one in the cities and fertile valleys, but Tibetans remain most numerous elsewhere (Spencer, 1998, 30).

The Uighurs of Xianjiang Province, China

China has some 35 to 40 million Muslims among its 1.6 billion people. There are some concentrations of Muslims, such as the smaller Hui group of Ningxia province and the much larger Uighur people of Xianjiang province. Most natives of Xianjiang speak either Turkic or Mongolian dialects, rather than Chinese. The Uighurs have been restless in recent years, often perhaps due to increasing cross-border communications of Islamic militancy. They had long resented the Han Chinese for using their province as a nuclear test site. Located just north of Tibet, the nominally "autonomous" province is a kind of "wild west" of China, an often arid area of livestock herding. Although the Uighurs, descendants of the Mongols, are not Islamic fundamentalists, they resent restrictions on religious proselytization in their home area, as well as prohibition of anyone joining a mosque (or any other religion) prior to age eighteen. Economic hardships such as recent droughts have added to discontents. China has not assuaged grievances by its very harsh repressions of any Uighur separatists it may identify. China often executes captured and convicted rebels.

The Moros of the Philippines

Toward the southwestern margins of several main islands in the Philippines, the Moro liberation struggle is one of Filipino Muslims who believe they are discriminated against among the predominantly Roman Catholic population of the country. Economic destitution dominates the principal places of insurrection. Guerrilla insurrection in scattered bands has been going hot and cold for decades. Even when a cease-fire is negotiated with one band, it may not be binding on other bands. Lately some of the holdouts have turned to kidnappings, whether as shields against air attacks or as means of securing ransoms. Primarily with an eye to destroying the 60-member Abu Sayyaf kidnapping gang, officially recognized by the United States as terrorists, the United States has recently sent the Philippine state military advisers and some $100 million of military assistance, including 30,000 machine guns. American strategic planners worry that a kind of archipelago of terrorist bases may arise across the Afro-Asian land masses, comparable to the al-Qaeda band in Afghanistan. But critics suggest that misguided military interventions at many sites may only encourage what American planners fear.

East Timor

When the Portuguese withdrew from Timor, in 1975 the Indonesian army invaded the small territory populated largely by Roman Catholics, unlike the predominantly Muslim population of Indonesia. Indonesia ruled the population of some 800,000 so repressively that a guerrilla rising broke out, making the occupation even more murderous. As the world turned against Indonesia on the issue, the Indonesian army finally withdrew and left interim administration to the United Nations. In an August 1999 referendum, the East Timorese voted massively for independence. In 2002 elections were held, and East Timor became the world's newest nation-state.

Aceh Province, Indonesia

The national motto of Indonesia, "Unity through Diversity," has not prevented autonomist or separatist movements of locally distinctive population groups. At the northern tip of the Indonesian island of Sumatra is Aceh Province, a region populated by people who have long prided themselves on an especially pure Islam, relative to the allegedly more corrupted Islam that dominates Java and most other regions of Indonesia except for largely Hindu Bali. The Aceh provincials were dubious about joining the new nation of Indonesia when it first became independent from the Dutch. The separatist sentiment continued to exist through the often economically troubled years of the leaderships of Sukarno (declared independence 1945, formally governed 1947–1965) and his successor, Suharto (ruled 1965 to 1999). When the central government began a policy of dispersal of the overpopulation of Java, sending large waves of migrants into Sumatra in general and Aceh Province in particular, which now holds about 4 million people, it encouraged an armed resistance from the local population, which continues to this day. The discovery of oil in the region added to the sense that secession was an economically feasible option, because Aceh accounts for about a fifth of Indonesia's oil and gas exports. But rebels assert that the foreign oil companies secretly help the Indonesian government repress their rising. In 2002 the Indonesian government and Aceh rebels were at least talking in Geneva and Stockholm, but the talks broke off in spring 2003.

In passing, some Papuans on Indonesia's western half of New Guinea, now called Irian Jaya, also dream of their independence from Indonesia.

The Tamils of Sri Lanka

The Tamils of India's Tamil Nadu state have wanted more autonomy, but their co-ethnics in Sri Lanka have waged a campaign for nearly twenty years for secession. The Tamil secessionists are strongest in the Jaffna region of the northern tip of Sri Lanka (formerly Ceylon, which had been colonially governed by the Portuguese, Dutch, and British in succession). Unlike the majority Sinhalese, who are largely Buddhists, the Tamils are largely Hindu, and they speak a distinctive language. When Ceylon was becoming independent in 1948, the Tamils, who had immigrated many generations before, asked for a power-sharing allowing themselves and other ethnic minorities half the seats in Parliament. The Sinhalese refused the requested accommodation and ignored a constitutional provision not to act against a minority interest in their 1948–1949 move to deny citizenship to many Tamils. They wanted to deport to India the Tamil laborers on the tea plantations in the southern part of the island nation, the "estate Tamils" who had been coming in from the nineteenth century (in a compromise with India, only some of these were repatriated to India). Tamils were further angered when the Sinhalese in 1956 declared their own language the sole "official" one, even if in 1978 they allowed that Tamil was also a "national" language. The Sinhalese also favored their own over the Tamils in weighting student test scores. During the later British colonization, the earliest immigrant Tamils had proven themselves culturally superior, more able to win administrative and professional careers (Horowitz, 1985; Taras and Ganguly, 2002, 209 n. 129). Sinhalese promises of more autonomy for the Tamils were insincere. By 1983 the Tamils, calling for their Tamil homeland (Tamil Ealam) and warring under the rubric of Tamil Tigers, began their struggle for secession. With the consent of Sri Lanka's government, India sent a military force to the region (1987–1991), intending to at once protect the Tamils but also prevent their secession, because that could stimulate separatism in India's Tamil Nadu state. But the Tamil Tigers refused to disarm. No initiative was able to stop a conflict that has continued since, although in cease-fire mode as I write. It is believed the Tamil Tigers were involved in the 1991 suicide bomb assassination of India's prime minister, Rajiv Gandhi. So far this conflict has killed some 27,000 combatants and 25,000 civilians (Taras and Ganguly, 2002, 182–208; cf. also Chadda, 1997, 145–74). A ray of hope arose in 2002 when a fifth cease-fire seemed to hold, unlike the previous four. Also, the main leader of the Tamil Tigers, Velupillai Prabhakaran, gave one of his very rare news conferences within rebel-held territory and said he could be receptive to talks. Sri Lanka is expected to offer them more autonomy.

Belief that their own nation has been insufficiently supportive of Tamil co-ethnics of Sri Lanka has generated anger among residents of India's Tamil Nadu state. India also has had some separatist sentiment among its northeastern hill tribes of Assam state as well as in Kashmir, a case examined at some length in chapter 7. The largely Christian (mostly Baptists) Nagas rebelled after British exit from India, but after a decade of military reverses they turned by the mid-1960s to accommodation with the government of India, which allowed more autonomy for Nagaland. Yet more skirmishing occurred from 1988 to 1992 (Bartkus, 1999, 52, 55–62).

African Separatisms

In civil wars, it is normally the weaker faction that most needs to look abroad for an ally. In cases of secessionist civil war, the seceding ethnic group most readily attaches to an irredentist state of the same ethnicity, but sometimes finds an ally in another kind of state that happens to at least partially share its goals, as when the East Pakistani Bengalis were supported by India in 1971 in becoming Bangladesh.

Africa has in the past weathered several secessionist efforts that failed.

Katanga

Moise Tshombe, principally backed by the Lunda tribal grouping, the white settlers in the province, the then white-dominated governments in southern Africa, and certain foreign mining firms, attempted during 1960–1962 to separate Katanga province from the newly independent Congo. Tshombe used rhetoric of anticommunism and sympathy for Christianity to court foreign support, but most states suspected a neoimperial conspiracy to control the richest mining region and backed United Nations forces, which suppressed the secession. Although a few other states did offer moral or material support, none extended diplomatic recognition to Katanga (cf. Saideman, 2001, 36–69).

Biafra

A far bloodier suppression involved the Ibo-Ibibio leadership of a secession from Nigeria as Biafra, a region poor in soils but rich in oil reserves and in the skills of its educationally advanced Ibo-Ibibio elite. Nearly two thirds of the population of Biafra were of that tribal grouping, but 90 percent of the whole population there was Christian, and the secessionists emphasized their shared religious tie, especially against the Islamic Hausa-Fulani on the opposed side. Yet the military leader of Nigeria, Yakubu Gowon, was also Christian if not Ibo (Saideman, 2001, 72). Only five other nations accorded diplomatic recognition to Biafra. The attempted exit was militarily repressed (1967–1970).

Other secessionist warring has occurred in Chad, in interior Morocco (Polisarios), and in Ethiopia's Ogaden (Somali tribesmen) in the horn of Africa. But other than Biafra, two of the bloodiest secessionist struggles have occurred in Eritrea and southern Sudan.

Eritrea

I have recurrently urged the view that ethnic minority policy choice by one group can shape the reactive choices of another. Sometimes an accommodation can degenerate into an aggressive assimilationism. Eritrea had been an Italian colony from 1890 to 1940, and the Eritreans developed some sense of their unity despite being about half Muslim and half Christian, and of nine distinctive ethnic groups. They had expected to become independent after a period of UN-granted trusteeship to Ethiopia, with assurances of autonomy in the interim. But during the period 1951 to 1956, Emperor Haile Selassie stripped away that autonomy.

When the emperor fell from power in 1974 and Ethiopia entered a phase of revolutionary turbulence, the Eritreans saw their chance to reassert their wish for separation, even if internally divided until 1981. The Ethiopian revolutionary regime of Mengistu Mariam continued the effort to quash the insurrection until the dictator himself fell from power when he lost crucial outside assistance due to the 1991 collapse of the Soviet Union.

Eritreans share their distinctive language only with the also restless Tigrayan province of northern Ethiopia. Although most Ethiopians are Coptic Christians, the Eritreans have a mix of Muslims and Christians, but both groups favored exit. Unless the beneficiary of total state collapse, as in the fall of Ottoman Turkey, Austro-Hungary, the Soviet Union, or Yugoslavia, it is rare for a relatively small ethnicity to succeed in secession without outside help, and Eritrea did get some. Eritrea holds some 4 million people compared to the rest of Ethiopia's some 60 million. But the rebels received some arms and monetary aid from Islamic states, and they fought their way to independence by allying themselves with Tigrayan and Oromo rebels against the Addis Ababa government, which fell to a sympathetic Tigrayan commander, Meles, who was able to seize power in Addis Ababa. In the overall violence, by press reports some 60,000 Eritrean guerrillas and 40,000 civilians died before the war sputtered to its end in 1991. One account estimates the dead at far more, close to a half million (Bartkus, 1999, 51).

Two years later, in 1993, a referendum in Eritrea opted for independence, and Ethiopia acquiesced in the exit of the province. But Eritrea claimed that

Ethiopia yet occupied some of its land. A boundary war occurred (1998–2000), which cost the lives of some 80,000 more soldiers and civilians, ending with Ethiopia prevailing (cf. Taras and Ranguly, 2002, 215–16).

Although there were also separatist tendencies within what remained of Ethiopia, it weakly held together by an ethnic power-sharing in the national assembly, under a one-party dominant system opposed by regionally based parties.

The Southern Sudanese

Another long and nasty conflict has pitted the largely Muslim population of northern Sudan (which controls the capital, Khartoum) against the majority black African population of the south. These consist of at least eleven distinctive peoples who are largely either Christian or animist and do not want the Islamic law imposed on them, as Khartoum sought to do from 1983, undoing an agreement not to do so, which had helped stop fighting in 1972. Among other demands, southerners had wanted English to be accorded official status alongside Arabic (not granted, but English was acknowledged as the principal administrative language of the south). They also would prefer the accommodations of a federal political structure and separate army in the south, both of which to northerners threaten secession (Bartkus, 1999, 22, 28, 133–42).

As in other scenes of guerilla warfare, often the Sudanese government is able to control the cities but the rebels dominate the countryside, especially by night. In one of the uglier aspects of the conflict, sometimes young southern blacks are captured and are sold as slaves to buyers farther north. Nearly 18 years of warring produced some 2 million dead and made homeless about 4.5 million.

By 1998 it became apparent that neither side could win, and with a ceasefire in one region, there was hope that a peaceful accommodation could be made in 2002.[1]

Angola's UNITA

Since Angola became independent from Portugal in 1975, one tribal grouping, the Mbundu, became dominant in the capital city. Jonas Savimbi led another people, the Ovimbundu, under an organization called National Union for the Total Independence of Angola (UNITA). During the Cold War, Savimbi enjoyed support from the former apartheid regime of South Africa (even a contingent of troops to counter Castro's supply of Cuban armed forces to the Luanda government) and from the United States CIA, because their leaders then leaned vaguely "Afro-communist" (Neto later warmed to Western capital investment in Angola's oil industry). With the collapse of the Soviet Union in 1991 and the collapse of the apartheid regime soon after, Savimbi's rebel movement no longer had crucial outside support. His movement degenerated into a de facto separatist effort in his region, until he was killed by Angolan armed forces in 2002. Surviving UNITA fighters quickly gave up the fight. They had caused some 36 years of destructive civil warring, which had killed about a half million Angolans and forced some 4 million from their homes. Some worry that remnants of UNITA soldiers may become local gang leaders.

In Africa, a kind of "warlordism" is becoming common when a local military leader assumes de facto control over some natural resource, such as diamonds or timber, snubbing his nose at central authority (Reno, 1998). But most true secessionist movements are more distinctively ethnonationally based, often linked to economic discontents. Per capita incomes are low in much of sub-Saharan Africa apart from South Africa. Per capita income correlates with happiness, increasing up to a plateau as per capita income rises. Most Africans are by subjective estimates highly unhappy, and the plateau is irrelevant to most (Graham and Pettinato, 2002; Veenhoven, 1984).

Economic suffering is widespread, made even worse by the HIV/AIDS epidemic in Africa, and it requires a high local concentration of a fairly large ethnicity, usually near a border, to make secession an attractive enterprise. Thus Donald Horowitz notes that Tanzania has 120 distinctive ethnic groups. This constitutes an ethnically dispersed as opposed to an ethnically concentrated society. In this case no ethnic group is big enough to break out if opposed by a coalition of many small ethnicities (Horowitz, 1985, 37–41). Notwithstanding other secessionist conflicts such as in northern Chad (boosted by Libya's Kadafi in the 1970s) and interior Morocco (the Polisarios), Africa has so far contained what would be potentially many secessionist strivings.

The potential problem is evident if one were to make a transparency of a map of Africa's tribal boundaries and put it over a map showing state boundaries. A map of African tribal boundaries can be found in Demko, Jerome, and Boe, 1992.

One is not surprised to learn that the Minorities at Risk Project identifies sub-Saharan Africa as the world region of highest percentage population at risk, 35.7 percent (Gurr, 2000, 12). It is also readily apparent why the existing states of Africa through the Organization of African Unity (OAU) have taken a strong stand in favor of preservation of the boundaries of all states as they existed at the moment of independence. Eritrea aside, secessionist efforts in Africa have been contained or successfully suppressed. But there will be many more of such efforts.

It has been argued by Viva Bartkus that a secessionist effort is predictable by linking a pair of cost-benefit calculations of a people. On the one side are the benefits of staying within the existing nation, as reduced by the costs of staying in. On the other side are the expected benefits of getting out as trimmed by expectable costs, whether in the course of leaving or later. Also, a dynamic analysis must consider all costs and benefits as variables, not constants. Thus Bartkus plausibly argues that the development of effective regional security communities or economic communities such as the European Union, along with the globalization of free trade, are reducing the benefits of being in big states, which are losing their capacity to make independent military or economic policy. That could make secession less costly (Bartkus, 1999, 167–201, 222).

Perhaps it could often reduce opposition to a secession as well. Note that in the past the politically dominant could avoid costly accommodations by the nearly costless threat of coercion, if it caused would-be secessionists to desist. But the paradox is that if deterrence fails, the resulting civil war can be extremely costly for both sides.

Bartkus concedes that a cost-benefit analysis must be an "as if" kind of analysis. Even if one were certain as to what consequences would occur, clearly not all consequences are measurable, let alone commensurable, say, by reducing them to monetary credits or debits. Also, it may be difficult to anticipate external actors as relevant to the feasibility of a secession. As Donald Horowitz wisely notes, "Whether and when a secessionist movement will emerge is determined mainly by domestic politics, by the relations of groups and regions within the state. Whether a secessionist movement will achieve its aims, however, is determined largely by international politics, by the balance of interests and forces that extend beyond the state" (Horowitz, 1985, 230).

There is as yet no theory that is highly predictive of foreign interventions. In the past many have speculated that states which are themselves vulnerable to secession are least likely to intervene in favor of secession in another state, often rather favoring suppression of a secessionist effort. The basis for the prediction is that favoring a secession elsewhere could justify one at home. However, Stephen Saideman's study of the cases of Katanga, Biafra, and Yugoslavia has concluded that in fact internally divided states are more likely to intervene. Alternative theory regarding relative powers of states is inconclusive, although more powerful states do tend to intervene more often, but their power position does not of itself predict which side is taken. Prior animosity with the other state, especially if a neighbor, is also somewhat predictive of intervention. But whenever relevant, the best predictor of a state's intervention in another state's secession is having in their own political community a significant presence of a relevant ethnicity, especially if that ethnicity is also an important part of the home-governing coalition. Thus if a state is largely Islamic, it would be more likely to oppose a secession of a non-Islamic region from another state with many Muslims (e.g., Biafra from Nigeria), and more likely to favor a secession of a relatively Islamic region from a primarily Christian state (e.g., Eritrea from Ethiopia). In other words, in accord with the pluralist school of international relations, domestic political pressures can significantly influence this aspect of a state's foreign policy (Saideman, 2001).

Not expecting in this an exact science, I offer a summary list of rather common predictors of secessionist attempts. A secession is more likely if:

1. a group comes to think of itself as a *distinctive "nation,"* whether by some shared civic identity or more often by ethnic identity, especially when a number of attributes are mutually reinforcing, such as sharing not only language but also religion, race, and so on;

2. the group is *geographically concentrated* or compactly settled, such that a line can be drawn on a map to demarcate where they are (a residentially dispersed minority such as African Americans usually fails to get any traction with a secessionist movement);

3. the concentration is *along a boundary of the existing nation-state* (with the prominent exception of the Armenian enclave within Azerbaijan, Nagorno-Karabakh);

4. the group *expects to be economically better off by exiting,* because it sees itself as unjustly disadvantaged in an economic way, less often because it is a more advanced region and feels held back than in the more common case of the region lagging behind the rest of the country;

5. the group also *sees itself as politically disadvantaged,* often underrepresented in political and administrative posts, and in no position to block the policies they do not want, let alone carry those they would prefer;

6. they *foresee no future corrective to their political weakness within the existing political community,* whether by a devolution of more powers to their region of concentration or by power sharing at the center;

7. they *expect no difficulties in implementing secession,* often because they expect to be allowed to leave in peace (sometimes mistakenly so, as was true of the South before the U.S. Civil War), or because they think the other side would quickly lose the will to continue civil war (often also mistaken, as the Eritreans, Tamils, or south Sudanese would know), or because they think another nation, perhaps irredentist, will come to their aid (Katanga got very little support); and

8. they *see future economic viability and military defensibility* if they secede, perhaps expecting restored commerce with the original nation, or their merger with an irredentist state, or an effective use of alliances.

A Closing Note on Secessions. A review of all wars fought in 1996 alone found that of these 40 wars, defined as violence taking the lives of at least 1,000 persons, 29 involved conflict between ethnic groups. Further, of the 40 wars, 16 were wars of secession, and every one of these was also a conflict of distinctive ethnic groups (Spencer, 1998, 18). In contrast, it is difficult to identify many internal wars that are primarily just on class lines, although a current Maoist peasant rebellion in Nepal may count as one. I have broadly used *ethnic* to compass identities of race, religion, language or cultural group. Many thinkers of the eighteenth and nineteenth centuries mistakenly believed that ethnic identities in politics would soon recede, either yielding to modern *individualism* or at most to group identities of personal economic function (the liberal theory) or would at least differentiate themselves to match *class* identities (as Marxists believed). Thus Joseph Rothschild has written of liberalism and Marxism:

The former has classically insisted that the basic problem of politics lies in the relationship of the autonomous individual to the state, and it rejects the notion that groups (other than purely voluntary associations) have corporate moral and legal rights. Indeed, since ethnic groups usually claim their members by ascriptive obligation rather than allow them a free choice, they are perceived by Liberals as quite menacing. Marxists, in turn, have long articulated a principled preference for analyzing society in terms of class interests and solidarities, and they continue to suspect ethnic allegiances as likely after all to turn reactionary, with their current leftward tilt in Europe proving ephemeral. (Rothschild, 1981, 24)

Once a secession has happened and been accepted as irreversible, then a whole new set of issues arise requiring accommodations of the now separated states. Most of these concern issues of fairness or justice in allocations of burdens and benefits, or what game theoreticians call "impure coordination problems," where both sides want to come to an agreement but have different preferences regarding desirable content. In addition to settling details on any border between them, how should they divide the benefits of some central treasury, foreign exchange, or military equipment? How should they divide such burdens as domestic and international public debt, any public pension obligations, any needed environmental cleanup, or the like? (Bookman, 1998).

Both those who would secede and those who would repress them may display similar fears behind their course of action: The seceding group often fears diminished physical security, economic life chances, or status unless they leave. Those who attempt to repress them may fear the same, that their reduced political community would not be militarily or economically viable or would suffer diminished world respect. The tragedy is that too often both sides, in experiencing sometimes protracted and destructive civil warring, bring on themselves the losses they set out to prevent.

NOTE

1. Nicholas Kristof, "The Bloodiest War," *New York Times International*, April 19, 2002, A-27.

CHAPTER 3

Assimilations as Controls: Strategies of the Stronger Ethnic Group

> We are frankly nationalists . . . and nationalism is our only factor of cohesion. In the face of a Turkish majority other elements have no kind of influence. We must Turkify the inhabitants of our land at any price, and we will annihilate those who oppose the Turks.
> —Ismet Inonu, prime minister of Turkey in 1925

Turkey began the last century in a series of moves against its ethnic minorities. The ethnically dominant Turks had genocidally destroyed many of their Armenian residents (some killing in 1894 and in 1909, but the main slaughter or death by hardships of about a million or more occurred 1914–18). Next, after territorially expansive moves of the Greeks in Thrace and the Smyrna area at the end of World War I, the new Turkish state warred with Greece in 1921–1922, and by the terms of the 1923 Treaty of Lausanne, they deported all of their Greek Orthodox while Greece exchanged their Muslims. In the next act, Inonu is speaking of the need to forcibly assimilate the Kurds of Turkey.

I. PLANNED OR UNPLANNED ASSIMILATIONS

There is a long history of that kind of aggressively assimilationist thought, which demands cultural uniformity and takes pains to create it, usually with an eye to improved (more efficient, more effective) social control. It does not matter if those who are to be standardized would like to be different. They are not even asked.

One may sympathize with a mildly assimilationist policy that merely smooths the integration of, say, new immigrants, if only because its success could curb sharp turns of voters toward the xenophobic right-wing parties, as witnessed in 2001–2002 in Austria, France, and the Netherlands. But an immoderately assimilationist policy merely replaces the specter of the segregationist's genocide with what some have called "ethnocide," the extinction of a cultural difference. When this is the intent, aggressive assimilators may sometimes even prohibit use of the name the target group gives to itself. Stop being different! Be like us!

To assimilate is to "make similar," which is in obvious contrast with the strategies of segregations discussed in chapter 1.

One thing common to assimilation as a strategy, whether chosen by the dominant (the often nonequalizing, nonconsensual form) or rather by the dominated (more equalizing, voluntary), is the denial that one deals with a fundamentally different human nature, at least for those who are the target of assimilation. There is no need for the common segregationist notion that targeted human groups are biogenetically almost a distinctive and inferior animal species. If ought implies can, there is here the assumption that the target group both can and ought to become like the majority group in certain key respects.

One could in principle unify a people either by accenting selective differences and related interdependency or else by such concentration on similarities and uniformity. Perhaps it need not be dichotomous. As the French sociologist Emile Durkheim knew, either differences or similarities can tend to make people feel solidaristic if in their contents they seem to imply complementary rather than antagonistic goals.

Often a dominant group—perhaps more often a class than an ethnic category—will claim that encouragement of differences, especially in the division of labor, tends to unify a society to the extent that each group becomes more dependent on the others. That sort of argument can be found in Plato's *Republic*, at least where he speaks of unifying his three classes, and it was to be repeated by Emile Durkheim in his concept of "organically" integrated society (Durkheim, 1933). Critics, usually further left, have argued that the division of labor rather divides us into asymmetrically exploitive categories (Beamish, 1992; Rattansi, 1982).

But as already apparent, another view holds that making groups *similar* is also unifying. Even Plato in his *Republic* held that view in some respects, as in wanting to promote broad similarities among his guardian strata, on the one hand, and among his trades stratum, on the other. In the paragraph that follows, Plato is talking about unifying his guardians in part by abolishing private property and families among them:

If, insofar as possible, a way has been devised to make common somehow the things that are by nature private, such as the eyes and the ears and the hands, so that they seem to see and hear and act in common; if, again, everyone praises and blames in unison, as much as possible delighting in the same things and feeling pain at the same things, if with all their might they delight in laws that aim at making the city come as close as possible to unity—then no one will ever set down a more correct or better definition than this of what constitutes the extreme as regards virtue. (*The Laws*, 739c–d; Pangle, trans.)

Is it virtue or rather tyranny to aim at such extreme unity? Yet Plato's ruler-guardians and auxiliary guardians would otherwise be largely segregated by residence, mating and lifestyles from the much larger trades stratum. But in the second best regime of his *Laws*, Plato accents assimilation of all of the citizens of his 5,040 landowning households, permitting all of them to have property and family. Durkheim, in the book just cited, calls such unification by assimilation rather than differentiation a "mechanical" similarity. It is this kind of unification that is addressed below.

Some processes of assimilation are unplanned by anyone. One case in point would be any assimilation by intermarriage of distinctive races, which some say would in the long run make skin colors no longer a badge of difference. Although some, such as Alexander the Great, may have sought to unify his empire through intermarriages, I know of no one who had a self-conscious plan to eradicate differences of skin color. Most ardent assimilationists have focused on making their subjects similar only in religion, political ideology, language, mode of dress, and so on.

Certainly some migrations and interminglings of population will tend to assimilate, as in the surely overstated theory of the "melting pot" of American immigrations.

De Tocqueville argued that the progress of democratization would tend to assimilate members of any society, both in some favorable ways and some deplorable ones, such as a kind of tyranny of public opinion, which John Stuart Mill also feared.

But from the nineteenth century to our time, others have argued that not some political development but economic development is the main engine of unplanned assimilation, as when globalization of market economies allegedly sweeps away many distinctive features of local cultures. The globalization of media, including the music and movies of the wealthier linguistic groups of the world, surely brings some assimilative tendencies. Not all agree, however. Benjamin Barber and Samuel Huntington have argued that any economic homogenization often encourages reactive resistances, sometimes taking militantly political forms such as anticolonial or secessionist struggles or even the spirit of holy war (Barber, 1995; Huntington, 1996). Also, to the extent that economic development passes by large groups, they are not made more similar to those enjoying development. On the contrary, they become more different, especially in being mired in low subjective happiness while those enjoying economic growth will show higher subjective happiness, at least to a plateau where the rise of expectations surpasses any real growth of individual capacities (Graham and Pettinato, 2002; Veenhoven, 1984).

However, aside from some anomalous outliers such as the United States, we do know that economic development does assimilate in the sense of making people more secular, less religious by such measures as the percentage who describe religious belief as "very important" to them (Wald, 1987, 1–2).

Leaving aside spontaneous processes of assimilation, this chapter next focuses on self-consciously chosen assimilation when guided by a dominant ethnic group.

Let us distinguish the policy as favored by the dominant from assimilation as favored sometimes by the weaker group, because the purposes are not identical. This chapter discusses only the first form, where at least in its collective form the purpose is to deal with a "problem" of control, often of possible crime or rebellion by the dominated. This seems to have been the aim when Spain's dictator Francisco Franco sought to exterminate the Catalan language, when Stalin sought to expunge Abkhazian or Chechen, or when governments of Turkey have sought to get rid of the Kurdish language. In some linguistic assimilations, the aim may be no more than administrative convenience or reduced costs, as when in the nineteenth century the anglophones who dominated Canada forced the francophones to use English in administrative procedures, even within Quebec. The well-being of the target group may often be loudly announced by the dominant ethnicity, but the sincerity of that aim is dubious, especially if the dominant group demands that the weaker ethnic group must surrender its identity, its pride in being distinct or different.

The sure mark of the kind of assimilation addressed here is that it does *not* intend to grant full equality to the weaker ethnics who are the targets of the assimilation. It is at best just a strategy of control, and at its worst, it can aim at cultural annihilation of the weaker group.

The dominant ethnic group's planned assimilation may have a limited target, sometimes coexisting with some continued segregation toward those beyond it. Thus during British rule in India, the rulers were pleased to have some of their subjects learn English and typically English contents of higher education. They would invite them to write civil service exams, but perversely force them to the great expense of traveling all the way to London to do so. But even those who excelled in the exams would find their careers bounded by a glass ceiling, because top administrative jobs back in India were reserved for the British (Kincaid, 1971). French colonial administrators were even more avid assimilators of the natives into French culture, but although the French liked to claim they lacked British racial prejudices, they, too, reserved the top administrative jobs for metropolitan French.

Less prejudice of blood or skin color was arguably found among some traditional empires, such as China and Rome, according to Dominic Lievan:

The Roman and Chinese empires were more assimilationist. What mattered were culture, behavior and lifestyles. Those who adopted Roman or Chinese culture and manners were accepted even into the empires' elite. By the early third century AD even Italians, let alone Romans, were no longer in a majority either in the Senate or in the equestrian order. Increasingly, emperors themselves were to come from outside Italy. No prejudice seems to have existed against Black Africans. Over the centuries the Chinese proved willing to assimilate barbarians, including barbarian conquerors of China itself. (Lievan, 2000, 27–28).

One may add that modern high imperial administrators also tended to practice a *social* segregation, rarely inviting natives to their dinners or dances. That is, in most assimilation policies conducted by dominant ethnics, the aims may be preventing secession or securing administrative conveniences, but the aims do not really include full equality for those assimilated. This chapter offers a number of other illustrations of that.

When pursued by the dominant, assimilation policy may be either selective or collective. I examine them in this order.

II. POLICY OF SELECTIVE AND LIMITED INDIVIDUAL ASSIMILATIONS

In the selective form, the dominant ethnics intend that only a few of the weaker ethnicity are to adopt the culture of the dominant. These select few will be coopted into usually lesser administrative or other leadership roles. It does open opportunities for some among the minority group, but the slots opened may be sparse. Also, there may be a heavy price for even the favored individuals in that they may have to sacrifice their prior identity. Any new one may be less satisfactory, if only because there may be little real respect from the stronger group members and possible contempt from the weaker group members. Thus in the United States during the 1960s, African Americans critical of black assimilators often spoke of Uncle Toms, just as some native Americans spoke of Uncle Tomahawks. In extreme cases, often when members of a group are engaged in an anticolonial or secessionist war, they may even kill members of their group who may be collaborators. Thus, when the Romans occupied Israel, the Sicarii, a subgroup of the Zealots, were fond of knifing not only Romans but fellow Jews, usually Pharisees or Sadducees who collaborated with the Romans.

Sometimes an implicit price to rise by such selective assimilation is for the individual of weaker ethnicity to express contempt for their own group's culture, accepting, or at least giving the appearance of accepting, the dominant ethnic group's not uncommon view that the subordinate group's culture is distinctly inferior to their own, even if offering rather vague and perhaps indefensible arguments for the superiority of their own culture. Thus that superiority may be claimed on the measure of economic development taken as higher growth, without considering that their way of life may be ecologically inferior, not sustainable, or perhaps exploitive. Or the claimed superiority may be merely in military arts, a superior capacity to slaughter one's fellow human beings.

Lost ethnic identity aside, although it may be true that the selected individuals become materially better off, it is by no means clear that their rise will help their group of origin. After all, they are only selected for higher office if attitudinally "sound," and their aptitudes and energies are denied for possible leadership of their own group. Further, in a theory articulated by Karl Marx even before Vilfredo Pareto, the circulation of elites can often prolong the existence of a regime, even a despotic one. As someone observed, in a sense the *circulation of individuals* in elite roles proscribes the *circulation of classes*, preventing social revolution. As I define it, a social revolution always entails a major if always limited restratification of society, whereby some class (or ethnic group, etc.) that was high becomes lower while some class that had been low becomes higher.

As noted, often the assimilation policy of a dominant ethnic will only be partial, being intermixed with the contrary policy of separation. Thus a sixth of the population of Israel (about 1.4 million people) is not Jewish but Palestinian, with these being primarily Muslim and secondarily Christian. A rather limited assimilation applies: They vote, and outside of the annexed East Jerusalem and Golan Heights where many reject Israeli citizenship, they have historically had high turnouts. Although Palestinian parties can compete, since 1985 they cannot if they question the existence of the state of Israel or its Jewish nature. They hold most legal rights, including a right to have legislation initially in Hebrew translated into Arabic as also an official language. They are supposed to get nondiscrimination in university admissions, if there has been discrimination against Arab student organizations. If Israeli Palestinians get university degrees, they can tend to be unemployed or underemployed. Israeli authorities early attempted to coopt traditional patriarchs and other notables among even the Muslim Palestinians because it served their purposes, offering them personal payoffs for assisting control by supplying information against dissidents, or helping to delegitimize them while lending legitimacy to Israeli authorities. But economic rewards for cooperators become increasingly costly as leadership shifts from traditional Palestinian elites to well-educated, younger people (Lustick, 1980, 200–9, 211–31). Israeli Jews accept Israeli Palestinians in many public or private roles, but they have drawn the line at national security matters. By informal rules, military recruiters will take Christians, Druze, and even those Muslims of the traditionally tent-dwelling Bedouin for mixed unit border police, with some non-Jewish officers but commanded by Jews. But Israel does not recruit other Muslim Arabs for a not unfounded fear that they could be security risks (Lustick, 1980, 93–94). There are other measures of their limited equality. For some time after Israel's founding, travel and residence permits were required of Palestinian Israelis, and travel permits may yet be demanded to visit the West Bank or Gaza. Lands of absentee Arab owners were expropriated, and eminent domain used for purposes of Jewish defense or settlements took more Arab lands or even houses, sometimes with the offer of compensation from the lands of Palestinian refugees, which many Palestinian Israelis have refused out of principle (Lustick, 1980, 181). Arab Israelis recognize an annual Land Day to commemorate their losses. Also, there is inferior spending on Arab Israeli schools or on infrastructure such as good roads, water, and sewers serving their villages or neighborhoods (Kretzmer, 1990; Landau, 1993; Lustick, 1980).

The incompleteness of an individual assimilation policy thus is one mark of an assimilation policy of a dominant ethnic group relative to that likely to be sponsored by a subordinate ethnic group. Again, it looks more to social control than real equality of opportunity, which could be more costly for the dominant ethnicity.

III. POLICY OF AGGRESSIVE AND COLLECTIVE ASSIMILATION

Now turning to the collective form of assimilation, in apparent direct opposition to the strategy of segregation is that of making the minority group as a whole more similar in at least some respects to the dominant ethnic group.

In an imposed collective assimilation, the dominant may attempt to remove the threat of some minority not by deepening its difference but on the contrary easing or even erasing it. If dominant group segregationists assumed innate evil and often turned to discriminatory practice or at an extreme physical genocide, here they are more likely to think of misshaping effects of bad environment or education. In principle, at least, the minority ethnicity (or other such group to be assimilated) may be redeemed, saved from its cultural backwardness, its heresy, and so on. Yet in some cases if redemption seems failing, they may attribute perverse will, and return to a punitive mode of thinking, as especially evident even now of those who—like Hitler—favor "corrective therapy" for minorities of sexual orientation.

Here many of the social distancing variables mentioned in chapter 1 may be reversed.

Far from opposing intermarriage, it may be tolerated, encouraged, or even commanded, as it was by Alexander the Great for his officers. He himself took two Persian wives (Green, 1970, 242). Claudius was said to have similarly favored intermarriage among peoples ruled by the Romans.

In a bizarre form for another group category, even gays or lesbians have sometimes been pressed into heterosexual marriages they did not want, or even abhorred—something that can still happen in a place such as Ethiopia.

Rather than encouraging separate residences, this logic sometimes shifts rather to residential intermixing of groups, sometimes even using forceful means to effect it.

The logic of collective assimilation, as an imposition of the dominant, can often bring punishment of either individuals of the group or of the group tout court for obstinate persistence in being different.

Zealous attempts at even "voluntary" individual or collective cultural assimilation may only seem to be egalitarian, because they always presuppose the superiority of the dominant culture. If the French were most eager to assimilate among European colonial powers, it thus need not have entailed any real egalitarian spirit among them, even if indirectly aiding some entry of natives into administrative positions subordinate to French officials (in contrast with the Belgian Congo, where university-educated natives were far too sparse at the moment of decolonization).

At its extreme, an imposed assimilation can become a kind of cultural genocide, destroying the richness of what is different. Although it is true that it usually has less physically murderous results than the extremes of segregation pursued by the dominant, it can just as effectively terminate the group, which is the target of such policy. They can no longer collectively seek other ways to better themselves, because neither they nor others can find them. There are many instances in history when even the name of the people becomes forgotten.

Assimilations through History

Obviously enough, an assimilation need not always be total. In 1644 when the Manchus took over China, starting the Ch'ing dynasty that would last until 1912, they were a minority ruling over the now-subordinated Han Chinese. The Manchus imposed their shaved head with queue hairstyle, their Manchu robe, and other assimilations, sometimes even killing any who resisted. But they did not ban the Han practice of foot binding of women. Some Han were even assimilated into military or administrative roles. Yet such assimilation was accompanied by some segregation: The Han were excluded from most high offices, especially from military commands. Further, the Manchu elite of "bannermen" lived apart from the Han and could not intermarry with the Han (Finer, 1999, 1132–33).

Most of China, about 93 percent, are Han Chinese, differing from each other moderately in language (they share the Mandarin script, but northerners speak Mandarin and southerners have spoken Cantonese, although Chinese communist schools have pushed even in the south a spoken Mandarin not unlike that of Beijing). Today the People's Republic of China, which has been rather accommodationist with some ethnic minorities not threatening secession, has been more militantly assimilationist toward those who do, such as the Muslim Uighurs and the Lamaist Buddhist Tibetans. Although China exempts its ethnic minorities from the one-child policy imposed on the Han, especially urban Han, there are indicators that Chinese leaders want dominance of the Han. Thus, in the Tibetan school system, whereas primary education is often in Tibetan, the Chinese prefer a mix of Tibetan and Chinese in secondary and higher education. More than in language, China precludes the two named religious groups from early training of the youth, or acceptance into membership of mosques or monasteries (cf. Goldstein, 1997; Schwartz, 1994).

In the 1536 Act of Union linking Wales to England, there was a directly stated intent "to Extirpate All and Singular the Sinister Usages and Customs Differing." This was especially focused on the end of any official use of Welsh: "Henceforth no Person or Persons that use Welsh Speech or Language shall have or enjoy any Manner Office or Fees with the Realm of England, Wales or Other the King's Dominion." Everyday Welsh was not banned, but it could be repressed by a "Welsh Not" game in the schools: "A piece of wood hung round the neck, was passed around among the children. A child could get rid of it to another child heard speaking his native language, and the child caught with it by the schoolmaster was caned" (Thomas, 1971, 33–34). In the course of time such means did tend to extirpate most use of the Welsh language, but that stimulated a Welsh nationalist movement focused around the limited objective of saving the language (Berresford, 1968; Davies, 1989; Sandberg, 1981).[1]

A more thorough assimilation policy may begin with separation of the different, especially at the borders. Note well that this involves a move of segregation to facilitate assimilation. In some countries, the dominant ethnic group may enact a policy offering a special right to immigrate to nearly all ethnic similars residing abroad, as Germany does for Germans, Israel for Jews, and Macedonia does for Macedonians. Before 1999, Germany made naturalization of its long-resident Turkish "guest workers" very difficult.

That ardent assimilators among the dominant do not really love the subjects of their ministrations is clear in that they do not normally encourage more immigration of a rival ethnicity. Although Britain had defeated the French in the Seven Years' War, anglophones were yet outnumbered in Lower Canada and in the early nineteenth century wanted increased immigration of their group to swamp the local French. Although later changing their announced standpoint, francophone leaders just as loudly stated their wish that anglophone immigrants were kept out (Chennels, 2001, 89, 92). Although some immigration restrictions could be charitably attributed to the costs of effecting assimilation of very different newcomers, it can rather be read as yet another evidence of their detestation of another culture.

Immigration policy can screen out ethnic dissimilars. Thus in the history of U.S. immigration policy, aside from the absence of any special prejudice against women, various enactments sought to screen out those who were politically or ethnically too "different." In 1929 Congress enacted a law setting quotas for immigration at 2 percent of members of a nationality who had been already here in 1890, which obviously was biased against latecomers such as Italians, East Europeans, and Jews (most of whom came from East Europe, including Russia). Prior to 1965, U.S. immigration laws favored entry of Europeans, and especially West Europeans, over other would-be immigrants. But after 1965 the policy shifted to a preference to reunite divided families and to admit especially needed job skills. U.S. immigration, which had been 90 percent European, became by the end of the century only 15 percent European. However, since the Cold War ended, the United States keeps reducing the number of refugees it is willing to accept, actually taking in even less than the allotted year 2001 quota of 70,000, perhaps in part because more applicants are now non-European. Many erroneously believe that most refugees head for economically advanced nations. As a matter of fact, most refugees, many produced in Africa out of ethnic conflicts, move only to a nearby nation with little economic capacity to sustain them. As Robert Went notes, beyond the some 23 million displaced persons yet within the borders of their own countries there were 17 million expatriated refugees in 1992, of whom 13.2 million were hosted in less developed nations. Only 5 percent of all such people uprooted from their homes were admitted to Western Europe or North America (Went, 2000, 32). Some older stock Americans are yet uncomfortable with newer immigrants from Latin America, Asia, or Africa. They feel unease when increasingly surrounded by many who are different. They should really worry more about an indescribably tedious scene when everyone around them would be precisely like themselves.

Encouragement of exits is another way to screen a population in favor of similars, as noted in chapter 1 of the early Nazi policy of favoring emigration of Jews rather than their later destruction. In white settlement societies such as the United States or Australia, the encouragement of emigration was not abroad but to remoter parts of the territory.

Recent Cases of Attempted Forced Enculturation

Also showing that assimilative policy need not be mutually exclusive, some groups may be first subjected to separations as segregation and then to partial assimilation, as true of Native Americans and the Aboriginals of Australia, who were first driven to and confined in reservations, then subjected to halfway efforts to assimilate them, usually without any intention of making them really equal. The cases of American Indians and Aboriginals show us phases of policy: segregation, forced but limited assimilation, and finally some accommodation.

In looking at any policy of social control, a common distinction concerns use of coercive, economic, or symbolic modalities, which can be subdivided into positive (rewarding) or negative (punitive) forms. To the extent we ourselves are targets of state control, there is a fairly clear preference ordering: (1) withdraw any use or threat of coercion, (2) economically reward compliance, (3) praise compliance, (4) dispraise noncompliance, (5) administer some economic deprivation such as a fine, and (6) threaten or use coercion. To the

extent that a dominant ethnicity in control of government reverses that ordering in attempting to assimilate an ethnic minority, one could call it an
aggressively assimilationist policy, which none of us would want imposed on
ourselves.

Native Americans in the United States

In the United States, segregation began in usually forceful separation of
Indians from both their lands and from white settlements from some of the
earliest seventeenth-century white settlements in Virginia and Massachusetts
Bay. It is shocking to find Adolf Hitler later cite this history on behalf of his
pursuit of *Lebensraum* in East Europe: "Neither Spain nor Britain should be
models of German expansion, but the Nordics of North America, who had
ruthlessly pushed aside an inferior race to win for themselves soil and territory
for the future" (Hitler, 1961, 44–48, as cited in Ingram, 2000, 113).

But American policy turned toward assimilation in 1879, and arguably began the first stage of accommodation from 1934.

Dominant ethnics bent on assimilation often fool themselves in rational-
izing that the weaker group members know its own culture is inferior. On the
contrary, often the natives looked at European culture as decidedly odd:

First contact with Europeans shocked both the Indians and the explorers. The Indians
watched without understanding as the residents in the European settlements bowed
before arbitrary authority with a meekness that the Indians loathed. They believed
that the whites had surrendered all moral substance in exchange for security in the
anonymity of institutional life. Many Indian nicknames spoke derisively of the whites
as "people who take orders," or "people who march in a straight line." And most
Indians had little respect for white military leaders who commanded their soldiers to
go to war while remaining safely in the rear. They might fear a white general, but they
respected very few of them. (Deloria and Lytle, 1984, 9)

General Custer did ride into the thick of battle, even underscoring his presence with a special hat, bandana, and golden long locks, usually with buglers
playing at his side. Yet although unscathed during the Civil War, Custer was
to have a rendezvous with Sitting Bull.

In an account offered by William Willard, himself a senior Native American
who has heard firsthand accounts of it, the turn to assimilation for American
Indians began with Lt. Richard H. Pratt, a Union officer who served from
1862 to 1865 in the Civil War, who would rise to brigadier general by 1904.
Not surprisingly, standard kinds of military discipline such as marching up
and down were central to Pratt's experience. After the Civil War, after an
unsatisfactory stint in civilian life, Pratt reentered the military and found himself in the southern Great Plains when the Indians of that region were defeated
after an insurrection. Having apparently fallen into bad grace with superiors,
Pratt eagerly accepted assignment to the role of attempting to assimilate a
portion of the defeated Indians. These men were selected randomly and

moved apart from the others, although later the wives of many were allowed to join them. The first model school was the U.S. Indian Semi-Industrial Boarding School founded November 1, 1879, on U.S. Army property near Carlisle, Pennsylvania. The style of training was that of a boot camp, with students ranging in ages from eight to their early twenties. There was much drill. The men ate in dining halls and slept in dormitories. Even the discipline was military, ranging across punitive drills, a public confessional for any who dared use a native language, lockup on bread and water, or even the ball and chain. Christian chapel attendance was compulsory.

Unlike white students at boarding schools, the Indian students had to do physical labor for half the day at menial jobs to supply basic food, shelter, or other needs of the camp. They also were by the "Outing Program" put out for several months at a time (usually in summers) to do similar labor for white families in nearby Pennsylvania or New Jersey. They were paid for Outing Program work, but the pay was substandard. Participating white families hence won the advantage of cheap labor in farm, housework, and maid service tasks. Beyond labor discipline, the separation from schoolmates and closer contact with whites was expected to aid assimilation. Many Indians pretended to accept it all in the hope it would end sooner rather than later, but most were never really brought into the white people's ways. Only a few of them went on through selective assimilation mechanisms to become well educated or enter important roles. Such individuals, like those who came up through other tracks, often praised aspects of the assimilative training, giving a misleading idea of how most natives regarded the experience.

The federal government took a large view of the assimilative program, creating a Pratt-inspired system of on-reservation day schools, regional reservation boarding schools, and off-reservation boarding schools for Indian youths. Eastern philanthropists and Protestant clergy seemed behind this last. Especially in the off-reservation boarding schools, modeled after Pratt's Carlisle school, Indian youths were forbidden to *look* like Indians—white hairstyles and not long hair, ornamentation without beads or feathers, and so on, clothing excluding a blanket, and shoes rather than moccasins. They were forbidden to speak their native languages. Even their diets were drastically changed, with a new emphasis on bread and sugar, among other foods unknown to traditional Indians. By the testimony of one native, Luther Standing Bear, about half of the often lonely youths initially taken from the southern plains died within three years.

When extended to reservations across the United States, a combination of verbal persuasion, blocked food rations, a display of federal troops, or even imprisonment of recalcitrant adults got most Indian parents to put their children in the schools. Often children involuntarily packed off to off-reservation schools, under pressure to fill up to capacity within constrained budgets, came down with tuberculosis, which would eventually kill many. Inadequate expenditures on the boarding schools often meant unhealthful water and poor sanitation, causing intestinal problems and skin diseases. Doubtless many were in a condition of depression at being forced to do unfamiliar kinds of work and at being separated from their parents and other familiars. If there were runaways, the Indian police of reservations would be enlisted to forcibly bring them back.

Wisconsin's Ojibwe, a people whose homeland had centered on the southern shore of Lake Superior, were to have their children dispersed to sometimes distant sites, a few even as far as Carlisle, Pennsylvania:

The boarding school experience did to Ojibwe culture what the General Allotment Act had done to Ojibwe land. As early as 1856, Ojibwe children were taken from their homes and placed in government boarding schools, where school officials discouraged them from speaking their language or practicing their traditional religions and customs. Through much of the late nineteenth and early twentieth centuries, Ojibwe parents had no say in which school their children would attend. . . . Most of the schools in Wisconsin patterned themselves after the Carlisle model, providing a half-day of academic instruction and a half-day of manual training. (Loew, 2001, 65–66)

Perhaps the idea of the boot camps was a rehabilitation for being Indian. In any event, in the later twentieth-century United States, boot camps returned as "shock incarceration" for juvenile offenders, and about half their inmates were African Americans, Hispanics, and . . . Native Americans.

The 1928 Merriam Report by the Brookings Institute, funded by the Rockefeller Foundation, was a thorough indictment of the deficiencies of separating children from their families. John Collier, regarded as a friend of the Indians, attended a Taos plateau Red Deer dance and had a mystic vision reaffirming the worth of the native cultures. In 1933 he was appointed by Franklin Delano Roosevelt as commissioner of Indian Affairs, serving to 1944. In that role he presided over accommodative policies in granting of some real self-governance to Indians by the Indian Reorganization Act of 1934. He also followed through on the Merriam Report in eventually ending the off-reservation federal boarding schools, on assuring full-day academic programs (not half-day menial labor) at even on-reservation boarding schools, and providing that bilingual education and Native American cultural materials were added to the educational curricula.

Although it is apparent that the boarding school movement meant at least for the young men the effort to make them into European-style farmers who grew their own wheat for the bread they were to eat, a somewhat later beginning sought to put them on privately owned farmland as part of the assimilation. Although variously titled, the agency since 1947 called the Bureau of Indian Affairs was in the War Department until 1849 and in the Department of the Interior thereafter. It would dominate reservation life, including the sales or leasing of individually or collectively Indian owned lands, until some real sharing with Indians beginning with the 1934 Indian Reform Act and especially the 1975 Indian Self-Determination and Education Assistance Acts.

From the Dawes Severalty Act of 1887, one assimilative initiative was to force the Indians to divide up communally owned land into 160-acre plots, ostensibly with the aim of making the Indians into white-style farm owners. But because many Indians could not make the farms successful, this often led to further sales of reservation lands to whites.

Once into the twentieth century it was apparent that the country would need fewer farmers, not more, so a new variant of "outing" was now pushed by the Bureau of Indian Affairs under the rubric of Adult Vocational Training, paying transportation for Indians who would leave the reservations in quest of urban jobs. This was just in time for the Great Depression, when such jobs vanished. Hence the program was terminated in 1938 until revived again in different form for supplying labor needs during World War II. Under the title of the American Indian Voluntary Relocation, after the war another variant offered subsidized one-way tickets to certain urban areas. As William Willard, from whom I have drawn most of this discussion, bluntly sums up: "The intent from the first Outing Programs was to permanently disperse Indians so that there would not be any Indian communities. American Indian identity would cease to exist. Human obstacles to the transfer of reservation land and natural resources would be permanently removed" (Willard, 1998, 57). Attempts at occupational assimilation of adults were often self-defeating. Thus Susan Armitage has noted that even for those Native American peoples who had done some agriculture, tillage was largely regarded as women's work rather than men's work. Attempts to make tillers (rather than fishers, hunters, herders) of Native American men only encouraged their turns to alcoholic despair.

In short, although proclaimed to be only for the good of the Indians, the educational programs, outing programs as well as the new reservation lands programs, were arguably aimed at separation of the Indians from both each other and their remaining land holdings.

Yet another assault on Indian land was to be the post–World War II "termination" movement (1945–1961), which sought to end some of the smaller reservations by selling off communally owned lands to the highest bidders (usually whites), even if the proceeds were shared among the Indians. This was again with proclaimed good intentions for the economic well-being of Indians but with the likely motive among some advocates of dispersing Native Americans, so they could not maintain any identity or constitute a political pressure group.

Recapitulating, for about two and a half centuries whites had used force, fraud, or pressured fire-sales to separate Indians from nearly all of their land, especially from the best farmland. The tribes that early sought to imitate the white farmers (the five "civilized" tribes of the South such as the Cherokee, as well as the western Nez Percé and Palouse) found that imitating European plowing and herding did not protect their land titles. Whites having already taken most of the farmland that Indians could have successfully farmed, in 1879 the boarding school movement sought to make Indians into farmers on what little and often inferior land was left to them on the reservations. That became even less when postwar reservation termination policy under cover of federal law opened some reservation lands to white bidding.

Because not many Indians became successful farmers on privatized reservation lands, Bureau of Indian Affairs policy, as noted, tried to prepare them for urban jobs for which on-reservation day schools had not adequately prepared them, with many cut off from their Indian communities, thereafter living marginally.

The acceptance of on-reservation gambling casinos in more recent decades has economically aided those reservation populations near large cities or destination resorts, but did little for those in more remote locations. The Native American population continues to suffer high unemployment or underemployment, high incarceration for crimes, high alcoholism and suicides, added to an unusually high rate of diabetes.

In 2001–2002 it was learned that the Department of Interior's system dating from 1887 to collect logging and grazing fees and mineral royalties had grossly mismanaged communal properties of the reservations. Accounting was a disaster. Interior's computer system was found to be insecure and had to be shut down for a time to prevent embezzlements. Lost funds supposed to have been distributed to individual Indians may amount to as much as $40 billion.

White assimilationists seem unable to learn. Although forced assimilation had largely failed for Native Americans, after repressing a nationalist movement in the Philippines (1899–1903), by 1912 the United States sought to assimilate an aboriginal minority there called the Agta or Aeta. The effort to make them into settled farmers clearly failed by 1923. Yet in 1975 Filipino dictator Ferdinand Marcos revised the same scheme all over again, with like failure. The outcome is not lovely, because disease, destitution, and homicide have continued to reduce the numbers of this already small indigenous people (Bain, 1986).

In passing, often the dominant ethnicity wants to obliterate what may be the more important aspects of the traditional culture, such as modes of family or economic organization, while sometimes patronizing customs of what could be regarded even by the minority culture members as of somewhat lesser importance. I am thinking here of, say, acceptance of the donning of costumes for certain ceremonials (although even here the U.S. federal government banned the more threatening ghost dancing of the Great Plains Indians).

Australian Aboriginals

In rough parallel to the American Indian experience, the Australian Aboriginals, now variously reported at 0.5 percent, 1.2 percent, or even nearly 2 percent of Australia's population of 16 million, experienced a similar shift of dominant ethnic policy toward them, moving from segregation to forced assimilation and finally toward accommodation.

By 1788 it was clearly a policy of segregation, for it was in that year that Australia's courts declared Aboriginally used land *terra nullius* (no one's land) because it was not tilled or improved. Writing in 1681, John Locke had held that plowing could justify conversion of a commons land into even extensive private property in land. Locke also admired the principle of contracts, but whites often did not keep treaties with nonwhites who got in their way. Like the American Indian reservations, original Aboriginal "reserves" were often cut back to make way for growing white settlement. But unlike American Indian reservations, even retained Aboriginal reserve lands were often not understood as *fully* belonging to them, not freeholds but perhaps Crown lands under lease, and white Australians with interests in grazing leases or mining have been especially vigilant against assertions of complete Aboriginal property rights.

A Commonwealth (federal) government turn toward assimilation policy was clear by 1937, for then and thereafter many official government documents acknowledged the new aim of mainstreaming the Aboriginals into the general population, showing no solicitude for preservation of Aboriginal identity or cultural differences. Here is the official joint statement of intent from the states and federal government in 1961:

The policy of assimilation means . . . that all Aborigines and part-Aborigines are expected to attain the same manner of living as other Australians and to live as members of a single Australian community, enjoying the same rights and privileges, accepting the same responsibilities, observing the same customs and influenced by the same beliefs, hopes and loyalties as other Australians. (Pittock, 1979, 18–19)

Note well the terms: "same," "single," "same," "same," "same," and "same." There was something monomaniacal in the phrasing.

The authors of that passage never considered that the Aborigines could want to remain in some respects different, and they would have been aghast if someone urged that all the "other Australians" should be made over to be the "same" as the Aborigines. Nor would they understand the possible accusation that they were practicing intolerance rather than striving for Kantian right. Instead of creating a more open society, they were trying to close off another option. As Michael Walzer has written, "It is the practitioners of religious persecution, forced assimilation, crusading warfare, or 'ethnic cleansing' who need to justify themselves, and they mostly do that not by defending what they are doing but by denying that they are doing it" (Walzer, 1997, 2).

As described by Scott Bennett, there was a clear white sense of cultural superiority, even if polite circles stopped assertions of biological or racial superiority. Supposedly to protect the Aboriginals from exploitation, from 1911 to 1953 special ordinances regulated white employment of Aboriginals or the having of sexual relations with them. In the past as now, many of the Aborigines are school dropouts and are illiterate or nearly so.

The intention of Australian assimilation was to end massive unemployment among Aboriginals on the reserves, in part by training them for manual labor within white communities, which is in rough parallel with the U.S. policy toward Native Americans. During this period many Aboriginal children were permanently removed from their parents, a group Aboriginal rights advocates call "the stolen children" or "the stolen generation." For in the years 1910 to 1970, about a tenth of Australian aboriginal children were removed from their parents to be educated apart from them. Many of these children were of mixed race, light-skinned enough to more readily "pass" into the social mainstream. Yet the mixed race individuals are often denied to be "real Aboriginals," especially when property rights and other special claims arise during the shift toward accommodation (cf. Vasta and Castles, 1996).

Scott Bennett notes that if some National Party supporters remained segregationist in thinking, most Liberal Party supporters embraced the new assimilationist emphasis. Yet many espousing assimilation for the Aboriginals persist in thinking that if they want full equality of rights they must stop insisting on claims to be *different*, especially if insisting on retention of their cultural differences or demanding some special Aboriginal rights, as in property claims or calls for reparations payments. Liberal prime ministers have offered only weak apologies for past abuses of the Aboriginals, fearing that stronger statements of regret would lend justification to a demand for reparations payments for past injustices.

U.S. reservation Indians were accorded full U.S. citizenship and votes in 1934, but two Australian states, Queensland and Western Australia, did not accord Aboriginals the vote until 1965. Although white rural voters—those more likely to support the rightist National Party—were less likely to vote yes, in 1967 a massive majority of 90.8 percent of Australia's voters supported a Commonwealth constitutional amendment according Aboriginals full equality of political rights. Mobile voting vans have helped boost their voting, especially in the outback, incidentally benefiting many whites also living in the remote interior. However, notwithstanding other important measures such as the 1993 Native Title Act to enlarge property rights for them, conditions for the Aboriginals have not shown much improvement: Aboriginals are twice as likely to experience infant mortality (their life expectancy is twenty years less), about three times as likely to be unemployed, and twice as likely to be in custody (they are about a seventh of the prison population). A recent and dangerous fad among Aboriginal children is sniffing gasoline for a cheap high.

The Laborites and Greens have tended to go beyond Liberals in favoring accommodationist special rights to further assist the Aboriginals, but this apparently costs them some white votes. Some think that Australia should add for its Aboriginals the equivalent of the five seats reserved for the Maori minority in New Zealand's House of Representatives (Bennett, 1999).

Romany and Magyars in Communist Romania

In Europe as elsewhere, militant assimilation sometimes extended to kidnapping of Romany ("gypsy") children from their own parents. The prince of Mecklenburg-Strelitz in 1710 decreed their removal to Christian parents, and such removal was for some cases also enacted in supposedly enlightened eighteenth-century Austro-Hungary under Maria Teresa and Joseph II, who also forbade Romany to move about, trade horses, or choose their leaders. Confiscation of Romany travelers' children occurred as late as 1973 in Switzerland (Fonseca, 1995, 230, 235, 240). Communist policy toward the gypsies of Romania pushed assimilation, forcing them to stay put in fixed residences before looking for jobs for them, but also punishing manifestations of their supposedly backward culture (Fonseca, 1995, 167). Sometimes the logic becomes self-contradictory, as when Romany children in East Europe were mainstreamed in the school system without any consideration of their distinctive language, which originated in India but became enriched by other vocabulary incident to the historic path of migration through Persia, Armenia, and Asia Minor. But this rejection of even transitional bilingual education caused most Romany children to become school dropouts, which frustrates eventual occupational assimilation. The high dropout rate remains a problem in most of Europe where Romany are numerous. Although open prejudice otherwise rages against the Romany, everyone in Europe seems fond of their music.

Romania has also contained a major ethnic minority of Magyars (Hungarians). The former communist leader Nicolae Ceaucescu outlawed any Hungarian-language schools, forbade public use of Hungarian, and restricted access to Hungarian literature. At an extreme, even gravestone faces were sometimes reworked to conceal the fact of past Hungarian residency in certain areas. When his regime collapsed, Ceaucescu and his wife were shot, after reportedly asking the gunmen to reflect on everything they had done for Romanians. Reportedly, there were lots of bullet holes in their corpses.

The Kurds of Turkey

Just before the birth of modern Turkey, in 1915–1917, Ottoman Turkish authorities caused the deaths by privation or outright slaughter of up to 1.5 million Armenians (Bartkus, 1999, 84–86). Soon Turkey would mass deport its Greeks, who were largely Orthodox Christians. Throughout the rest of the twentieth century, one of the harshest assimilationist efforts was visited on Turkey's Kurdish minority, which Turkish officials have denied existed, sometimes calling them "Mountain Turks" or claiming that they had simply forgotten their Turkish language. Both ethnically dominant Turks and Kurds are Sunni Muslims, which is why the Ottoman empire did not regard the Kurds as a distinctive *millet*, or religious community granted some autonomy. World War I had defeated and dismantled most of what was left of the Ottoman Empire, and key leaders of the new Turkish republic were emphatic in demanding that the Kurds give up their language and learn to speak and write only Turkish. After Mustafa Kemal (or Atatürk), one key leader was Prime Minister Ismet Inonu, who in 1925 made the policy line clear as cited in the epigraph to this chapter.[2]

Constituting some 6 to 12 million people, about half the Turkish Kurds no longer live in the separatist region in the southeastern corner of Turkey. Not surprisingly, many of these emigrated Kurds have become assimilationist rather than secessionist. As an old saying holds, where you stand depends on where you sit.

Turkish state policy long banned even oral use of the Kurdish language, not to mention rigorous exclusion from mass media, from educational institutions, and the like. As already observed in chapter 2, this linguistically repressive policy proved counterproductive in encouraging a violent secessionist movement, costing over 20,000 dead. It also proved to be a liability for Turkey's application for membership to the European Union. In recent years Turkish governments have retreated in at least the cultural rather than the military side of their effort to repress Kurdish nationalism, now allowing the language to be spoken and reappearance of some Kurdish schooling and media (cf. Barkley and Fuller, 1998; Chaliland, 1980; Ciment, 1996; Ibrahim and Gürbey, 2000; Kíríci and Windrow, 1997; McDowall, 1985; O'Ballance, 1996). Linguistic group repression surfaces elsewhere. Having in May 2001 lectured at an American Studies conference in Khmelnytsky, Ukraine, one of my four talks elicited the remark from one native Ukrainian speaker that in the Soviet Union the Russians had been repressive toward the Ukrainian language. I quickly asked him if some Ukrainian native speakers were not now being somewhat repressive toward those who grew up speaking Russian in Ukraine. He recoiled in silence, then said, "No!" He and others like him then laughed nervously.

Past or Recent Cases of Religious Assimilations

Throughout history, aggressive assimilations have often been applied to deviants from monopoly religion. Often those who did not convert were executed. In the Spanish Inquisition, even converts to Roman Catholicism were later subjected to torture to find out if they had feigned conversion. In the early seventeenth century, the Moriscos or the Moors (Muslims) who had converted to Roman Catholicism were deported en masse from Spain.

The early Protestant reformers were also intolerant. In 1543, just three years before his death, Martin Luther is openly anti-Semitic in his essay, "On the Jews and Their Lies," repeating common slanders while urging that their properties be confiscated, their synagogues and prayer books destroyed. In one of his sermons he had urged that if the Jews refused to convert to Christianity, "we ought not to suffer them or bear with them any longer." Note how an aggressive assimilation can easily convert into segregation, here stated with ominous overtones.

John Calvin was so intolerant that he even tipped off French Catholic officials about the presence on their territory of anti-Trinitarian Servetus, who, when caught passing through on his way to an Italian sanctuary, was executed in Calvin's Geneva. Although Calvin thought himself generous in having recommended decapitation rather than burning (not granted) and that his tongue not be cut out as sometimes done to prevent dying utterance of heresy (granted), his real service was inspiration for Sebastien Castellion's critical book, *On Heresy* (1555), apparently the first book in history dedicated to religious toleration. Castellion, like Calvin originally a refugee from France, himself had to flee Geneva, writing his fine book in Basel.

Although some Muslim regimes such as the Ottoman empire can be accommodationist toward minority religions, especially those that have a book of revelation, they can be severe toward infidels, atheists, and especially apostates from Islam. Also, there are some currents of Islam that are strongly intolerant of any difference.

The mystical tradition of the Sufis is not regarded by Muslims as a separate school of Islam, unlike the Sunnis and the Shi'as. Even this last pair did not have deep differences of teachings, sharing among other things the Five Pillars of Islam. There have been historical occasions when adherents of one group attempted to aggressively assimilate the other, but they have, like Western Catholics and Protestants in many contexts come to a live and let live outlook, at least at the official level.

Often impulses of aggressive assimilation arise among distinctive teachings within the same school of Islam, Sunni or Shi'a, depending on which outlook has become dominant in a specific nation. The most extreme teachings may thus be doubly or even triply intolerant, toward other tendencies within their own school of Islam, toward the opposed school, and toward infidels. What are these distinctive teachings that may arise within any one school of Islam?

In his interesting book, *The Failure of Political Islam*, Olivier Roy notes that the Islamic community is not supposed to be divided:

The ideal Islamic society is defined as *umma*, an egalitarian community of believers. The political concept that expresses *umma* for Islamists is thus *tawhid*, "oneness," the negation both of social classes and of national, ethnic, or tribal divisions. All differentiation is inherently a negation of *umma*. At the very worst, this leads to *fitna*, a rupture, separation, splitting of the community. . . . Segmentation is perceived as a sin and not as a sociological fact. Which is why Islamist thought denies whatever may result from divisions, first and foremost the division of religious schools . . . the four traditional Sunni schools . . . as well as the division between Shiism and Sunnism), but also the divisions between countries, ethnic groups, tribes, classes, social categories, interest groups, and so on. (Roy, 1994, 71)

Roy later adds,

Since Islam has an answer to everything, the troubles from which Muslim society is suffering are due to nonbelievers and to plots, whether Zionist or Christian. This obsession with the internal enemy and the homogeneity of the Muslim community is more reminiscent of a sect with its concern for purity than of a society confident in its identity. It thus becomes necessary either to convert or to expel. (Roy, 1994, 85)

But among both Sunni and Shi'a, in Roy's view, intolerance grows as one descends this list:

1. *Most religious teachers* (or *ulema*) have links to nonrevolutionary or even secular governments, sometimes being supportive even when these are secularizing. In the spirit of the Ottoman Empire, most are tolerant of other religions. They accept many traditional teachings of Islam not directly from the Quran or early recorded sayings and practices of the prophet *(hadith)*. Roy indicates that this group tends to be of higher education and specific education in Islamic traditions. Although not said, they are by implication of a higher class background.

2. *Moderate Islamists* have views originating among such figures as Hasan al-Banna (1906–1949), founder of the Muslim Brotherhood, or on the Indian subcontinent, Abdul-Ala Maududi (1903–1978). They are critical of *ulema* who get too cozy with secularizing governments. They also want to return to the sources, to go back to the Quran and *hadith*, while stripping away from Islam a later accumulation of dubious traditions. These moderate Islamists do not want to debar women from education or out-of-home employment, or agitate much for *jihad* in the militarist vein. Their teachings, like those of neofundamentalists, may attract those who are fairly well educated yet unemployed or underemployed. These Islamists often criticize state corruption, but they usually do not try to subvert their state. In some cases such Islamists have assassinated specific *ulema* they regard as having sold out to secularism, however. Roy suggests that moderate Islamists are more middle class, often with higher education in technical fields such as engineering.

3. *Neofundamentalists, the immoderate Islamists* who take their religion as beyond debate, are intolerant of religious difference. They think the full Islamic law (or *shari'a*) needs no development or reform and should be imposed as a whole and at once. Further, men should grow long beards and women should be excluded from education and work outside the home. Roy virtually says that neofundamentalists for the most part are of lower class, and that they are poorly educated (often at rote memorization schools called *madrassas*). He depicts their spokespersons as largely "Lumpenintellects," a term with obvious linkage to the Marxist Lumpenproletariat, the "rag proletariat" who live by hook or crook in the ghettos of cities and often get caught up in low projects. The Islamic neofundamentalists have much appeal for the young unemployed or underemployed men of many Islamic area locales.

Yet he also suggests that neofundamentalism can appeal to poorly educated peasantry in rural areas, too. (Roy, 1994)

Revolutionary Iran

As already suggested regarding attempts to assimilate minorities of sexual orientation, it is often true that frustrated assimilators reverse themselves and turn toward segregationism at its worst. Thus when Roman Catholic Inquisitors could not convert schismatics from their faith, or assure themselves that Jews, Muslims, or Protestants had not recanted their errors, they were less inclined to deport them than to turn them over to the state for execution. Under the Ayatollah Khomeini's influence in revolutionary Iran, his former allies in the overthrow of the shah in 1979, the Mujahedin, were denounced as spurious "Islamic Marxists" and imprisoned in massive numbers. Often under the guise of killing pimps or prostitutes, many were later executed. Islamic women were returned to segregation and required to wear suffocating *chadors*. The regime was especially repressive toward the Bahai faith, which regards all religious teachers as prophets of God, denying the special role Islam accords to Mohammed as The Seal of the Prophets.

The Ayatollah posted a state bounty on Salman Rushdie, a Pakistani novelist who had allegedly slandered Mohammed. Even now, Saudi Arabia not only prohibits proselytization of any religions rival to Islam but also threatens public execution of any Muslim who is an apostate from Islam, that is, who has been a Muslim but came to reject the faith, unless the accused recants the apostasy.

Afghanistan

In 1973 a cousin overthrew the king of Afghanistan, Zahir Shah. After the King's deposition, Noor Taraki and Babrak Karmal became principal leaders. When Karmal was challenged by his generals, he called in Soviet military assistance in 1979, and the Soviets were not to leave until 1989, a decade later, having lost some 15,000 dead Soviet soldiers and with no victory in sight. Their last client ruler was Najibullah, who, in the absence of Soviet military support, was overthrown and executed in 1992. The Pashtun warlord Gulbuddin Hekmatyar was prime minister of Afghanistan (1992–1996) but rained artillery shells on much of Kabul in his bid to have all power to himself.

Out of the emerging anarchy, the Taliban would eventually come to power in Kabul in 1996. The principal leader was an obscure village mullah, Mohammed Omar. Journalist Dan Freeman has reported that Omar first drew attention to himself in 1994 by leading a vigilante group to catch and hang a local warlord who had kidnapped and sexually assaulted two girls. Omar became a symbol of restored law and order. With a following of young men from the *madrassas*, many of them located within Pakistan but enrolling Pashtu-speaking tribals from both Afghanistan (Pashtuns) and Pakistan (Pathans), he eventually became leader of an apparent majority of the Pashtun tribe, who constitute 38 percent of the Afghanistan population of some 25 million. He led the Taliban against all rivals, including his fellow Pashtu, Hekmatyar.

Once in control of most of Afghanistan, Omar despotically required women to wear tent-like *burkas* and men to wear long beards while banning television and films. Women were basically sequestered, forced to quit most jobs outside the home, leave schools, and required to have relatives escort them when walking on the street.

Why are the most severe oppressors of women often so prominent among oppressors of minority ethnic groups?

Omar's regime seemed to be especially harsh on the Hazaras, a minority group whose members are some 19 percent of the total Afghan population and are prominent among the some 15 percent of Afghans who are of Shi'a faith. Like many other Afghans, they speak a dialectic of Farsi (Persian), and have lived in central Afghanistan from the thirteenth century. They have distinctive Mongol facial features. The Taliban, regarding them as allies with their enemies, the Uzbeks (in the northwest) and Tajiks (in the northeast), launched murderous raids into their region, leaving much death, destruction, and destitution in their wake. According to Human Rights Watch, in 1998 some 8,000 Hazaras were murdered by the Taliban. Several hundred more were murdered in 2000–2001. As late as summer 2002 new mass graves of Hazaras were being discovered.

Non-Muslim religious minorities were also harassed, with Buddhists finding not only the great stone Buddhas of Bamian but even their home statuettes destroyed (cf. Marsden, 1998; Mousavi, 1997).

Omar was militarily opposed by Uzbeks and Tajiks in the north who wanted less Pashtun dominance and a less severe Islamic regimen, even if predominantly Sunni Muslims like Omar. The Taliban eventually faced an American-led invasion because they had shielded the al Qaeda terrorist organization of Osama bin Laden, believed behind the September 11, 2001, destruction of the World Trade Center towers. The United States and European allies, mostly by air war, joined with Uzbeks and Tajiks on the ground to oust the Taliban. The interim regime was headed by Mohammed Karzai, a Pashtun whose father had been murdered by the Taliban. Hekmatyar had after 1996 settled into Iranian exile, but he also became an enemy to this new regime, and many alleged co-conspirators against the interim regime were arrested in April 2002. The aging exiled king Zahir Shah was welcomed back to Afghanistan in April 2002, and he refused candidacy before the traditional council of tribes, the *loya jirga*, which by June voted a two-year term for Karzai.

Communist Attacks on Religion

Officially atheist communist regimes have sometimes been hard on all religious believers. In The People's Republic of China, for example, one cannot belong to a church that retains fidelity to a foreign leader such as the pope, so China forces its Catholics to adhere to a strictly national version of the faith. For any religion, one may not proselytize door to door, conduct Bible or Sunday schools, or make a minor a member of a religious organization. Because it mounted large public demonstrations and had some suicide protesters when these were repressed, China has simply banned the Falun Gong movement, which intermixes traditional forms of Chinese religion with physical exercises. Although the movement had claimed to be nonpolitical, the elite fears its subversive potential.

But the most severe persecution of religion was practiced in the now deposed communist regime of Albania. Although Albania's population was just before communist rule about 70 percent Islamic, 20 percent Orthodox, 10 percent Roman Catholic, most Albanians were not zealous in their faith (unlike the ethnic Albanians living within Kosovo or Macedonia). Albania's brutal and mendacious communist leader, Enver Hoxha, was not initially as severe on Islam, in part because he fancied himself something like Mohammed, the Seal of the Prophets in Marxism-Leninism (Pipa, 1990, 140–42). But he was harsh toward Roman Catholicism, because it gave allegiance to the pope in Rome. He imprisoned an archbishop in 1947, with prison hardships contributing to the cleric's death not long after. In 1946 the Jesuits were banned, followed by the Franciscans in 1947. Some twenty Roman Catholic priests were executed and forty more imprisoned.

Hoxha had decided to go beyond communist official atheism and make everyone in his society atheist, stamping out religion to create the first fully atheist state in history. The public rationale was that religion was exploitive and divisive. Hoxha was fond of citing an earlier Albanian nationalist, "the religion of Albanians was Albanianism." All 2,169 churches and mosques were eventually closed down (O'Donnell, 1999, 142). The mass media and public schools were used to teach atheism. Even personal and place names had to remove any references to religion, such as names of Christian saints. Writing before the collapse of communism in East Europe, one analyst notes, "Unlike all other Communist East European countries, Albania has outlawed the practice of religion, celebrating herself as the first atheist state in the history of mankind" (Pipa, 1990, 225). The 1946 Constitution of Albania had guaranteed the right to religious worship, but the 1976 Constitution's Article 37 stated, "the State recognizes no religion whatever and supports atheist propaganda for the purpose of inculcating the scientific materialist world outlook in people." Hoxha's measures against religious buildings and clerics were severe (detailed by the Minnesota Lawyers International Human Rights Committee, 1988). Hoxha was so tyrannical that he even required police registration of private typewriters with a typed sample, so people could not produce carbon-copied manuscripts. Also, to attempt to leave Albania without state permission was a crime minimally punishable by ten years in prison but maximally punishable by death (O'Donnell, 1999, 131, 136). A 1994 survey in postcommunist Albania found that by self-reports people were 45 percent Muslim, 21 percent Albanian or Greek Orthodox, and 4 percent Roman Catholic. But 30 percent reported themselves atheists (O'Donnell, 1999, 139). This suggests that the antireligious campaign did make a difference. Yet Hoxha, who died in 1985, had failed to annihilate religion.

Notwithstanding Hoxha's failure, there is little doubt that any officially disseminated viewpoint on religion can make a difference. A nice example is offered in the contrast of West Germany, which offers publicly funded religious education (your choice, Catholic or Protestant) in its public schools, whereas East Germany did not, and also encouraged atheism. Even allowing that Catholics were far more common in West Germany whereas Protestants abounded in the East, and Catholics tend to be more tenacious in their faith unless it is attacked with Albanian severity, a 1991 poll found that in the formerly communist East Germany 75 percent disbelieved in God and 86 percent disbelieved in an afterlife, compared respectively to only 33 percent and 45 percent in West Germany.[3]

Speaking to Fears. Why would boundedly rational people subjected to an aggressive assimilation sometimes choose a strategy of quiescence before it, rather than some more active option? An opportunity by some tactical maneuver may be passed by if an agent expects an equal or larger gain by

a. *pursuit of the same tactic at a later, even more opportune time:* Timing is crucial, in politics just as in sport or business life. Often agents see that implementation will be easier or returns would be larger if they bide their time. Of course any expected future benefit could at some crossover point be discounted by rising uncertainty of getting it (cf. Racklin, 1980, 221);

b. *pursuit of another tactic within the same strategic field:* Especially in the strategic fields of influence, recruitment or restructuring, the fields subsume a range of tactical alternatives. Often when an agent passes up one kind of tactic, it is only because another tactic within the same field looks more promising and resources do not permit choice of both;

c. *pursuit of an advantage by another strategy:* Moving to a yet larger perspective on the whole of the political game, an agent may pass up an opportune maneuver within one strategy only to pursue a better one in another strategic field;

d. *pursuit of a direct payoff in policy or social outcomes:* In the largest perspective of all, a rational agent would often trade off some tactical advantage in power-seeking for what such power is wanted for, namely, winning wanted policies or social outcomes. After all, a political agent would put resources at risk of loss or attrition only with the expectation of culminating with a more valued stock than was held before, or if diminution is inescapable, at least suffering as little loss as possible. Why play the game if your rivals will concede it? Or why play the game if you are certain to lose the larger contest, and losses can be minimized by not playing at all?

Merely to identify such standard trade-off considerations does not tell us where the thresholds occur, but awareness of their presence at least prepares us to watch for them. A cynic could charge that the list of standard trade-offs offers an easy out to save the hypothesis for any specific forecast of action. But any valid theory of politics will have to include them. Inattention to trade-offs has led many theorists of isolated strategic or even tactical fields of choice to posit unbounded maximizations that simply do not fit known facts of political life. As I have recurrently emphasized, the parts must be viewed within the whole or they will not be correctly understood.

As I have elsewhere illustrated in the case of women (Cook, 1983), those who perceive that present and potential resources of friends will be exceeded by those of rivals tend to avoid the strategies of the stronger (or influence, recruitment, structures) and the expected defeats in them. Given a bad situation, the basic aim is to make those choices that adapt friends to uncontrolled official decisions. Often such a choice is forced when no coalition of friends is possible at all, when agents must as isolated individuals confront the political system. Yet the unfortunate consequence is that the more friends pursue only such strategies of the weak, the weaker or more vulnerable they may become. Temporarily at least, they will be in a defensive rather than offensive posture toward the political contest. Unable to adjust the authorities to themselves, they must somehow adjust themselves to uncontrolled authorities. In this it is something like the "income effects" of economists: the higher the costs of all options, the fewer of them they can buy. But there is also a "substitution effect," for when the cost of one option gets too high, they must shift to a cheaper one. For the resource-poor, even the least costly option uses up most of whatever available resources they have. Usually this suggests a hopeless situation, at best recommending to many of its targets an alternative strategy of evasion, of concealing who you are or what you are doing.

Most aggressive assimilationists not aiming at mere administrative convenience or curtailment of costs seem to fear loss of control. They fear that the different may rise against them, perhaps even defeat them by taking power at the center or by seceding from the political community.

Sometimes they even fear cross-border threats linked to fifth columnists at home. Hence sometimes aggressive assimilations operate internationally. When a revolution emerges, there is often a rough sequence such as follows: (1) the revolutionaries, be they English Puritans, American patriots, French revolutionaries, Marxist-Leninists, or Islamic revolutionaries, proclaim the universality of their ideal, and they attempt to disseminate their ideas to subvert other regimes, usually with limited success in it; (2) the status quo or counterrevolutionary powers around them take umbrage and alarm, and they counter the revolution with economic sanctions or usually ineffectual military intervention; (3) the revolutionaries react to this by taking up arms to impose their truths on the recalcitrant old regimes, sometimes at least temporarily successful in it; but (4) now even more foreign states align against them, and a Thermidorean reaction may set in at home, too, and the revolutionary cycle has completed its course (cf. Halliday, 1999, esp. 56–132).

NOTES

1. I owe the nice examples of Welsh assimilation to my student, Michael E. Johnson.

2. I owe this citation of Inonu to my student Kyle Bauer, "Turkey's Internal Conflicts."

3. The poll was conducted by Erwin Scheuch, Department of Sociology, University of Cologne, under direction of the German Central Archive for Empirical Research.

CHAPTER 4

Assimilations as Integrations: Strategies of the Weaker Ethnic Group

Assimilate, not be assimilated.
—Léopold Senghor, first president of Senegal and poet

Although African, Léopold Senghor (1906–2001) became an accomplished poet in French as well as a Roman Catholic leader of his people, who were over 85 percent Muslims. Although he would have opposed any aggressive French policy of assimilation, such as any attempt to wholly supplant native languages or convert everyone to Roman Catholicism, a personal choice to partially assimilate to another culture was quite acceptable. For Senghor believed that voluntary exchange can enrich cultures as well as economies. He himself studied the cultural riches of France at the Sorbonne, but as an exponent of *négritude* ("blackness") he also took pride in what Africa gave to Europeans, such as more of a social sense, soul, the roots of jazz, and inspiration for many modern art forms.[1] Exploring such voluntary assimilation, eagerly embracing the opportunities of integration, by a situationally weaker ethnicity is the concern of the present chapter.

One kind of assimilation, not much addressed here, is that of ordinary persuasion without meaning to either extirpate another ethnic distinctiveness or to promote social climbing by aping the dominant. Much effective persuasion begins by the speaker explicitly or implicitly invoking something similar or shared with the audience. It recalls Cicero's conception of rhetoric as involving three phases: conciliate the audience, instruct them, move them to action. Thus Hans Hut, an Anabaptist who would apparently die in prison charged with that heresy, described Christ in his 1526 essay, "On the Mystery of Baptism," including elaborate scriptural citations here deleted:

Jesus taught the gospel to the gardener by using the trees, to the fisherman by using the catch of fish, to the carpenter by using the house, to the goldsmith by using the smelting of gold. He taught the gospel to the housewife using the dough. He taught the gospel to the vinekeeper by using the vineyards, vines and grapes; to the tailor by using the patch on old cloth; to the merchant by using pearls. He taught the gospel to the reaper by using the harvest; to the woodcutter by using the axe and tree; to the shepherd by using the sheep. He taught the gospel to the potter by using the clay; to the steward and overseer by using their accounts; to the pregnant woman by using the act of birth; to the thresher by using the winnowing fan; to the butcher by using the slaughter. (Liechty, 1994, 69)

This eloquent portrayal suggests that Christ was by no means adapting rhetoric to his audience in a manipulative way, but with respect for the person addressed. Yet he also wanted to be effective in persuasion, perhaps touching each of Cicero's phases. He meant only the good of the person addressed. As a carpenter's son who lived in voluntary poverty, he had no wish to flatter others to advance his economic fortune.

But among those of less saintly disposition, often the seeming of similarity is rather aimed at this-worldly progress for its practitioners. It is sometimes true that the policy favored by the dominant may in part accord with that favored by many among the dominated, as is especially common for at least individual strategies of assimilation.

I. INDIVIDUAL ASSIMILATIONS FOR PERSONAL SUCCESS: OPPORTUNITIES AND OBSTACLES

There are cases when some of the members of a weaker ethnic group will vigorously oppose voluntary assimilation to the culture of the dominant as a kind of sell-out. Often these will be members of a religious group, who decry the drift of some of their number into either skepticism or into assimilation to the religion of the dominant ethnicity. They may therefore segregate themselves, but not necessarily in such forms as going into exile, going into remote boundary areas, or seeking secession as discussed in chapter 2. They just choose to keep themselves apart. Thus were the Essenes among the Jews at the time of Christ, who were thoroughly described in Josephus's *The Jewish War*. So were many ascetic monastic orders who remained within the Orthodox or Roman Catholic churches. There were also those who chose to exit such churches and live as if despising worldly advance, as illustrated by Anabaptist pacifist sects such as the Dukhobors in Russia or Canada, or the Mennonites or Amish in West Europe and the United States. In modern Israel, where they are some 10,000, and even in the United States, where they may be 100,000, the devout Jewish Haredim live as an antimodernist group never quite comfortable with the secularist goals of the original Zionists (Armstrong, 2000, 204–12). All of such groups regard either individual or collectivist voluntary assimilation, no less than capitulation before an aggressive assimilationism imposed by the dominant ethnics, as a profound betrayal of everything important.

When upward mobility is possible by making oneself like the dominant, or at least *to seem* like them, many among the dominated will want to choose this.

Although their strategy may seem convergent with selective assimilation sometimes accepted by a dominant ethnicity toward a subordinate one, it differs in several respects: First, the dominant ethnic group often maintains a glass ceiling, thus not according full equality of opportunity. Second, dominant ethnics may not offer to the subordinate ethnicity quality education or other resources needed to compete effectively for the roles for which they could be accepted. Third, any examinations or other screening procedures could be biased against the weaker ethnic group. Fourth, the dominant ethnic group may often fail to accord full respect to the upward mobiles from the weaker ethnicity, especially when they do not wholly abandon changeable attributes of their group of origin.

Put otherwise, when the dominated choose individual assimilation, they hope to be eligible for even the highest positions. They will want access to the best educational and other resources that could assist their rise. Also, they wish to be respected as equals, and many of them may be unwilling to disparage their ethnic group of origin.

Yet would-be upward mobiles may tend to avoid any *challenge* to the dominant, which would almost surely block any attempt to rise by individual initiative. For many this may require hypocrisy, following Balthassar Gracian's dictum, "Be all things to all people." Perhaps by cognitive dissonance mechanisms, many assimilators may actually incorporate key attitudes of the dominant group. As it has been said of Catholic converts, some become "more papal than the pope."

Perhaps some voluntary assimilators carry it through to completion and really do become ashamed of their own prior acculturation. But one suspects that more often they have to fake it. But faking it can bring a sense of shame, a hidden freight of guilt that may make them lash out against any critics from their group of origin.

Voluntary assimilators may express some criticisms of their group of origin even if any of their remarks could be turned against themselves as well as others from that group. Members of their own group could attack them for such verbal betrayal.

Without attempting to pass as other than they are, a form of evasion, those seeking advancement may try to correct or modify themselves to at least appear to be like the strong. As noted earlier, one variant of an enduring strategy of a weaker ethnicity before a stronger may be a personal attempt at assimilation. Not necessarily groveling before the strong, they expend energy on trying to make themselves more *like* the strong.

Examples would be strenuous attempts at change of personal appearance (grooming, dress, etc.) to look like those more advantaged, sometimes extending to such extremes as cosmetic surgery. Asian Americans living in the West used to have alterations in the almond shape of their eyes, just as many living in the East, such as children fathered by American servicemen in South Korea or Vietnam, have pondered the advantages of getting rid of their rounded eyes. Further assimilation may involve earnest self-improvement in the way of learned skills of "correct" diction or social manners, or more substantive practical educational attainments.

The Arab scholar Ibn Khaldun noted that a vanquished people quite typically imitates the ways of the victors, as if that would be enough to remove the conditions of their defeat (Khaldun, 1963, 53). Nothing has changed in this, as illustrated by Crawford Young:

Where incorporation is not possible, individuals and groups may seek to raise their status by emulation of traits identified with higher status communities. Within the colonial context, persons adopted the dress and language of the colonizer. In extreme form, exemplified by the Straits Chinese of Singapore, this extended to the total adoption of English language, dress, and Victorian mores. More often, the emulation was selective and partial. (Young, 1976, 100)

In Sri Lanka, two groups of the Hindu Tamils are living among the largely Buddhist Sinhalese population of the island. Several centuries ago, the first immigration from the nearby Tamil-speaking part of India settled in the north and points south rather than on the coast. In time these became quite well educated and could aspire to professional jobs. The other group consists of more recent immigrants arriving to become tea pickers on the northwest and western coasts. In the account of Donald Horowitz, the first group of culturally advanced Tamils were eager to be assimilated and given access to better opportunities. However, the Sinhalese blocked them from public jobs by requiring Sinhala rather than English, and they eventually also restricted their numbers in the universities, in part by weighting exams in favor of Sinhalese. It was these frustrated would-be assimilators who first turned toward rebellion and dreams of secession of Tamil-concentrated parts of the island. They naturally coalesced in this shift of strategies with the more recently immigrated tea-picking Tamils (Horowitz, 1985). Once again it is apparent that preferred ethnic minority policy of one ethnic group can be shaped by policy choice of another group.

Some individualist assimilationists accompany it with a practice of evasion, of concealing who they are and attempting to pass as an ethnic group of higher status. Sometimes such passing may be dual, trying to pass before dominant ethnics to maximize opportunities while also passing before one's group of origin to avoid any exposure or recriminations for surrender of the group identity. Thus it seems likely that when Spain enjoined deportation of the nonconverted Jews (1492) or Muslims (1499), many *conversos* were only pass-ing as such to avoid deportation. The Spanish Inquisition sought to find them out from details of their diets, behavior on religious special days, or through torture. Interestingly, when Enver Hoxha was attempting to stamp out all religion in communist Albania, as discussed in chapter 3, his agents also used dietary observations to see if some were yet secretly religious.

One can imagine that in predominantly Sunni Islam nations, some Shi'as would attempt to pass as other than they are, trying to remember to pray with their arms folded as do Sunnis when standing rather than with arms and head hanging down as typical among Shi'as. They would also dispense with the hardened piece of clay from Kerbala on which a Shi'as may put the forehead rather than directly on the prayer mat. They would avoid speaking too well of the *hadith* reported by Ali or Fatima, and avoid any display of enthusiasm for Shi'as holy days, such as celebrations of the martyrdom at Kerbala of Hussain and most of his family. For as Olivier Roy notes, "In countries such as Lebanon, Iraq, Afghanistan, and Pakistan, not to mention in the oil mon-archies, the simple fact of being a Shiite made a career in the army or gov-ernment nearly impossible" (Roy, 1994, 53).

In our own time, many ethnic Koreans in Japan attempt to pass as ordinary Japanese, but this, when known, can cause them to be sharply criticized by other resident Koreans who rather want all members of their group to strive for naturalization and equality of rights. Sometimes what is best for personal assimilation may impede longer run collective assimilation. It must be tempt-ing for many assimilating individuals to conceal their Korean ethnicity both from dominant ethnics and from their own subordinated ethnicity. Because so many of the latter could personally know one from one's past, this second kind of passing has to be more difficult than the first.

I here offer some broad remarks on evasion as a political strategy, used not only to assist one's assimilation but in other contexts also to aid one's emi-gration or secession strategies as discussed in chapter 2.

Evasion, like enduring or emigrating, is another strategy of the weak. In part it may involve concealment of where you are or what you are doing, but in a second form it may involve concealment of who you are. There are obviously rough parallels of both among strategies for life pursued by non-human forms of life. Thus either thick cover or camouflage may conceal the location of a form of life from possible predators, and sometimes camouflage (as well as vocal mimicry, etc.) may even conceal what kind of an organism it is, as when moths evolve on their wings snakelike eyes to frighten away pred-atory birds.

The strategy of evasion involves a de facto but hardly de jure shift of de-cisions to oneself or one's friends, putting some powers with friends but with-out sanction of law. As such we can understand it as the counterpart of the strategy of institutional restructuring, which normally requires more resource strengths to *legally* relocate powers of decisions with friends. Evasion often involves disobedience of law or decrees of authorities, and usually but not always such disobedience is covert. An exceptional case of overt evasion could be a robber band or guerrilla army that locates itself in some virtually inaccessible terrain, from there flaunting the law with impunity.

Although evasion is most commonly a strategy of the resource-weak, occasionally it will also be followed by those of more considerable resources who yet are unable to advantage themselves by changing the law and choose instead to secretly disobey it. Most criminal behavior involves some evasion. There are two main forms of evasion, which are not exclusive in use: (1) concealment of membership in a certain category likely to bring deprivations on those known to belong; or (2) concealment of actual behavior other than such belonging when that conduct is contrary to law.

The first kind of evasion, concealment of a group membership, could also be understood as passing as something other than what one may be. This is unlike the enduring mode of assimilation in that it works not at the being of similitude but only at the *appearance* of conventional memberships. Instances of this sort of evasion could include the attempt of illegal aliens to pass as citizens or lawful immigrants. If much criminal behavior involves some evasion, including that of the tax evader, we here pass over from what may be punishable static group identities to those group memberships that are inseparable from conduct. Note well that concealment of a group membership may sometimes extend even to suppression of a personal identification with a category. Although it is often claimed that under great stress most agents deepen their commitment to more "primordial" identities such as race, ethnicity, and the like, there are cases rather where agents actually abandon such identities. Perhaps the very behavior of passing as something other than you are may at some point lead many agents to lowered identification with what is concealed.

Laws contain not only references to classes of persons but also to classes of behavior. The more dynamic side of evasion concerns concealment of some activity that would be punishable if known. Throughout history gays and lesbians would necessarily conceal their unorthodox behavior when being caught could bring punishment ranging to death. Or the concealed practice may rather be involvement in some prohibited religious service (any non-Muslim service in Saudi Arabia, or any religious service at all in Enver Hoxha's Albania) or participation in an illegal political movement trying to subvert a political order it cannot openly enter. Secret meeting places, codes, passwords, and the like, have often characterized such evasions, which here relate to the management of sensitive messages as part of what I have elsewhere broadly defined as the influence strategy. Perhaps especially in self-interested criminal activity, a strategy of evasion is often accompanied by influence of lower level officials or police, as in bribing them not to enforce the rules. What is here an evasion strategy before higher officials is an influence strategy before lower ones. Forms of evasion are various, however, sometimes not involving violation of law so much as mere commands of lawful superiors, as in the elusive behavior notorious among exploited slaves, serfs, or even modern peasants (cf. Scott, 1986, 1989, 1990). Slacking off work when the authorities are out of sight, pretending to misunderstand directives, are some among many of such forms.

Like other strategies of the weak, evasion is often workable by isolated individuals, but perhaps collective uses of evasion more often portend an attempt to turn to the more active strategies requiring more coalesced resources to win. Thus in the histories of illegal labor unions or revolutionary parties and movements, extralegal, covert activity often preceded an attempt to legitimize such organizations by plays of the influence, recruitment, or structures games. When eventual overt activity runs into the extreme of revolutionary overthrow, it may involve simultaneous plays of the influence, recruitment, and structures strategies. Often a first move is operation of some decision-making body in parallel, but illicit form before it eventually may operate openly and perhaps displace the opposing public bodies. Thus a guerrilla band's rebel first "extols stealth, evasion, planned retreat, and nonattachment to territory." But after a period of activity ("retreat, evasion, escape, hiding, evacuation of territory") that conventional military doctrine may hold demeaning, that same band may cross over to a structures strategy of pulling all power to decision units where friends prevail (Leites and Wolf, 1970, 152–53). What had been an illegal usurpation of authority becomes then the legal authority.

Friedrich Nietzsche (d. 1900), like his follower Michel Foucault (d. 1980) much later, emphasized a *will to power* in all of us, which may in part reflect liberal society, as comparable remarks are found in Thomas Hobbes (d. 1679) or John Locke (d. 1704). But the strategies of the weak show that sometimes a will to power is merely an effort to attain more personal (or favored group) autonomy, without necessarily reducing the autonomy of others. In the more active strategic fields of political action, such as influencing, recruiting, and restructuring, agents while seeking enhancement of their own autonomy more often do so by somehow reducing that of others. That is one way to make others more predictable. As Alasdair MacIntyre somewhere observed, in human society everyone would like to be less predictable to others while making those others more predictable to themselves.

Primarily writing of what I call evasion, James C. Scott lists some forms of "everyday forms of resistance" of the relatively weak as including "foot dragging, dissimulation, false compliance, feigned ignorance, desertion, pilfering, smuggling, poaching, arson, slander, sabotage, surreptitious assault and murder, anonymous threats, and so on" (Scott, 1989, 5). He argues that often such action must be viewed as really political. It may not only be defensive but actually create some gains for those turning to such tactics. Also, although it normally cannot be called "collective behavior," it not only has some consequences similar to Marxist class struggle but also involves much cooperation or complicity across the stratum, as when one peasant winks at the poaching of another peasant in the landlord's forest.

Lying easily crosses the borders between a strategy of mere evasion before an authority and that which attempts some influence over an authority: "There are two forms of lying: concealment, leaving out true information, and falsification, or presenting false information as if it were true" (Ekman, 1985, 41). Only the first form is usually evasion. It offers many possible escape routes in excuses, but the second form, which is necessary if one is frontally challenged and does not remain silent, is a riskier recourse to persuasion, part of the influence strategy is more likely to be used in an accommodative frame by the weak, as addressed in chapter 6.

Peasants are not always ethnically unlike the higher strata in their context, but they often have differed a great deal by acculturation. Historically, peasants have been viewed by some analysts as existing in a "moral economy" of caring and sharing, as opposed to the "market economy" of individualistic self-seeking. Eric Wolf suggests that whereas the former outlook often underlay past peasant rebellions (even if usually repressed because insufficiently organized beyond localities), modern peasants have tended to assimilate into the modern market economy, and they have been unlikely to participate in peasant rebellions (Wolf, 1969). Yet especially within liberal democratic contexts, often such peasants have turned to what I call the influence and recruitment strategies, using pressure tactics or voting, to secure aims such as lower taxes or protection against import competition in their commodities.

Occasionally focused less on their own condition than on better lives for their children, the assimilators may often exaggerate their success by recourse to a narrow range of reference within the stratification system. Even if they cannot enter the higher stratum, at least their effort may further differentiate them from a stratum just below their own.

But consider the whole system of stratification. One may identify cross-nationally comparable understandings of socially disadvantaging attributes, using as indexes economic deprivations (e.g., less than equal pay for equal work, greater unemployment or underemployment) or an actual or aspirational attempt to correct or conceal the attribute in pursuing conventionally acceptable goals such as getting good jobs (cf. Cook, 1983). That understood, there are predictable patterns in political recruitment results. Sparing the reader some obvious qualifications, *the percentage incumbency of a socially disadvantaged attribute tends to thin out as the importance of office rises.* The pattern prevails in public and many private hierarchies, such as corporate leadership. If anything, it can be worse in the latter, for among the Fortune 500 CEOs in the United States, one sees only a few women and but one African American.

Further, in the historical development of such tapering and often vanishing wedges, the order of first entries of a socially disadvantaged group into various roles roughly inverts the importance of office, if "importance" is understood by such conventional criteria as scope of decisions made, by career pathway preferences (most politicians would give up a less important job for a more important one), and " stepping-stone" value for increasing chances of attaining an important office as measured by the first criterion (perhaps one could measure the stepping-stone value of office A as the higher of two values, the percentage of office A who go on to B, or the percentage in B who were previously in office A).

Of course one could turn this about and *measure* importance of offices by absence of disadvantaging attributes. A top office such as the presidency of the United States or prime minister in Canada tends to less formally than informally screen out socially disadvantaging attributes. One concedes some exceptions, as when by an informal norm, most Canadian prime ministers will be not only from Quebec but also francophones.

As so often noted, often there are "glass ceilings" that keep a disadvantaged attribute out of the topmost roles, as experienced not only by ethnic minorities but women or other socially disadvantaged categories. The cross-national similarities of such stratified results of recruitment politics are at least as interesting as any national differences of the details of such systems.

As already apparent, struggles over eligibility criteria may occur at either the formal or informal aspects. Formal criteria are those that are publicly avowed, usually not only announced but also written up in constitutions, statutes, administrative regulations, or association bylaws. Among the many rhetorics that may focus on these, the formal criteria may often be argued through tendentious statements of the purpose of the organization to which the written rules apply. As Stanley Hoffman once put it, "'Who governs' may well be one of the key questions of politics, but 'what for' is the other one. The wrong 'who' cannot reach the right 'what'; but depending on the 'what,' the right 'who' will not be the same" (Hoffman, 1970, 177–78). Thus, as the old aristocratic argument went, if the purpose of government is to promote virtue, obviously the more virtuous should rule. Or, as the later "stake in society" theory maintained, if the purpose is protection and expansion of property, taxpaying or property-owning criteria of eligibility would seem to be appropriate to higher office, as well as basic citizenship. But note that even aside from arguable understandings of the purpose of government, discussions of potential contribution tend to conceal a circularity. One's capacity to give to society is in large part a function of what one has got from it.

Arguably the informal criteria of eligibility are more resistant to argument or change precisely because they are not formally announced. These informal selection criteria are not only typically unwritten but usually unacknowledged by those who tend to win by them. Their appropriate verbal strategy is either silence or loud emphasis on the *formal* openness of the affected offices. In contrast, the losers will demand both acknowledgment and elimination of the *informal* closure of office to their friends, claiming that the biased selection modality or prejudice in its application accounts for the pattern of adverse recruitment results.

The formal-informal dimensions crosscut the three basic types of recruitment criteria. The basic types are (1) *ascriptive* (broadly, who you *are*, tapping attributes literally or virtually fixed by birth), (2) *achievement* (what you can *do*, or measures of "competence" or "merit," most often some combination of educational attainment, examination performance, experience, and effectiveness), and (3) *attitudinal* (where you stand, including personal loyalties as well as ideological "soundness"). Most practiced recruitment can be understood as progressive reduction of the potential pool to the charmed overlap zone, meeting all three sorts of criteria from which recruitment actually occurs and for both formal and informal criteria.

If formal ascriptive criteria for the U.S. presidency are sparse, the informal ones are formidable, judging by actual recruitments of the presidents to date.

As for age, presidents typically have been in their 50s, but only three of them have been over 65 in office. Further, informal screens require that one be white, of pronounced Northwest European ancestry, of the male sex, and typically taller and with a full head of hair (only a few presidents such as Gerald Ford could be called bald). Although the founders rejected Charles Pinckney's suggested specification of a property requirement, and against the grain of the log cabin myth, most presidents have come from somewhat higher class origins, if Nixon and Clinton are recent exceptions. Indeed, most recent serious candidates for the presidency have also been millionaires.

In part a consequence of prejudice in application as well as antecedent resources working their way through procedures, such results illustrate the yet high importance of informal ascriptive criteria. In the example of the U.S. presidency, such criteria on one side predict candidate resource positions, whereas from the other side, they guide both presidential kingmakers who shape nominations as well as voters who may choose them in primary or general elections with expected policy bias of candidates. Often voters will tend to favor at least some of their own kinds on the premise that those ascriptively like themselves may more likely share their views. The syllogistic chain runs something like this: If X is of my ascriptive attribute, then X has shared my conditions of life; if so, then X shares my learning experience; if so, then X must share my attitudes on political and other issues. Hence if X is like me, X would choose as I would choose.

However reasonable in the absence of more specific information on policy preferences of politicians, there are many obvious weak links in that chain, and a chain is neither weaker nor stronger than its weakest link. For one thing, the predicted behavior may fail because the higher the office the more office-holders tend to have been closely screened on attitudes (regardless of ascriptive origins). Writing in 1850, De Tocqueville suggested that electoral system details such as the scope of suffrage influence more the types of persons elected in lower level offices, including assemblies, more than higher level offices, such as cabinets and chief executives (Tocqueville, 1970, 104). Office-holders are subject to special learning or incentives once in the office, in any case. Yet those who feel excluded by one of their salient ascriptive attributes, such as African Americans in the United States, will make a proportional presence of their attribute in offices of all levels a central meaning of what they regard as "representativeness."

I have been suggesting that a weak ethnic group such as those of a minority religion, race, or native language will, when assimilating, have a difficult time attempting to rise very high. I am also suggesting that rising high will not only require unusual achievement attainments but also a strong willingness to make oneself attitudinally conforming to the dominant ethnics or their relevant leaders. For whatever the details of local recruitment rules, the results usually look *cooptative*, that is, as if those who are already high really select who else can rise, and they prefer to help rise those who are most like themselves. If rising in the world requires for most of us a bit of toadying to superiors, individuals of ethnically subordinate groups almost surely have to do more of it, at least if trying to rise in organizations run by dominant ethnicities.

The consequence is that ambitious members of a subordinate ethnicity must in effect suppress their own identity, and many of them in their behavior may quite literally betray the best chances of their ethnic group of origin. They may begin by faking their similarity of thoughts with dominant ethnics, but they may end up actually thinking just like them. As my friend John Donnelly once quipped, those who cannot speak truth to power end up lying to themselves. They "sell out."

Often individual assimilations cannot be controlled by a group. Many immigrants of North European continental origins found that their children quickly abandoned their native Swedish, German, and so on. Also uncontrollable are the many marriages of American reformed or secular Jews to non-Jews.

Yet if most of their own ethnic group rather favor a strategy of accommodation involving a greater measure of group rights, or even a strategy of separation such as a secessionist effort, many among the dominated may in some way attempt to punish "traitors" to their ethnic group, at an extreme, sometimes even with murder.

One supposes the sharpest division within a group when some of them are economically and educationally retarded but live within a regional concentration of their group, whereas others live outside that region of concentration, have sought assimilation, and have been substantially accepted by the dominant ethnics. The former could be thinking of secession, and the latter would think it a threat to their interests in advancement by integration. But as the Horowitz warning about Sri Lanka Tamils warns us, any closure of opportunities could cause the latter group to reverse its position (Horowitz, 1985). The secessionist struggle for Tamil Eelam killed over 62,000 people 1983 through 2001. No talks have occurred since 1995, but in 2001, the principal leader of Tamil secessionists known as the Tigers said he could talk of an autonomist accommodation if the Sri Lankan government ended its proscription of his organization as terrorist.

Assimilation as voluntary integration is not working well to the extent that the society remains quite obviously stratified. As noted, one can quickly grasp the stratification system of a society by examining patterns of power (what attributes thin out as the importance of office rises?), patterns of economic privilege (which attributes predict higher unemployment or less than equal pay for equal work?), or status (what attributes would people like to "correct" or somehow "conceal" when pursuing an otherwise acceptable goal, such as pursuing a good job?). All known societies have been stratified, and as long as systemic inequalities remain, one can expect some recourse to assimilation by ambitious individuals, and, given the importance of the choice in question, it is quite plausible that an instrumental but boundedly rational reasoning may explain the choice.

If one were to attempt a list of the kinds of individuals of an ethnic minority most likely to turn toward personal assimilationism, one may suggest the following as plausible, while awaiting empirical evidence:

1. they do not live in any place of regional concentration of their ethnic group, but are rather dispersed;

2. the above dispersion is over a long period of time, such that they may even be a second or third generation;

3. they do not live in some new residential concentration of their ethnicity, such as an urban ghetto, but rather are scattered about among members of the dominant ethnic group;

4. they perceive clear rewards in assimilating, whether for self-protection or for self-advancement in their careers (this usually supposes that the dominant ethnics are not following a thorough segregationist strategy against them, even if exclusion may emerge in the roles of highest prestige and rewards);

5. some of them are enough alike in appearance or speech that they could "pass" as if members of the dominant ethnicity, at least if they are not identified on mandatory ID cards.

Apart from some residential concentration such as in Osaka, most of the preceding seem to characterize the Koreans attempting assimilation within Japan, although they are handicapped, in danger of being exposed, because ID cards read "Japanese National of Korean Descent" (cf. Hicks, 1997; Lee and De Vos, 1981).

II. COLLECTIVE ASSIMILATION FOR GROUP SUCCESS: BUT AT RISK TO GROUP IDENTITY?

Unplanned collective assimilations occur. Thus the children of German or Scandinavian immigrants to the United States did not learn the language of their parents, unlike many Hispanic immigrants. Or some Native American groups (Cherokees, Nez Percé, Palouse) took up herding and farming or even the Christian religion. As earlier noted, the farming did not save their land, but the Christianity gave some one privilege: After the 1876 Nez Percé rising—just three years before the Carlisle school opened to assimilate Indians—and its consequent suppression, Christian Nez Percé were allowed to settle on Idaho's Nez Percé reservation, but non-Christian Nez Percé were moved far from their homeland to the Colville reservation in northern Washington State, there intermixed with other tribes.

Chief Joseph of the Nez Percé was a spiritual rather than war chief. But he was so disgusted by the belated theft of Nez Percé land and the brutal repression by white soldiers (such as aiming high but shooting directly into native tents, which contained women and children) that he renounced his prior Christianity. When one considers other examples such as a turn of many African Americans to Islam from the 1960s, it is apparent that reversed assimilations are also important and deserve study.

If many among a weaker ethnicity favor collective assimilation, it is not forced down their throats by the dominant ethnicity, as in some examples in the prior chapter. If any pressures are acceptable at all, it may be only parents or other relatives leaning on their own children, out of concern for their future security and economic prospects. Thus I have met Chicanos who speak almost no Spanish, who sometimes volunteer that they have a strong mental block against learning Spanish now. For when they were small children, their parents punished them for using any Spanish words, pressuring them to master English as the key to better opportunities. There is something tragic in that.

Normally any voluntary choice of collective assimilation also will be limited, not culminating in the kind of ethnocide such as reviewed in chapter 3. In some contexts, those of a weaker ethnicity may also regard the dominant ethnicity's assimilation-for-control as merely a way *to rationalize denial of some group right.* This was illustrated in chapter 3 by the assimilations aimed at American Indians or Australian Aboriginals, as arguably strategies to whack back the reservations or cut public welfare expenditures going to natives.

Normally collective assimilative strategies are not out of some unanimous concurrence by members of the weaker ethnicity. Yet there are occasional instances where a whole group becomes assimilated due to a choice by its leader. One thinks of how the conversion of Vladimir of Kiev in 988 c.e. to Orthodox Catholicism led to the conversion of virtually all of the Rus people.

Assimilation may also be *recommended* as a collective strategy for the weaker ethnicity, sometimes more in hopes of security than of major economic gain. Note that group *status* (social prestige) ceases to be in question if the group is wholly assimilated, which usually obliterates any distinctiveness, any identity. But some leaders of a group may reluctantly concede that they must let important parts of their distinctiveness go for the sake of the group's security or economic livelihoods.

Some advocates of collective assimilation, focused on improved livelihoods, clearly assume goodwill among the dominant ethnics. One finds that uttered in 1884 by Booker T. Washington in his National Education Association address in Madison, Wisconsin, where he says, "The black man is beginning to find out that there are those even among the southern whites who desire his elevation" (Washington, 1900/1970, 111). He was saying that just as Jim Crow laws were being put in place across his South (Woodward, 1974). Most of the weaker ethnics favoring separatism would by no means speak of the goodwill found among whites, as becomes evident throughout the contrasting, often bitter *Autobiography* of W. E. B. Du Bois (reviewed in chapter 2).

As one reads the second installment of Washington's autobiography one looks in vain for any expressions of pride in his African cultural heritage or even the African American cultural achievements such as the black spiritual. On such things there is a sonorous silence. But one does find him expressing shame that African Americans had failed to improve themselves, had let themselves be edged out of jobs by whites who offered better service as barber, nurse, and so on. For Washington, the head of the Tuskegee Institute in Alabama, African Americans had to assimilate to rising standards in technical skills and take pride in good work as farmers or mechanics rather than dream of leaping into the learned professions. Writing in 1900, he proudly cites a long 1853 letter from Frederick Douglass that had advanced much the same viewpoint (Washington, 1900/1970, 133–39). At its best, one may say that perhaps in Douglass's day it was sound advice, even if it also seems to pander to white bigots whom were known by Washington to look askance at newly emancipated blacks who had grown too "uppity."

As Joseph Rothschild notes, African American policy alignment went through two phases: "Initially they expected no more than an end to civil, political, and social discrimination against their members as individuals, that is, an end to unequal treatment violating the universalistic and regulative values that the dominants themselves purported to profess. Only after this expectation was disappointed did they recoil into collective strategies stressing group rights and group autonomies—sometimes to the point of reversing their original integrationist aspirations" (Rothschild, 1981, 114).

Avoiding Cultural Suicide. Some assimilationists differ from Booker T. Washington in aiming at the best of two cultural worlds, that is, assimilating to the stronger culture in part for its riches and in part for chances of career progress, and yet preserving much of their own cultural tradition. One example is Léopold Senghor, the first president of Senegal (1960–1980) (after being also the first to voluntarily relinquish office in sub-Saharan Africa, he lived on to die at age ninety-five in 2001). As earlier noted, Senghor wrote excellent poetry in French, yet he also espoused the idea of *négritude*, or taking pride in his African cultural heritage. This included closeness to nature, identity with ancestors, and contribution to jazz. Other prominent advocates of the concept included Aimé Cesaire of Martinique and Léon G. Damas of French Guiana. Recall Senghor's motto as cited in the epigraph to this chapter: "Assimilate, not be assimilated." He seemed to be saying, welcome another culture but do not lose your own.

When dominant ethnic groups are in segregationist strategy, they may punish imitation of themselves, but they may sometimes shift to accepting at least assimilation of individuals from a weaker ethnicity. But that becomes full integration only if the more advantaged group members accept the assimilators as no longer "other," at least when according opportunities.

But sometimes those who are increasingly integrated, whether by intention or unplanned processes, may at some point fear loss of their group identity. It is interesting when many members of a group have come to recognize that price of its assimilation and shifts to efforts to preserve at least some threads of what distinctiveness remains to its members. Assimilation sometimes means a purely personal view of the problem and its resolution, but the practice of assimilation by many often may eventually awaken a heightened return to a sense of group identity precisely because of the shock of recognizing that it is being lost.

Recall from chapter 2 that W. E. B. Du Bois once attended Fisk University, a black-enrolled university with poor facilities that had been a military barracks. A Public Broadcasting Corporation documentary of early 2002 described how the attempt to field a chorale group singing European songs to raise funds foundered until the discovery that what really attracted big audiences was not a repertory of European classics but of black spirituals. Not making themselves similar to white choruses but revitalizing what was distinctive to their group was what worked. Through exhausting work on the part of the directors and singers, the Jubilee Singers funded new buildings and programs for the young university. For the rest of us, they helped preserve a cultural treasure for civilization. One wonders what both Du Bois and Washington thought of that.

To have to forego one's ethnic identity out of fear for one's security or economic prospects has the certain consequence of obliteration of any pride in that origin, and it may not assure the safety or economic gains expected from the sacrifice. When Spain expelled its unconverted Jews (1499) and Muslims (1502), any insincere *conversos* may have bought some time to retain their place and possessions, but they immediately sold their pride. Some would also lose their lives to the Spanish Inquisition. Also, 275,000 Muslim *conversos*, the Moriscos, were forcibly expelled from Spain (1609–1614), losing their landholdings in the process.

Group identities are not only a means to self-respect but sometimes important as a means to mutual protection or economic assistance. Perhaps at least if not targets of physical genocide, many would usually be wise to preserve their ethnic identity. It is a necessary condition for working out any collective accommodation with the dominant ethnic group. Only a widely recognized group can expect to negotiate any group rights, including even *official* recognition.

NOTE

1. Alan Krebs, "Leopold Senghor Dies at 95," *New York Times*, Dec. 21, 2001, p. A–25.

CHAPTER 5

Accommodations as Minimal: Strategies of the Stronger Ethnic Group

> If you offer them your hand, they will take your arm.
> —a commonplace heard around the world

I have heard much the same bigoted remark in such varied places as South America, East Europe, or India. Usually it is uttered by members of a dominant ethnic group who hold that a local ethnic minority is not only greedy and ungrateful, but perhaps treacherous as well.

In prior discussions, we have normally assumed that a dominant ethnicity effectively controls the state apparatus, in which the subordinate ethnicity has little or no voice. The possibility of the state assisting accommodation depends very much on how one views the state. Thus Terry Nardin says, "Much of the disagreement and confusion about the concepts of violence and conflict management which characterizes political discussion stems from conflicting conceptions of the state and of its role in political conflict. On the one hand, one can regard the state as a manager of conflict; on the other, as a party to conflict" (Nardin, 1971, 12). Although Nardin notes that this classic opposition appeared between the Hegelian and the Marxist concepts of the state, which focused on the question of class domination of a state, one could as readily extend analysis to ethnic group domination. Nardin himself takes the position (which I share) that the state can be both manager of conflict and party to conflict, and to the extent the latter is true, one may sometimes have to look outside the state for a solution.

When the dominant and subordinate ethnic groups each is relatively unified and pursue their ethnic policies, when they choose very different directions in separation, assimilation, or accommodation, there can be expectable problems of moving at cross-purposes, as indicated in some of the cells of Figure 5.1.

But even when they may seem to be on the same page, as when both look to separation, or when both look to assimilation, there can be important differences in their specific aims. This is so when both give at least lip service to accommodative policy, as this chapter and that which follows attempt to show.

I. THE MINIMALIST MENTALITY OF DOMINANT ETHNICS

This chapter assumes that the dominant ethnic group and the state controlled by them are inclined toward at least a gesture of accommodation with the weaker ethnicity. As a residual category, neither separation nor assimilation, I now turn to variants of the strategy of accommodation, once again looking at it when sponsored by the dominant or when initiated by the dominated. Every form of accommodation avoids the extremes of either seeing the weaker ethnic group as wholly different or as at least potentially wholly alike. Rather, it views the group as in some ways similar, in others different, and it gives due recognition to both as somehow appropriate in political arrangements. It accepts the idea of pluralism in its strongest sense, of public acceptance of some group prerogatives, whether by informal norms or even in law. Accommodations look to some often negotiated compromise between rival ethnic group positions. However, forms of accommodation will rarely succeed if not ultimately embraced by both sides.

As suggested by the epigraph, it is quite common for dominant groups, whether classes or ethnicities, to think that the appropriate resolution of any conflict is for the subordinate groups to trim their aspirations toward what they are already getting. Hence usually leading members of a dominant ethnicity, especially those lacking in moderation (one could call them the intransigents, militants, or ethnic chauvinists), tend to be *minimalist* in any offered accommodation accorded to grievances of an ethnic minority.

The *least* that a dominant ethnic can offer is nothing at all, ignoring any grievances of the weaker ethnicity. This is no accommodation but perhaps accompanies a policy of either segregation or aggressive assimilation. But next to giving nothing is any offer not really meant to be kept, but either (1) never implemented, or (2) revoked at the earliest opportunity. In the spirit of the analyses of Murray Edelman, what weaker ethnics are given is but a merely symbolic reward that is a substantive deprivation, whereas dominant ethnics are incurring a merely symbolic (unreal) deprivation for substantive rewards (cf. Edelman, 1964).

In the latter case one finds a long history of treaty settlements with Native Americans, often followed up with revocations. Quite typically a native group was offered a reservation, but then either they were later displaced from it

Figure 5.1
Paired Ethnic Minority Policy Choices and Possible Consequences

	Choice by Dominant		
	Separation	**Assimilation**	**Accommodation**
Choice by Subordinate **Separation**	1. If their labor is not needed, emigration by the weak is no problem. But if they attempt secession, the dominants may repress it.	2. If the weak want to remain apart or secede, they may punish their own members who succumb to assimilation by the dominant.	3. Here the strong may be making concessions to preserve the community while the weak are attempting to secede, as Slovaks in 1992.
Assimilation	4. Here the weak may be frustrated in their ambition to compete for jobs and other benefits, facing either thorough segregation or at least glass ceilings.	5. When the dominant assimilate select individuals, they weaken the subordinate group, without giving the latter desired equality. They could even aim at an aggressive assimilation or ethnocide.	6. The strong may here accord to subordinates minimal rights, even merely formal equality of opportunity to those meeting certain assimilations.
Accommodation	7. The dominants may have no interest in negotiating a "social contract" with the weaker ethnicity, who want one.	8. Although the dominants select some subordinates, they accord no real equality. They may even try to erase the cultural difference.	9. Concurrence here may be difficult because the dominants usually make *minimal* concessions, the dominated look for *maximal*.

farther westward, or else the initial grant of reservation land was whacked back as soon as frontier whites coveted its good farmland or other resources. Any compensatory promises of off-reservation hunting or gathering rights often went unenforced in the sequel, if sometimes partly recovered in rather recent federal court rulings.

Often an impermanent concession was only intended to avert conflict with a weaker group, or perhaps to head off a future coalition of weaker ethnic groups. In the latter case was an early grant in South Africa of voter rights to two nonwhite groups, the Asians (mostly Indian subcontinentals in origins) and the Coloureds (a mixed race population concentrated in the Cape vicinity), expecting them to support the white regime against any challenge from the much larger black African (Bantu) population. However, as they gained strength, Afrikaner Nationalists eventually rescinded such voting rights entirely, not offering to restore them until 1983, when the apartheid regime was threatened. Consider these other examples. In 1960 the Greek Cypriots granted a power sharing or consociational constitution to placate the Turkish Cypriot minority, but they were trying to rescind that by 1963, and by 1974 many Greek Cypriots sought merger (*enosis*) with Greece. In another case, in 1972 the northern Sudanese Muslims bought peace by promising to back off from their wish to impose the Islamic law, the *shari'a*, on the southern Sudanese black Africans, but they revoked that promise in 1983, starting two decades of renewed warring.

Often dominant ethnicities in a political system will be more attached to the status quo. In noncommunist systems this makes them more rightist in terms of standard left-right policy space, as has been true in the United States and Canada. As Harry Jaffa correctly notes, throughout American history the more conservative party (Federalists, Whigs, Republicans) has received more support from the English ancestry voters, and the more liberal party (Democratic-Republicans, Democrats) has been backed more by the non-English (even Jefferson was of some Welsh ancestry), especially newer immigrant waves (Jaffa, 1959, 72). Most Canadians would concur that the Progressive Conservatives, the Reform Party, and the newer National Alliance have been less willing to accommodate Canadian francophone aspirations, especially in Quebec, than have Liberals and New Democrats. In Europe, conservative parties often tend to be slightly more xenophobic than parties to their left, if not as shrill as extreme rightists of a near-fascist or fascist leaning. However, in some political systems, ethnic identity is a separate dimension of ideological space, not reducible to the left-right divide (cf. Laver and Schofield, 1990, 131–42).

It has been noted that in coalition formation, if any coalition can be stable at all, it will tend to have a leader who for all salient issues can cover the median left-right issue space among those they lead, for otherwise a rival candidate for leadership could defeat them by at least one vote simply by covering any uncovered median (Laver and Shepsle, 1996). But there are different reference sets for medians. Although there could be other coalition spans, one could imagine a dominant ethnic group coalition as consisting of the intransigents only, of a broad spectrum of the whole group inclusive of militants and moderates, or of the moderates only. The first coalition, likely to offer nothing or very little to the weaker ethnic group, could be outvoted by someone pitched to the median of a more inclusive spectrum. If leaders cover the median space of a broad spectrum of their group, those at the center of the distribution of opinion will tend to dominate, inclined at best to minimal concessions. Although moderates could also sometimes threaten to bolt that coalition, an extremist wing that loudly declaims against offering anything at all, or offering too much, to the demands of an ethnic minority may often have more weight. If such ethnic chauvinists succeed in persuading more of their ethnicity to their hard-line positions, the existing leadership will lose its median position and perhaps have to either become more intransigent, too, or risk loss of leadership to someone who is.

Even if such threats from hard-liners from within or without their program coalition were not objectively present, a leader of a dominant ethnicity could *say* that this is so, if only to bolster resistance to larger demands of some ethnic minority. Such a leader does not want to be painted as "selling out" or "appeasing," especially when costs of any substantive accommodations to the dominant ethnicity may run high for the support base. Personal costs may be high, if such leaders are either removed from office or assassinated by hard-liners, as in some illustrations of my introduction. For whenever one or both ethnic groups is sharply divided, sometimes the level of conflict over ethnic minority policy can make one or both factions of a group violent toward members of their own group. If hard-liners are not attacking compromisers, sometimes the moderates may have to accept military or police force to contain the excesses of the intransigents.

At worst, the extremists may effectively dominate *each side* when two ethnic groups are in conflict, such that the conflict situation often approximates the game of Chicken, a one-shot game of nearly simultaneous moves. It becomes a zero-sum game if only one driver swerves, but a Doomsday game of mutual destruction if neither does, at least if driving cars of equal vulnerability. As Thomas Schelling famously noted long ago, in such a game it may be the best strategy to seem or even be totally rigid. If one were to throw one's steering wheel out the window, it is more likely that the opposing driver, if seeing that move, would turn out. Sometimes in the real world two ethnic groups fall into mutual destruction, as when an ethnic minority moves toward secession and the other group vows to repress it. Although the ensuing war can do much damage to both sides, it may do its worst when they are nearly equal, unless one gets an advantage through strategic surprise. As Vishnagupta Kautilya's *Arthashastra* noted, as two sides approach military equality, war between them would be mutually ruinous: "A fight with an equal brings losses to both sides, just like the destruction of two unbaked mudpots hitting each other" (Kautilya, 1992, 566).

It is at least plausible that certain arrangements of the regime may make a difference on the probability of situations of either rigidity or flexibility. It is arguable that many traditional emperors or monarchs were often more ethnically accommodative than are some modern military dictators, especially fascist ones, who are characteristically most xenophobic. Crawford Young saw little that was accommodative in military dictatorships (Young, 1976). Donald Horowitz, too, notes that military regimes tend not to be multiethnic, and often there can be a back-and-forthing of central power as several ethnic groups through their own military brass compete for power (Horowitz, 1985,

472–508; also, Horowitz, 1980). I would add that states may tend to deploy different kinds of public employees as the main force depending on favored ethnic minority policy: A formal segregationist policy may emphasize enforcement by the military, police, prosecutors, and judges, as in apartheid South Africa. An aggressively assimilationist policy, as in Turkey toward the Kurds, could add some weight to ministers of education or the approved press. But an accommodative policy usually requires people skilled in political negotiations, especially civilian politicians. Even more than educators or specialists in mass media, they are experts in two-way talk, or dialogue.

If open societies may take the lid off public expressions of ethnic animosities, they may be better at resolving them. Relatively democratic societies seem to be best in working out accommodations, but as Eric Nordlinger argued, not when (1) a dominant ethnic group holds majority status and (2) insists on pure majoritarianism. He itemizes six often effective "conflict-regulating practices," which rather would require any majority ethnicity to practice restraint, to make some sacrifices, as in forming a stable coalition with the weaker ethnicity, following proportionality in allocating offices, institutionalizing mutual veto, depoliticizing a divisive issue, making compromises, or yielding unilateral concessions (Nordlinger, 1972, 20–36).

I suggest in Figure 5.2 some contrasts of nondemocratic and democratic situations as related to factional or party systems, influenced in this primarily by Donald Horowitz (1985).

If anticipating the beginning or continuation of mutually ruinous ethnic conflict, even a stronger ethnic minority can choose to seek a deal. No deal happens, of course, if either or both reject talk, keep the discussion only at a level of noncommittal "cheap talk," or really do talk of some possible accommodations but fail to concur on any result. Fortunately, this game now is normally not like Chicken.

If both sides are really sincere in wanting an agreement, the game is not what game theorists call "a *pure* coordination problem," which by definition would mean that they value the agreement more than its content, as often illustrated by noting when good friends quickly agree on a place to have lunch. All it takes is communication, if they are not fussy about food type. No, the usual problem form is what game theoreticians call "an *impure* coordination problem." That is, all want an agreement but differ in preferences as to its contents, usually concerning (1) what each side gives and (2) what each side gets. Most of the giving and getting would be direct exchange of the two parties, but occasionally some third parties get somehow involved, as when the United States offered billions of dollars of aid to both Israel and Egypt after Menahem Begin and Anwar Sadat concluded peace in 1979.

To those not game theorists, "an impure coordination problem" is more familiarly known as typically disagreements over what has been called from the ancient Greeks "distributive justice." Familiar in allocations of grades in

Figure 5.2
How Regime and Party Variables Affect Chances of Ethnic Accommodation

Regime Type	*Nondemocratic* (usually tends to be less accommodative, if a modern military dictator or civilian autocrat)	*Democratic* (tends to have more open expression of group grievances and produce more accommodations, especially if parliamentary and federal in form)
Party or Factional Variables	1. Least accommodative if the autocrat gets nearly all support from just one dominant ethnicity, such as the Taliban in Afghanistan.	1. Least accommodative if the electoral system is plurality, which may sometimes yield a one-party dominant system (which could be of one ethnicity), but more often a two-party array, unless a third party has a local concentration of voters.
	2. More accommodative if the autocrat has put together a program coalition including at least two ethnic groups, including one that bears grievances, provided this is not a coalition to oppress a third group in a tripolar system.	2. A proportional representation system may often be more accommodative if every ethnicity finds a party voice (this could be a tripolar system with a "swing" party between two larger ones). But if each of two large ethnic groups divides its voters between two parties, there may be a polarization if militants of each ethnicity gain high influence. If a militant faction monopolizes central government power, it is poorly accommodative.
	3. Perhaps most accommodative if the autocrat is not of the dominant ethnicity, or not even of two ethnic groups in coalition but from some weaker third ethnic background, permitting more impartiality.	3. Most accommodative if the major party or parties are multiethnically based, or else if there are many small ethnic parties that must coalesce to form a governing majority.

an academic context, this looks to proportionality of deserving and getting, as in this form:

A's desert/B's desert: A's rewards/B's rewards

Such a problem is most manageable if each took the other as fully equal in desert, often as measured by contributions of something to the society, and hence deserving of absolute equality of rewards, as in the familiar problem of two children dividing a piece of cake, best following the rule, "one divides, the other chooses." But it quickly becomes complicated when this does not apply.

Sometimes population will be the sole measure of contribution to a political community, but problems may arise because groups then exaggerate their numbers or because retaking censuses becomes politically impossible. Thus in a recent armed conflict between ethnically dominant Macedonians with some among their Albanian-ethnic minority, the latter contended that they were 40 percent of the population, whereas census data had indicated only 23 percent. Albanian-ethnic demands included integration of local policing, a local university using their language, the right to use Albanian in official contexts, including the Macedonian parliament, and power sharing in the central government. Perhaps because of outside pressures by the United Nations and the major powers, the dominant ethnics conceded most of these demands, which was unusual.

Sometimes two ethnic groups are roughly the same percentage of the population, and they regard their relative numbers as the only appropriate measure of desert. But often a somewhat less numerous group may insist on parity even if anywhere close to the more numerous group. Slovaks were insisting on that even if less numerous than the population of the Czech lands of Bohemia and Moravia just before Czechoslovakia collapsed in 1993. This demand for parity could sometimes be more acceptable if the less numerous ethnic group is demographically rapidly gaining on the larger ethnic group, as when the Northern Ireland Roman Catholics are yet less than a third of the population but by projection of their higher fertility can be expected to eventually overtake the Protestants. One hopes that the 1998 power-sharing accord will be successfully implemented, having thus far been hung up for failure of the IRA and Protestant "loyalists" (the pro-British group unlike the "unionists" in having links to paramilitary forces) to give up their arsenals of weapons, as the accord stipulated. The 1998 prisoner release agreement has been extended by Britain's declaration that it would no longer seek extradition or prosecution of those legally accused who remain at large in regard to the Protestant-Catholic conflict.

The impure coordination problem becomes much more difficult if two groups in conflict are not about equal in population, or if population is by at least one side subordinated to some *other* criterion of "contributions" or "desert."

Not surprisingly, groups tend to emphasize anything they've got, or at least claim to have, in relative abundance as the appropriate measure of merit, but this almost inevitably puts them in tension with other groups having something else in more abundance.

Thus in the time of Plato or Aristotle, upper-class Greeks countered to the mere numbers of the many (the democratic party) the greater wealth or asserted superiority of "merit" of the upper classes, insisting these had to be weighting factors in allocating political power within the framework of the "mixed regime," which is elaborated a bit later in this chapter.

But the estimate of the justice or fairness of a distribution is difficult even for one measure of desert. How much difference on the measure of contribution should yield how much difference in the reward, as in share of public offices?

Solution becomes almost intractable if there are other measures of desert to be somehow weighted in, because there may be no plausible yardstick of commensurability.

The rhetoric of "balancing" considerations contains some wisdom in recognizing that two good aims can be in conflict, but it is usually hollow if it pretends that the balancer has some real "knowledge" of how to resolve such conflict of aims without conflict in acts (Hampshire, 2000; Rescher, 1966).

Thus an impure coordination game or problem of distributive justice may find it difficult for parties to concur on the terms, on who gives what and who gets what. Fortunately, it is not usually a one-shot game and need not always involve simultaneous moves, so even a present failure need not preclude one or more future negotiations that could succeed. Thus in the Arab-Israeli conflict, Al Fatah and Israeli officials or their proxies have had recurrent meetings in quest of more common ground, even if yet unable to secure a stable accommodation to their conflict exceeding a half century. But each side wants to give as little as possible and get as much as possible, so negotiations can be difficult.

Although dominant (usually majority) groups are rarely very generous to subordinate groups, there are cases when they perceive their advantage in accommodating subordinate groups rather than segregating them (deepening differences) or aggressively assimilating them (erasing their differences). The otherwise subordinate groups are recognized as having a right to remain different rather than to assimilate, and their differences as such are not singled out for punishment. On the contrary, the dominant ethnics now want to make the *minimal* concession to the ethnic minority necessary to create or preserve community. Broadly, the dominant favor this strategy only when it is quite clear that segregation or aggressive assimilation are not feasible alternatives. One can distinguish cases where they grant rights with far less than equality to the weaker ethnic group from cases where they accord a bit more, often because somehow constrained.

II. MINIMALISM IN FOUR FIELDS OF ACCOMMODATION

Perhaps the major forms of accommodation can be defined by this list, where the labels assume a tendency of dominant ethnics to grant the least possible:

1. Minimalist Basic Rights
2. Minimalist Justice in Other Policy

3. Minimalist Devolution of Powers

4. Minimalist Power-Sharing at the Center

Later I will say something about each type of policy, reviewing what could be "minimalist" concessions typically offered to minority ethnic groups by dominant ethnic groups, unless severely constrained to yield more by economic boycotts, riots, long civil warring, threat of foreign military intervention, or the like.

Minimalist Basic Rights

Very minimal rights include the right to be left alive, the right to change residence, the right to change place of work, and in modern societies the right to marry or divorce according to one's choice. But I here dwell on the granting of bare toleration of the language or the religion of the minority ethnicity as the object of the minimalist accommodation.

Many traditional empires practiced some kind of accommodation with cultures (languages, religions) different from that of the core ethnicity group, but normally without pretense of full equality for the subordinate cultures. Examples include the Babylonian or the Roman empires. More recent cases include not only some sea empires (the British or the French more than the Spanish) but also the last great land empires (the Ottomans and Austro-Hungarians, more than the Russians).

When the accommodation is linguistic, a minimalist concession may permit the language to be publicly spoken, but perhaps with denial of any educational, media, or official-use rights. A slightly more generous minimalism may concede that a language may have local official use, but only in defined areas of ethnic group concentration. Thus the Sinhalese-dominated Sri Lanka government conceded that Tamil is a "national" language that can be officially used along with Sinhalese in certain areas of high Tamil population concentrations. Quite obviously this is far from Canada's nonminimalist concession that both French and English are official languages across Canada. The official status of languages becomes most heated with urbanization and expansions of basically urban organizations. Thus Eric Nordlinger has written,

Language is part and parcel of the competition-conflict for governmental and private employment which is most viciously pursued in the cities, it is in the national and regional capitals that language issues are decided, it is in the cities that the speakers of different languages compete for scarce economic rewards, and because of segmental intermingling it is here that slurs upon a man's language are most often (inadvertently or purposefully) made. (Nordlinger, 1972, 115)

In religion, a very minimalist position may be bare toleration of a religion, if its practitioners keep it private, avoiding any public worship or proselytization, as in the earliest Dutch Reformed toleration for other Protestantisms or even Roman Catholics. A bit less minimal is conceding some protected public worship for at least some minority religions.

One author suggests great equality among the religious communities protected by the Ottoman *millet* system, and it is true that just as peoples could speak their native tongues, at least the peoples of the book (such as Jews or Orthodox Christians), were able to practice their religion without significant hindrance (Karpat, 1985). However, because they were Sunni Muslims, the Kurds were not granted *millet* rights as a separate community, even if a very distinctive people from the Turks and Arabs who were also Sunnis. Membership in one's *millet* was ascriptive, not a voluntary choice, and Ottoman officials designated *millet* leaders. Even peoples granted *millet* system rights in religious worship, marriage laws, and so on, could suffer a number of disadvantages: If a slave, a non-Muslim could not expect children to be freed from slavery as true of a Muslim slave parent, even when only the mother was a slave. A non-Muslim could not ride a horse or carry a sword, but enjoyed exemption from military service. A non-Muslim had to pay a special tax (*jiyaz*), which was some fifty times the alms (*zakat*) collected from Muslims. Non-Muslims could not proselytize their faith (even if it had been permitted, by the *shari'a*, apostasy from Islam to either another faith or to atheism—charged of Salman Rushdie, despite his disavowal—is a capital crime). Non-Muslims could not serve in any high office (even the originally Christian janissaries were converted to Islam before holding offices, sometimes as high as Vizier before the corrupted order was abolished in 1826).

Michael Walzer notes that Israel has continued portions of the *millet* system, as in according to Israeli citizen Jews, Christians, and Muslims separate courts for their distinctive family laws or in certain matters of education. But sometimes relative seculars of such involuntary groups find this system alien to them (Walzer, 1997, 41–42). As Mehta Spencer notes, recently some have advocated a revised system whereby people could freely choose their ethnic group identities, then these groups could be given formal representation in democracies (Spencer, 1998, 34–36). One assumes that these groups would either be recognized as absolute equals or would be weighted only by their relative numbers.

The Ottomans clearly gave some primacy to the Muslims who were Turks or secondarily, Arabs, just as the Austro-Hungarians favored Roman Catholics who were germanophone by rearing or by later acculturation (especially Germanized Bohemians and Magyars). The czars favored Orthodoxy over other religions, and the Great Rus over the White Russians and Ukrainians, with other peoples of lower status. Under Stalin, the Soviet Union turned to a nearly genocidal collectivization of agriculture in the Ukraine, where some 7 million may have died (Conquest, 1986). Also, during the war Stalin revived the ancient Assyrian policy of forcibly relocating lesser peoples who could be possible collaborators with the Nazi invaders.

Minimalist Justice in Other Policy

Another sort of minimalist accommodation would be to offer by law equality of opportunity, for often formal nondiscrimination is all that would be needed for educationally advanced ethnic minorities to succeed. Note that segregationist policy makes law enforcers and judges work at *implementing* official discrimination, whereas a policy fully open to voluntary assimilation requires that they rather work in good faith to *prevent* discrimination, at least in defined matters such as public university admissions, public or private employment, public accommodations, and so on. Mere legal prohibitions against discrimination are nothing if not enforced. But even when enforced, they mean less than meets the eye if relevant conditions of life are so unequal that some groups cannot successfully compete. Thus to get ahead of ourselves, Donald Horowitz shows that educationally backward groups may ask for far more, perhaps special remedial programs on their behalf (Horowitz, 1985).

But if a dominant ethnicity were to concede some compensatory or remedial program to allow for past injustices and for inequalities of resources now, the dominant group would of its own accord often tend to make this minimal. The most minimal is just verbal encouragement not to discriminate, which may yield the thin results of some token hiring of previously excluded groups. For some, going beyond that would involve "reverse discrimination" in law and its enforcement. Yet if dominant ethnics were to concede something like affirmative action, their more militant faction would tend to want it limited in scope or range of jobs to which applicable, to function as targets rather than quotas entailing some specific percent of hires or resultant staff, and to be limited in time, as in a "sunset provision" for termination of the policy.

A minimalist program could concede a narrow legitimate purpose as a kind of breaking the ice of total exclusion, a kind of "glass ceiling" that once went nearly all the way down to even employments of rather modest socioeconomic status, as when earliest American affirmative action programs finally opened up the municipal garbage workers, firefighters and police forces to previously excluded racial minorities as well as women, the physically disabled, and so on. In India, like attention is given to lower caste and outcaste statuses.

The obvious benefit of such policies lay in opening doors previously closed, although a price may have been some racial backlash in the United States (especially in the 1970s) and more severe riots over college admissions in India (1980s and 1990s). Doubtless such policies sometimes give an edge to protected categories, and they may lower performance standards. But one must keep in mind that they only became necessary because such categories were formally (by segregationist law) or informally (by practices) excluded in the past. Minimalist critics counter that one cannot really quota some groups in without quota-ing other groups out, as argued by some Jewish Americans and Asian Americans who fear among other things that their groups' high presence among students or even faculties in the best universities could be threatened. Those of such groups not needing such compensatory mechanisms may, if conceding the case for breaking the ice of total exclusion, see every reason to keep the programs closely confined. Others argue that once one begins such "group rights" laws, it may be difficult to ever end them, and it tends to prolong such sensed rivalries among groups. They may note that affirmative action falsely assumes internally uniform categories, as if all individuals in non-protected categories are socially advantaged and that no individuals in the protected categories were so. In fact, in the case of the United States, some white male Anglos come from very poor backgrounds without college-educated parents, whereas some African Americans or Hispanics come from affluent, well-educated origins. Hence affirmative action could unfairly impair chances for the former but bolster existing advantages for the latter. Such argument may add that such programs may tend to stigmatize as inferior all members of the protected categories and preserve racial tension by artificially creating zero-sum situations (some of these arguments and counters can be found in Ingram, 2000, esp. 149–73; also Ingram, 1995).

Those of a dominant ethnicity may fear that if they permit some affirmative-action type program for any one ethnic minority, a number of other minorities (along with women, the handicapped, etc.) may demand the like. They may not be wrong to see such imitative and often competitive mobilizations. Thus by the 1980s in the United States, the WASP male found that a massive majority of his society now found themselves in "protected categories," and that he would not himself attain any such status until he should become a senior or a disabled person. He was in the meantime an unprotected category, who could be attacked but never counterattack. Major censorship arose to silence any discourse in criticism of what had developed, such as asking whether jobs were being competently performed (cf. Hentoff, 1992).

In India few have protested the reserved parliamentary seats for *dalits* (untouchables, Harijans) or Tribals, but quotas for university admissions or for hiring in civil service jobs have caused upper caste Hindu youths to riot (cf. Mitra, 1987).

Minimalist Devolution of Powers

Minimalist devolution of powers may aim at more efficient/effective governance or even at curtailment of secessionist strivings, but refuse to accord locally concentrated ethnic minorities everything they could want.

British imperial policy emphasized "indirect rule" though local traditionalist leaders (sometimes really elevated by the British), which was another variant of inegalitarian accommodation. It was inegalitarian in that it was mostly for administrative convenience. It could handle a dispute over ownership of a cow but in many colonies would rarely extend to the most important, all-colony issues. It was largely abolished by the British when passing central power to new, native elites with independence (residual authorities in India's princely states or in the Kingdom of Baganda within Uganda were eventually removed by their successors).

Applicable when disaffected ethnic groups are locally concentrated, passing certain powers downward and outward from the center increases "home rule" for the group. Usually as responses to some secessionist noises, regionalist measures have been pursued by Spain, France, and Italy, all of which have some regions that have demanded at least more home rule. A devolution ceases to be minimalist at some cusp, as it draws close to the demands of the weaker ethnic group, as illustrated by Canada's shift of even more powers to its already strong provinces, with much of that reflecting a wish to placate Québécois nationalists.

If devolutions go to an even more local level, such as to states or provinces in a federal system, to the extent that these states or provinces are ethnically homogeneous, this could reduce interethnic conflict at the center while creating more intraethnic conflict in these states or provinces (Horowitz, 1985, 619–20). Not all federal systems give really high autonomy to their states. The former USSR was a largely a sham federal system, although the defined units became very significant in defining boundaries when the Soviet Union collapsed in 1991. Or, as in India, state governance can be overridden by central imposition of emergency powers through President's Rule, as often overused and abused by Prime Minister Indira Gandhi.

However, both larger regions and such smaller states could also contain some local, embedded ethnic minorities. Thus if devolution reduced central inter-ethnic conflict of ethnicities A and B, it may shift the problem to inter-ethnic conflict between local ethnicities B and C. Local minorities could join dominant ethnics in fearing that devolutions could assist secessions.

Minimalist Power Sharing at the Center

A fourth form of accommodation aims at concession of some power for a disaffected group at the center.

The most minimal form of this could be viewed as just "tokenism" or symbolic politics, as when a few seats in parliament are reserved for ethnic minority groups, as in India or New Zealand. Perhaps this would be unnecessary but for largely English-influenced systems using plurality voting, which is unlike proportional representation in cutting out likely representation for weaker parties, except where they enjoy unusual local concentrations. New Zealand has shifted in part to proportional representation.

The minimalist model of central power sharing in constitutional forms was originally evident in "mixed regime" postures of nobilities in the history of Europe. The main idea was that, given that regimes could be by the one, the few or the many, and in moderate or immoderate versions of each, a regime could be more stable and moderate in policy if it avoided any single form, such as the monarchy, aristocracy, or moderate democracy, or their corrupted forms such as tyranny, oligarchy, or immoderate democracy. The key thought of theorists identified with social elites was, where necessary, to make a very minimal concession of a democratic or popular element in the constitution, thus conceding something to the claim of the many. However, they arranged the constitution such that a "democratic" power unit would be checked or countered by other, nondemocratic institutional units of monarchic or aristocratic tendency. Such regimes of institutionalized vetoes were indeed sometimes long lived, as illustrated by ancient Sparta, the Roman Republic, or arguably even the United States under the constitution drafted in 1787. But it served best those most committed to the status quo, especially in economic policy, because they could block any change adverse to themselves, such as redistribution of land or wealth. Yet such a constitutional arrangement becomes less acceptable to the popular element to the extent that they have not just negative demands on the political system (protection against being harmed) but have positive demands (want to be helped, as in having major budget categories oriented toward their welfare) (elaborated in Cook, 1991, 53–89).

Another, recent historical kind of power sharing has also been present in *neo-corporatist* or *liberal corporatist* regimes of Europe, whereby representatives of labor, business owners, and government representing consumers negotiated wage policies to avoid inflation. That is, if the mixed regime dealt with *class* conflict, this system rather worked with economic *sectoral* tensions. This system arose across parts of West Europe, ranging from Switzerland and Austria northward into the Netherlands and Scandinavia (cf. Lijphart, 1984). But arguably due to GATT-WTO lowering of at-the-border trade barriers of tariffs and quotas, thus increasing competition for both domestic and export market shares, most manufacturers no longer accept the system, and neocorporatism has been waning. Labor has not been equal in the system, because it cannot veto its demise.

Another variant of minimalist ethnic power sharing at the center was illustrated by the last two constitutional efforts of the waning apartheid regimes in South Africa. The 1983 version restored votes and even separate parliamentary assemblies for Asians and Coloureds. Whites sought to have their cake and eat it too in wanting to permit the white fifth of the population to veto any adverse policy favored by nonwhites, yet they wanted whites (or the two other ethnic categories) to be able to legislate "own affairs" of their group, as if that had any clear meaning. Neither constitutional project could survive growing unity among nonwhites and foreign economic boycott pressure on the apartheid regime. The apartheid constitutions in question amounted to a truly minimalist, indeed, bogus, power sharing that secured no lasting accommodation (cf. Adam, 1985).

A nonminimalist power sharing goes further and would look to either population proportionality or even parity of groups for central government power sharing, a discussion I reserve for chapter 6, when I return to the same four variants of accommodative policy.

As long as dominant ethnic groups are only willing to grant minimalist concessions in accommodation and as long as weaker groups ask for maximalist concessions, no meeting of minds seems imminent. Often there is a long history of "gaming" between a dominant ethnic group and a weaker one, and part of the game may often be an unwillingness of either side to move too fast toward the middle ground, which often but not always could be the moral high ground. Dominant ethnic groups fear loss of control if they are generously accommodative, hence may use any available means to avoid that.

Although strongly convinced that republican institutions, or popular government, was the way toward a more peaceful world, Immanuel Kant once said in despair, "Nothing straight can be made of such crooked wood as men are made of." Yet political sociologist Max Weber, in concluding his essay, "Politics as a Vocation" with its warning against approaching politics with moral absolutism, said with slightly more optimism, "Politics is a strong and slow boring of hard boards."

CHAPTER 6

Accommodations as Maximal: Strategies of the Weaker Ethnic Group

> The costs of consensus are paid by those excluded from it.
> —Alasdair MacIntyre, *Against the Self-Images of the Age* (1971)

Although he himself has taken many different political stances over the course of his life, British social philosopher Alasdair MacIntyre recognized that when a consensus forms in a community but leaves some group out of it, they will be the losers. Thus costs of consensus were paid by African Americans as long as the white-dominated political parties were in consensus on continuance of slavery (to 1860), or later when they shifted their consensus to continued segregation (to the 1950s). In the present chapter I shift the vantage point to the direct involvement of the weaker ethnicity in seeking a consensus with the ethnically stronger group or groups. How do things differ when they, too, must give their yes to any arrangement?

Perhaps one key contrast of the stronger and the weaker in accommodation policy preference is that the dominant group tends to wait until there is a clear crisis (e.g., the threat of economically dislocative strikes or riots, civil war, or foreign economic or military intervention) before choosing to initiate some attempt at accommodation. Even then, as I argued in chapter 5, the dominant group may look for *minimal* concessions. They follow the old farmers' maxim, "If it ain't broke, don't fix it."

I. THE MAXIMALIST MENTALITY IN SUBORDINATE ETHNICS

In contrast, leaders of a weaker ethnic group, who perhaps think of the system as *chronically* in crisis (definitely "broke"), may be pushing for accommodation in the absence of any acute crisis, and they look for the *maximal* opportunity for themselves. I use "maximal" as a figure of speech, because only irrational activists would really try to maximize their gain, which would often lead nowhere in the way of accommodation.

However, some activists may play a sophisticated game: Some may not really want any accommodative arrangement, as may be true of those among an ethnic minority who are attempting secession or else attempting a complete seizure of power at the center. Thus Peruvian Indians launched the Shining Path guerrilla movement of the 1980s, apparently hoping in vain to win central power. In addition to economic grievances of the Indians, there were surely questions of respect. In 1973 I saw a mestizo police officer in Cuzco whip an Indian on the public square for having washed his feet in a fountain pool. Once a rebellion is launched, guerrillas may make punitive moves toward any of their own group who advocate or practice negotiation with the "enemy." The militants of the weaker group will insist that leaders be maximalists. Even if such people did not exist, however, a dominant ethnicity attempting a minimalist strategy will often assert this is the real game of those who advance a list of utterly unacceptable demands that could not plausibly be trimmed by good faith negotiation.

A lesser but more common form of bad faith among an ethnic minority may involve exaggeration of each demand in the hope of thereby ending up at least closer to their real expectation. The obvious risk here is overshooting, such that they may not get a wanted agreement at all. The other side may either refuse to start negotiations on such terms or may terminate any negotiations already started.

I suggested in chapter 5 that negotiations typically involve problems philosophers have called distributive justice or game theoreticians call impure coordination. I doubt there is a real "science" of their solution, although more able mathematicians may disagree (see Brams and Taylor, 1996). But one practical measure of sensed unfairness is when at least one party clearly rejects a scheme of accommodation. No deal! Of course some walkouts from negotiations are often pure theatrics, and I am thinking here of more emphatic negations. Thus in India the better educated upper castes have rioted when lower castes or *dalits* (Harijans, untouchables) were allotted university slots or civil service posts in rough proportion to their numbers, even though their educational credentials or test performances were far lower. But what if the latter groups were to riot if they did not get posts at least proportionate to their numbers in the population? In 1999–2000 Yasser Arafat walked away from peace offers made by Ehud Barak. But would he have done so if he could have anticipated the mess that ensued in the *intifada* of 2001–2002?

Whenever one finds a great distance between the minimal offer of the dominant ethnic group and the maximal demands of the weaker ethnicity, this disparity often means that ethnic groups in conflict may often not be willing to talk at all, or demand that the other side uniquely announce generous concessions before the talk. If they do talk, the negotiations may go nowhere. Or even if they did reach some kind of accord, it may not be fully implemented. A famous maxim of public administration notes that the odds against successful implementation increase with the number of bureaucratic units that must concur (Pressman and Wildavsky, 1979). Even if an accord is successfully implemented, each may look for opportunities to amend or subvert the arrangement to their own advantage. Thus in 1996 during the Boris Yeltsin presidency of Russia, his prime minister Lebed had granted the Chechnyans a cease-fire and promise of a plebiscite on either remaining within Russia or seceding after five years. But when Vladimir Putin became president, after charges of organized crime and terrorist actions in Russia planned in Chechnya, he rescinded the deal. He made a second invasion of Chechnya.

II. REVISITING THE MAIN FORMS OF ACCOMMODATION

Recall that dominant ethnic groups tend to offer minimal concessions, whereas the weaker group may look for maximal. Often the weaker groups look only to formal equality of rights or for proportionality of reward by relative population. But as noted earlier, sometimes when there are but two ethnic groups in question they may demand full parity, or full partnership in any shared political community, even if not precisely equal in numbers (let alone military power, wealth, etc.) to the dominant ethnic group. In parallel with the review of dominant ethnic group concessions advanced in chapter 5, let us review some common forms of accommodation.

Maximalist Basic Rights

Sometimes an ethnic minority aims at only the same legal right already enjoyed by all members of a dominant ethnicity. An example of equalization of rights by outside imposition consists in the following action by Prussia, under pressure of Napoleon's France:

Wherever the French occupied German lands, Jews were the beneficiaries of the rights of Man, winning emancipation in most of southern and western Germany. In some places under French command, the obligatory extension of equality to Jews enraged the Germans even more than French domination. Nevertheless, the trend toward emancipation reached even into the stronghold of Prussia. In 1812, as part of a sweeping program of legislative and economic reform, Minister Karl August von Hardenberg, himself under the influence of the ideas of 1789, persuaded the reluctant Frederick William III to grant the Jews citizenship and political rights. (Dawidowicz, 1975, 25–26)

The Prussians did not complete the liberation, because they yet required Jews to convert to Christianity to hold a public office, such as when the father of Karl Marx became Lutheran to become a Prussian state lawyer. Yet Prussia retained its reform even when freed of Bonaparte. In other German lands, local elites had made but a temporary assimilation to the conquering French, because they revoked rights for Jews after Napoleon was defeated.

Another kind of equality of rights may involve an agreement to depoliticize a question, such as the U.S. Constitution's First Amendment commitment not to have any established church, thus avoiding any future conflicts over which of many faiths should be established. Any single church establishment would be a monopoly right.

As dominant ethnics may fear, sometimes demands of a weaker ethnic category may grow with any concessions made to them, as most groups tend to expand their claims with increased plausibility that they will be gratified. This can be through their own power or alliance with some outside force. Sometimes a group can evolve to the point of asking not just equal but superior rights. One can sometimes discern some stops along a continuum: (1) no demand even for minimal justice or freedom, (2) demand minimal rights, (3) demand full equality or parity, (4) demand privileges, and (5) demand supremacy, a monopoly right.

Thinking of the history of Christianity within the Roman Empire, Friedrich Nietzsche (1901/1914) classically noted that a group that begins by asking for bare toleration may go on to demand parity, or full equality in state recognition. But once it obtains parity, the group may eventually go on to demand superiority or even a monopoly status: "In the first stage, one demands justice at the hands of those who have power. In the second, one speaks of 'freedom,' that is to say, one wishes to 'shake oneself free' from those who have power. In the third stage, one speaks of 'equal rights'" (*The Will to Power*, I, lxxxvi). He later adds, "First step: they make themselves free. . . . Second step: they enter the lists, they demand acknowledgment, equal rights, 'Justice.' Third step: they demand privileges (they draw the representatives of power over to their side). Fourth step: they *alone* want all power, and they have it" (*The Will to Power*, II, ccxv). His is the dominant group's voice, recalling the epigraph to the previous chapter, "If you offer them your hand, they will take your arm."

Nietzsche may overgeneralize the matter, but he hinted that one could foresee such overreaching in other movements, including feminism, as if he anticipated Catherine MacKinnon. Although granting her virtues in exploring law regarding working women and in opening attention to comparable worth as a standard for pay, MacKinnon does sometimes tend to demand superior rights for women. She takes almost any male initiatives in sexuality as an affront while carefully protecting women's right to signal that male "attentions are wanted." She recurrently merely asserts against abundant empirical studies invalidating the claim that dissemination of pornography causes increased aggression toward women (cf. Strossen, 1995; see also Hentoff, 1992, esp. 283–99). On that and some other questions, she seems to be disinterested in factual evidence. Thus MacKinnon variously asserts that the percentage of women who have done prostitution is 13 percent, 20 percent, or unknown (compare MacKinnon, 1987, 25; 1989, 143; 1993, 7–8). In an outrageous denial of equal juridical rights for men, she apparently holds that in rape cases only the testimony of the supposed victim should be heard (MacKinnon, 1987, 113). Unless one were sure that women never have faulty memories or lie, or that any false accusations by them could otherwise be revealed, she would permit any woman at her discretion to destroy the reputation of any man and put him in prison, too. Some rapes of men do occur, but with one highly publicized exception when a jilted lover tied her man to a bed, they are almost never perpetrated by women.

An old French proverb holds, "The appetite comes while eating." Surely one can say that the anglophones of Canada, after defeating the French in the battle of Quebec, began as accommodative toward the francophones, then soon evolved away from that. As David Chennels holds, by the 1890s they tended more to "privileging an English, Protestant way of life" (Chennels, 2001, 76). But after the 1990 failure to recognize Quebec in the constitution as a distinctive society due to the failures of Nova Scotia and New Brunswick to ratify, the near vote of Quebec to secede in 1995 was a wake-up call. It turned many anglophone leaders back toward a more accommodative stance. Even the Supreme Court in 1998 weighed in with the assurance that Quebec, if it so chose, could depart in peace, although not without fair negotiation of economic impacts on the separated sections of Canada.

Governments of Quebec have declared themselves a distinctive society on their own and have taken major measures to protect the locally predominant French language. They passed a law in 1974 requiring that only French be used in Quebec province government offices, adding in 1976 that it should also be used exclusively in business, even on business signs. This disturbed many of the anglophones of the province, who are themselves a minority there of about 20 percent. Some anglophones, especially those who have emigrated in disgust from the province, may see a move toward cultural supremacy. After all, bilingualism or the rule of reciprocity had become law, at least for the rest of Canada. Francophones could retort that, unlike later immigrants, they were a conquered people who had experienced anglophone cultural tyranny in the past. Use of French was vanishing outside of a few pockets in the rest of Canada, and their cultural survival was at stake, which would be unlikely with bilingual reciprocity within Quebec.

Quite surprisingly, a recent study finds that ethnic violence increases with increased duration of democratic regimes, a finding that appears inconsistent with prior research holding that democracy correlates with less domestic political violence (Saideman, Lanoue, Campenni, and Stanton, 2002; contrast Rummel, 1997). Rather than reflecting a will to power regarding ethnic group rights, my suspicion is that many older democracies are also more economically advanced, and their growth stimulates competitive mobilizations of juxtaposed groups of ethnic dissimilars. Thriving cities bring in-migrations from their countryside, sometimes ethnically distinctive. Also, the nations as wholes become immigration magnets, often drawing in ethnically dissimilar groups, especially when the old stock populations have had low fertility, not even replacing themselves in the labor force. That also explains the surprisingly high xenophobia found in some West European states. If my hypothesis that it is not the democracy but an effect of economic growth is correct, what should one observe? One would *not* find comparable increases in ethnic violence with duration of democracy in nations with only modest levels of development, such as much of Latin America (although even Argentina has attracted ethnically dissimilar immigrants such as Bolivians and Paraguayans to Buenos Aires slums).

Maximalist Justice in Other Policy

Dominant ethnic groups may resist compensatory justice for the legacy of past wrongs, especially if claims involve return of or payment for lands stolen, say, a century or more ago, as in the case of the Native Americans. Often whites may retort that sometimes prior Indian possession was the fruit of their own rather recent stealing from other Indian tribes, as could be illustrated by the expansive Sioux. Although one may cite some instances of arguably successful land reforms, such as in the Mexican revolution's redistribution of land in favor of the peasants, in independent India's takeover of the estates of the *zamindars*, or in the Kuomintang redistribution of land on Taiwan, it can damage production. The philosopher David Hume urged that any society needs to give some presumption to stability of present possession if an economy is to thrive. A poorly managed takeover of white farms in Zimbabwe in 2001–2, if quite arguably just (a minute minority of whites had gained control of most arable land), caused needless violence and severely disrupted agricultural production. If a policy may move in the correct *direction*, it can yet go either too far or too fast.

In another kind of reparations, justice may look for monetary compensation for past land grabs or labor exploitation. Swiss banks, which have already had to pay compensation for profitable investments in Nazi slave labor factories, are recently facing a lawsuit over investment in South Africa's apartheid system, when the United Nations had declared a boycott. Some African Americans are urging civil suits against surviving insurance or like businesses that had done business with antebellum slaveowners.

Chapter 5 noted that dominant ethnics tend to oppose affirmative action programs. Accenting individual rights and "equality-as-sameness" of standards for individuals, they see something wrong or illiberal in any scheme involving *group rights*, at least for weaker ethnic groups. However, they may be inconsistent in accepting other sorts of group rights, as in subsidies to some nonethnic economic grouping, such as farmers or business owners. Or they may accept preferential university admissions or scholarships by region of residence, athletic ability, or prior attendance of the university by their parents.

A weaker ethnicity backing affirmative action programs may want them (1) sooner rather than later, (2) applied to a broader range of cases as when regulating both public and private hiring or promotion, and (3) kept indefinitely in being, or at least as long as the category to be protected predicts lower life chances.

Dominant ethnics were in the past often beneficiaries of their own "group rights" at their expense while they themselves were subjected to group disadvantages in law. Thus laws prohibited teaching literacy to slaves in some antebellum slave states. Also, past disadvantages leave a present legacy of socially disadvantaged status for their group, such that only a compensatory group advantage could compensate. Without it, any formal equality of rights for individuals in, say, taking tests for college or job entries, would create an inequality in results adverse to themselves. It is good for society to remove the legacy of ethnic or like discriminations, promoting social harmony.

Another kind of remedial justice could involve special public expenditures to help the ethnicity of a backward area. Thus the Berbers are about a tenth of the Algerian population, and many live in the Kabylia region in northern Algeria, where unemployment is about 30 percent. Although the ethnically dominant Arab government has recently made some concessions regarding protection of the Berber language, it has remained unyielding to their request for unemployment compensation and a program of development expenditure for their region.

Among many problems with implementing a reparations justice, it becomes difficult to ascertain what is "fair" in setting the amounts of restitution, the appropriate beneficiaries, as well as on whom the burden of the correction should fall. Thus if the Australian Aboriginals were to claim remedial justice, should it be from all other Australians, even recent immigrants not descended from the land thieves? Or if U.S. descendants of slaves were to be paid reparations, should it be only at the expense of the descendants of past slave-owners, or should one tax even descendants of Union soldiers who fought to abolish slavery, sometimes dying in that cause? Or should one focus only on the easier targets of surviving insurance or other corporations that did business in the region? If it is not feasible to tote up their profits by it, just *how much* compensation is due from them? As in most issues of distributive justice, it is often easier to state such questions than to find persuasive answers.

Maximalist Devolution of Powers

Comparative empirical study has found that the constitutional choice of having a unitary rather than federal system makes a difference in ethnic politics: Federalism increases the amount of ethnic protest, which can focus attention on solving issues, but federalism *decreases* the amount of ethnic violence. This is plausibly because an ethnic group need not worry about losing everything if unable to win control of the central government, because it can yet be strong in the state or province government, especially when the boundaries of such units reflect local residential concentrations of ethnicities, as in India's recognition of linguistic groupings (Saideman et al., 2002).

Some regionally concentrated ethnic groups, if not seeing any feasibility in secession, may yet demand more autonomy for their region, province, or state. Sometimes this could involve advocacy of change from unitary to a federal government, or even to a confederal model (Abkhazians of Georgia, Turks of Cyprus). In contrast, the dominant ethnic group may want to retain the unitary form of government, but yet be willing to devolve powers to regions with more limited political autonomy. Dominant ethnics may assert, and perhaps really fear, that high regional autonomy or federalism could be just transitional to a secessionist effort, as illustrated by the former Soviet Union, Yugoslavia, and Czechoslovakia. There are no obvious ways to know for sure in advance.

With far less political muscle than Quebec behind their demand, the Inuit of northern Canada won local autonomy as Nunavut ("Our Land," in the local language of Inuktitut). Even though the whole population of the territory is only about 25,000 people, they now govern about a fifth of all Canadian territory. In addition, the Canadian government allocated $1.1 billion per year to defray expenses of their home rule (cf. Cameron and White, 1995; Duffy, 1988).

In multinational states, sometimes the central government could largely restrict itself to foreign affairs (or high politics) while deferring most local policy matters such as economic policy (low politics) to the regional level. Thus Ariel Rothschild noted that this was roughly how the Austro-Hungarian imperial government related to Hungary, which was granted considerable home rule (Rothschild, 1981, 11). This can be done even without any *uniform* devolution of powers to all regions, even to those that do not demand it. David Lilienthal noted that those who make a dogma of uniformity or standardization of policy are unlikely to be able to devolve much power to local governance. The solution is not centralization of power but abandonment of such rigid thinking (Lilienthal, 1953).

Often in ethnically divided states, especially newer ones, the political parties or factions will tend to be ethnically based, even where two or more parties may compete for the leadership of any one ethnicity. As Donald Horowitz notes, political parties are ethnically based to the extent that party supporters disproportionately reflect ethnic categories, even when no one party has preponderant allegiance of its group (Horowitz, 1985, 293 and 295 n.14). Yet sometimes ethnic groups do tend to support but one party or faction, as in an ethnically bipolar state. This form may have distinctive problems from other power constellations (cf. Milne, 1981).

Thus when Angola belatedly became independent from Portugal in 1975, there emerged among other ethnicities two principal factions, the more northern Mbundu people, led by the leftist Agostinho Neto, and the south-central Ovimbundu people, the largest ethnic group long led by Jonas Savimbi, who headed the National Union for the Total Independence of Angola (UNITA). After initial civil warring, Neto held the capital city of Luanda as well as the oil wells, the leading source of foreign exchange, and he accepted the patronage of the Soviet Union and Cuba during the Cold War. During that time, both the white South African government and the United States supported Savimbi in his military struggle to hold his territory and to potentially take power in Luanda. But after the end of apartheid and the Cold War, outside support was no longer forthcoming, and eventually elections were arranged by mutual agreement of leaders of the tribal groupings. However, Savimbi resumed fighting after losing what he charged were fraudulent elections, a view not supported by foreign observers. He was finally killed in battle in 2002, and ragtag remnants of his followers seem to have finally made peace with the Mbundu. The point is that long years of civil warring and economic dislocations could perhaps have been avoided by a special home rule arrangement comparable to that of Austro-Hungary vis-à-vis Hungary, or else by a consociational power sharing at the center. Winner-take-all national elections may not be wise when a nation is ethnically polarized between two roughly equal groups.

Unlike the more repressive government of Franco's Spain, governments of democratic Spain have been much more accommodative to the demands of special cultural regions such as Catalonia and the Basque territory. Thus the latter region now enjoys extensive taxing powers and a voice in the content of the Spanish constitution. Perhaps most Basques find it a fair deal, and the more isolated Basque Land and Liberty (ETA) movement increasingly turns to desperation assassinations, which are unpopular with most Basques as well as with other Spaniards.

Maximalist Power Sharing in the Central Government

Maximalist power sharing at the center either demands proportional power for groups or the even greater demand for parity (absolute equality) among them. It sees a greater threat in a tyranny of the majority than any alleged tyranny of the minority receiving special power.

Often a weaker group may be content with bare proportionality of in rewards, such as allocation of representation or public offices. A recent pooled time series analysis of cross-national data not surprisingly found that proportional representation electoral system rather than plurality voting correlated with less ethnic violence (Saideman et al., 2002). This is almost surely because a plurality system by the so-called cube law converts party ratios of votes into exaggerated ratios of their parliamentary seats, which can mean underrepresentation of an ethnic minority of dispersed rather than concentrated residence. Further, more ethnic diversity in public offices plausibly contributes to more dialogue about tensions.

In other allocations of offices, census collectors or other studies may identify relative proportions of groups. Even in power-sharing arrangements, as noted, when a group is yet considerably less than half the population it can sometimes demand half of the offices. One thinks of the case of less populous Slovakia relative to the Czech lands before shifting to separatism, or of the Catholic minority in Northern Ireland (Ulster) even now. Given higher natural increase, one may reasonably expect the Catholics there to equal and then surpass the numbers of Protestants.

Arend Lijphart has coined the term "consociationalism" for nonmajoritarian arrangements of democracy to accord more protections for ethnic minorities (Lijphart, 1975, 1977, 1984, 1999). Although he extends the concept to devolutions of power to regions, I address it here only in terms of central government power sharing.

In the consociational model, there is rather clear recognition of ethnic "pillars" topped by recognized leaders who fear disintegration of the system, want to preserve it, can communicate across ethnic boundaries, are able to work out consensus on practical arrangements, and usually make it stick. It typically involves institutionalizing unanimity or mutual veto, proportional division of offices, and sometimes more direct compromise on policy. It helps if leaders' followers can back off from violence and allow discretion to the leaders of their pillars.

The case of Lebanon began from 1943 with a reasonably fair allocation of central power among the various religious communities of the country, in rough relation to the perhaps already dated census report of 1932. But as demographics changed over time, the holding of a new census was impossible because it was too politically sensitive. The Christian Lebanese, here the minimalist accommodationists, knew they were being surpassed by higher fertility among the Muslim Lebanese, especially the rather low-income Shi'a minority. Unwilling to rewrite the rules of the social contract, they found themselves mired from 1975 in many rounds of often savage civil warring. Even now a reconstituted central government is extremely weak, for a time unable to control a southern borderland dominated by Christian militias in alliance with Israeli forces (who are now withdrawn, but threaten to return if Hezbollah attacks from there increase). Neighboring Syria polices much of the country with a presence of its armed forces.

Other cases were more successful because they went beyond the bare minimum. Among such relatively successful consociational regime cases one may cite the Netherlands, Switzerland after 1848, and Canada, at least since repatriation of the constitution. The dominant ethnics in each case (respectively, the Dutch Reformed, the Swiss Protestants, the Canadian anglophones) began as minimalist but conceded more, once recognizing this would not be enough to maintain a political community at peace with itself.

In the Netherlands, the rough parity of Protestants (mostly Dutch Reformed) and Roman Catholics within the United Provinces led to the early religious toleration, something only partially achieved (excluding Catholics) by two rounds of Dissenter challenge in England during the seventeenth century. Although secularization there has been reducing its urgency, the Dutch into modern times have sought to balance the secular (socialist), Protestant, and Catholic political forces.

In the Swiss case, this has been worked out through a seven-person plural presidency, which as practiced gives proportional weightings to not only linguistic groups (four to five German, one or two French, and perhaps one Italian) but also religio-partisan strengths (a traditional 2:2:2:1 ratio of secular Social Democrats, nonobservant Protestants or Catholics of the Radical Democrats, observant Catholic Christian Democrats, and observant Protestant Social Democrats (Lijphart, 1999, 34–37).

In Canada, the accommodation has been worked out in a kind of "consociational federalism," more than by formal power sharing at the center. Thus far the some 80 percent francophones of Quebec have been placated with much home rule, including their legal system inspired more by the French code system than the Anglo-Saxon common law models. Quebec's exercised autonomy extends to educational and linguistic policy, favoring supremacy of French within the province, even on road and business signs. As earlier noted, the all-Canada or federal policy includes official bilingualism as well (cf. Doran, 2001).

One kind of accommodation is informal only, that underlying selection of the prime minister. As Hudson Meadwell notes: "For twenty-eight of the last thirty years, the Canadian prime minister has been from the province of Quebec, and for twenty odd years, the prime minister has been Francophone. Despite this inclusion, the likelihood of secession is higher in Quebec than in any other part of the developed West" (Meadwell, 2001, 13). The francophone cases included St. Laurent (1948–1957), Trudeau (1968–1979 and also 1980–1984), and Chrétien (1993 to the present). Yet Meadwell argues, against Lijphart, that increased feasibility of secession means the disgruntled group may demand more rather than less in power sharing, in part because threats become more credible, even if not always sincere (Meadwell, 2001, 16, 18). Yet as overall voter support for secession in Quebec has retreated from nearly a majority to just over 40 percent (depending on question wording), bargaining leverage may have declined.

The importance of Canada's kind of linguistic accommodation was illustrated recently in Macedonia, where concession by majority Macedonian speakers that Albanian would also be an official language has permitted an end to the Macedonian-Albanian communal warring that blighted the year 2001.

The limits of consociationalism are clear with references to places where it seems beyond practicable implementation (Israel and the West Bank) or where it has failed, especially in Lebanon after civil warring began in 1975. Another failed consociational project occurred in the local government of Abkhazia province, in newly independent Georgia (Kaufman, 2001, 116–23).

Whatever their stake in power, ethnic minorities often demand that their share in any past accommodation be increased if their numbers increase, as illustrated by the Shi'a demands in Lebanon before the 1975 collapse of that system (Younis, 1978). As Aristotle long ago noted, rapid change of the relative size of two groups often leads to political upheavals. The main causes of such shifts can be their differences in (1) net natural increase (excess of births over deaths), (2) net migration, or (3) net conversions when relevant. Demography is destiny, and it often destines likely conflict of ethnic groups that generate insecurities through their competitive mobilizations.

When ethnic tensions rise, the most militant ethnic and other minorities may often speak of securing their liberation "on their own terms," which can be quite reasonable if only construed to mean rejection of the dominant group's typically belated and minimized concessions. But sometimes the less reasonable view denies that even their own demands may require some constraint to curb violence and restore community with the adversary. That was central in the teaching of Mahatma Gandhi.

Whether accommodation arises from the initiative of the stronger ethnic group or of the weaker ethnic group, it does not arise without some costs, even beyond the protracted negotiations often involved. One argued cost of power sharing is an institutionalization of the tensions among ethnic groups rather than real transcendence, comparable in this to the most extreme case of splitting rival ethnic groups into separate nation-states. However, a consociational arrangement may be transitional to a time when the ethnic animosities cool down.

The Dutch became sharply divided on both class and religious lines just before World War I. The class issue concerned extension of equal suffrage to male workers. The religious issue concerned whether taxpayer funding should aid only the secular public schools or also accept funding of religious schools (chiefly Roman Catholic). By bargaining they worked out a deal whereby the Social Democrats got workers' votes but had to reluctantly concede public funds for religious schools, whether Catholic or Protestant. Arend Lijphart argues that the three "pillars" of the socialists/seculars, the Protestants, and the Roman Catholics thereafter governed successfully by institutionalizing mutual vetoes on policies and by balancing office holding as well. Many saw Dutch consociationalism as in retreat by the 1960s as an increasingly secularizing society tended to become depillarized (but for some surviving issues such as gay rights or death with dignity), but Lijphart believes that more than its spirit lives on (Lijphart, 1989).

Belgium is another apparently successful accommodation on consociational lines. The Belgian people are largely Roman Catholic. This is in part because when it was yet part of the Spanish Netherlands, many of its Protestants migrated northward to the rebellious seven northern provinces, where Calvinist Dutch Reformed were stronger and dominated the United Provinces (Netherlands). But one historic cleavage of Belgian politics became that between clericals (pro-Catholics) and anticlericals, the latter consisting in either Protestants or nonreligious who wished removal of Roman Catholicism from the public school curriculum. Although that has waned as a public issue, the originally Roman Catholic Christian Democratic party has tended to occupy the median space and hence most post–World War II Belgian coalitions, even if its voting base has retreated to about half of its historical high. Another division of the Belgian people concerned the typical left-right cleavage, with the largely anticlerical left consisting of communists and socialists.

As if the Belgian party system were not already fragmented, another divisive issue arose in the 1960s concerning the Flemish, who speak Dutch, and the Walloons, who speak French. Many of the parties already differentiated as clerical or anticlerical, left or right, further split into their respective linguistic subgroups. In a 1963 allocation of public offices, Belgium aimed at this breakdown: 40 percent to Flemish speakers, 10 percent to a bilingual person whose mother tongue was Flemish, 40 percent to French speakers, and 10 percent to bilinguals whose original language was French (Covell, 1985, 248). They later worked out special provisions: Since 1970 their constitution requires that, apart from the prime minister, the cabinet (Council of Ministers) consist of half Flemish and half Walloon. Also, the Belgians turned to a major devolution of powers to the respective regions dominated by the two linguistic groups. Further, to pass any constitutional amendment, a majority of present members of each linguistic group parliamentarians must vote yes. Any constitutional amendment must be approved by two-thirds of both the lower and upper houses of the Belgian parliament. In short, a set of constitutional protections was worked out such that neither linguistic group could feel threatened in remaining within the political community (De Winter, Timmermans, and Dumont, 2000).

Although most consociational solutions adopt formal commitments in constitutions or statutes, in other cases they can be worked out by more informal and hence flexible "rules" of allocating cabinet or other important offices in rough proportion to the sizes of ethnic groups in the population. That can work just as well, and it may be found even in democracies that are majoritarian rather than consensual, such as the United States. This calculated inclusion of all ethnicities developed in some big city governments such as New York before becoming prominent in the U.S. federal government.

I summarize some common contrasts of dominant ethnic groups and weaker ethnic groups on accommodation policy in Figure 6.1.

Figure 6.1
How Stronger and Weaker Ethnic Groups Approach Accommodations

Dominant Ethnic Group	Subordinate Ethnic Group
Often uninterested in making an accommodation, unless pressed by some unusual crisis, such as a national security or economic emergency.	Unless firmly bent on secession, often wants an accommodation, because from their perspective the status quo is in chronic crisis.
An initial mental set toward making no more than minimal concessions, the least that can keep the subordinate ethnicity from rioting, rebelling, etc.	Once stimulated by initial gains, tends to frame demands in terms of maximal concessions. Militant demonstrations may help.
Often thinks it reasonable to offer the subordinates less than formal equality of rights, as true of the *millet* system of the Ottomans respecting non-Muslims. If pressed to grant full formal equality, no help with educational access, other resource distributions, etc., necessary for *effective* equality.	May start with a simple demand for formal equality of rights, but may want some special rights, too, to permit them to better compete. In a rare case of high confidence, like Christians in the Roman Empire, they may ultimately demand a superior or monopoly right.
With regard to impure coordination policy problems (distributive justice), quite content to have the subordinate ethnic group give more, get less, than is proportional to their presence in the population.	In distributive justice questions, they would prefer to give less and get more, the latter preferably at or even above their numbers in the population, allowing for remediation.
Tends to favor the unitary regime, fearing that federalism or even strong devolutions to regions, could tend to secession. If adopting a regionalist program, tends to want it the same for all regions, with no special allowances for distinctive social groups such as the *Québécois* or the Inuit.	If they have a regional concentration of their group, they may demand federalism or in rare cases even confederation to enhance their local autonomy. Special devolutions may be asked, too, which may accord less than equal rights to local residents of the nationally dominant ethnic group.
If turning to power sharing, prefers just tokenism, as in allowing a few parliamentary or cabinet seats. If going beyond that, prefers to overweight power shares of the dominant ethnics, even if a minority, such as South Africa's apartheid regime schemes.	May express contempt for tokenism, demanding a share in power at least proportional to their numbers in society, and possibly higher, at parity, if they come anywhere close to the numbers of the dominant ethnicity.

III. SOME DIFFICULT CASES FOR ACCOMMODATIVE SOLUTIONS

It may be useful to consider some especially hard cases for any accommodative agreements. I look in turn at Nigeria, Rwanda and Burundi, the Israeli-Arab conflict, and Afghanistan. I reserve a longer analysis of the Kashmir conflict to chapter 7.

Nigeria

With some simplification, Africa's most populous nation finds itself divided into three major peoples or families of peoples, namely, the Igbo or Ibo-Ibibio coalition toward the southeast; the Yoruba, divided by religion and by principal city, toward the southwest; and the Hausa-Fulani coalition to the north. A classic problem of tripolar power situations is that, whenever the system sinks into Realpolitik terms, there is a strong temptation for two to coalesce against the third. In 1966 the Hausa-Fulani felt aggrieved, apparently thinking the Yoruba and Ibo-Ibibio were united against them, and they threatened secession. But then they seized power by military coup in Lagos. In 1967 communal riots and murders forced many of the educationally advanced Ibo-Ibibio group to flee to their relatively backward homeland region, which suffered from poor soils due to erosion but could potentially control some local oil wells. The Ibo-Ibibio then attempted to secede. Their attempt was in 1967–1970 ruthlessly suppressed by an opposed coalition of Yoruba and Hausa-Fulani.

Currently the Hausa-Fulani in the north, who are largely Muslim, have been attempting to apply in their region the Islamic law, the *shari'a*. The first state did that in 1999, but by 2002 the whole northern region—encompassing 12 of Nigeria's 36 states—has done so. Most of the Ibo-Ibibio had fled the region in 1967. But this development has angered many Yorubas who reside in the north, especially those who are not Muslim but Christian. This has led to communal violence between Yoruba and Hausa-Fulani. If these last persist in their Islamicization, one could anticipate a possible scene of conflict that will find most Yorubas and the Ibo-Ibibios united against the Hausa-Fulani pole. The latter could then again talk of secession, as they threatened to do in 1966. A forceful repression would be less likely, because the Yorubas and Ibos have little economic need for the Hausa-Fulani region.

Added complications concern the shifts between democracy and the military, because either tends to produce a top leader who represents one of the three communities and may tend to gather too many co-ethnics into the ruling cabinet. Another complication is that in the politics concerning the three main groups, there are recurrent schemes to change the numbers and boundaries of the states, causing each group to perceive ulterior motives of divide and rule.

One could conceive of central power sharing in Nigeria, perhaps with a rotating presidency, but one doubts this would be very successful, especially in view of internal divisions over religion and subregion among the Yoruba. As I write this, the president of Nigeria, Olusegun Obasanjo, is a Christian Yoruba but of a very minor tribe, whereas the army is more Hausa-Fulani. Nigeria cannot be regarded as stable. It is not obvious how some accommodation such as a strong regional devolution of powers (at the risk of secessions) or consociational democracy (at the risk of military coup) would work out.

Nigeria is really three nations pretending to be one, and it could in the longer run fall apart.

Rwanda and Burundi

In Rwanda, the population is about 80 to 85 percent Hutu (or Bahutu) and some 10 to 15 percent Tutsi (or Batutsi). Burundi is similarly populated by a very large Hutu (or Bahutu) majority and a Tutsi minority.

By oral traditions the Hutu people first entered the region and lived primarily by cultivation of the soil, whereas the Tutsis came in later and were a more pastoral people. On average the Hutus are shorter, darker, often with a flatter nose, and the Tutsis tend to be taller, lighter, and with a more pointed nose. But they speak the same language, Bantu, and share other cultural traits, to such an extent that many have intermarried and further contributed to closure of group differences, although cross-marriages can subconsciously raise sexual rivalries.

In the precolonial period, there were no known expressions of major intercommunal violence. In fact, none are known before 1959. Both Burundi and Rwanda had been long ruled by Tutsi monarchs who enjoyed the confidence of the larger Hutu populations.

The two territories were annexed to German East Africa in 1899, then relinquished after Germany's 1918 defeat in the First World War. Belgium, notwithstanding its history of rather brutal rule in the neighboring Congo, thereafter replaced the Germans and continued ruling the territories as a United Nations trust after World War II.

Both German and Belgian colonial authorities held special admiration for the Tutsis, who were regarded by them as a biologically superior people of supposed "Hamitic" ancestry. They followed a frequent tendency of colonial authorities to favor minorities in local military recruitment (the tactical reason should be obvious enough). They encouraged continuation of Tutsi leadership in each state. In short, they introduced a kind of bolstered segregation and stratification not much present in the Tutsi precolonial monarchy. The Belgians also introduced identity cards that defined the bearers as either Tutsis or Hutus, which made it difficult to "pass" when genocidal rages later arose. Also, eventually the Belgians could foresee their exit from the colonies and decided to introduce democracy, which if majoritarian rather than consensual in form would obviously favor the Hutus over the Tutsis, reversing their historical relationship. The first outbreak of intercommunal violence occurred in 1959 in Burundi, preceding independence for both Rwanda and Burundi in 1962.

Both nations have populations that are primarily rural (about 95 percent) and quite densely settled in relatively small national territories. Tutsis have been more prominent in urban employments. The population growth rate has been 3.1 percent a year, which is *very* high by world standards but not much above the sub-Saharan African average, at least before the HIV/AIDS catastrophe.

One plausible account of the underlying roots of the conflict emphasizes increased population pressure and the increasing Hutu demand for tillable farmland, which puts them into conflict with the more characteristically Tutsi pastoralism. If corn and cattle are rivals, so are Hutu and Tutsi. If valid, it is apparent that as long as most of the population remains in extractive employment, there is a zero-sum conflict of interest. Any winnings of more cornfields by Hutus must match losings of pasturelands to Tutsis.

The Tutsis historically have more skilled military commanders, and against a Hutu-dominated democratic regime, in 1972 they seized power in Burundi and did nothing to stop a genocidal destruction of some 200,000 Burundian Hutus. This was well known to Hutus in neighboring Rwanda, because there were among them many Hutu exiles from Burundi. In 1993 Burundi Hutus counterattacked that nation's Tutsis, killing over 50,000.

In Rwanda a few hundred thousand people died in spasms of communal violence in 1990 and 1992, but the major slaughter began in 1994. The triggering event of the 1994 genocide in Rwanda was the shooting down of an airliner that killed the Hutu president of Rwanda (Habyarimana) as well as the Hutu president of Burundi (Ntaryamira). Although the crime was blamed on the Tutsis, it is possible that Hutus could have done it, out of opposition to the presidential willingness to accommodate Tutsi demands as a price for ending a guerrilla war. Without waiting for clear evidence, the state-directed Rwanda public radio began to openly urge the slaughter of all Tutsis. In the course of the murder of some 800,000 Tutsis, they also killed some 2,500 Hutus who were married to Tutsis or who sought in any way to protect them (for elaborations, cf. Adelman and Suhrke, 1999; Gourevitch, 1998; Jennings, 2000; Nyankanzi, 1998; Peterson, 2000; Prunier, 1995).

This slaughter was long planned by some of the Hutu political leadership. Including open incitements on the radio, it differed from the Nazi genocide in more mass involvement of ordinary people (but cf. Goldhagen, 1996). Hutus wielded machetes against their Tutsi neighbors. Because of the earlier communal violence, there were some UN French troops on the ground in Rwanda, but because they were not a large force, they were not permitted by their commanders to directly intervene. These troops eventually created a small security perimeter, but it was not extensive enough to offer refuge to many Tutsis. The United States and other great powers refused to launch a military intervention to curtail the genocide, even if it could have been feasible to deploy troops by air. The chaos caused about a million displaced persons within Rwanda, and another million exiled, with Tutsis then most likely to flee abroad.

Rwanda Tutsi exiles launched a military counterattack on the Hutu authorities in Rwanda, and they were soon victorious. Many Hutus, especially those much involved in the mass killings of Tutsis now took their turn at slipping into exile, but many others were imprisoned to await expected trials. Too many Tutsi judges and prosecutors had died in the 1994 genocide, and the Tutsis were slow to arrange trials for the Hutus sweltering in crowded prisons. In 2002 they shifted many of the cases to informal, traditional tribal courts, called "justice in the grass" (or *gacaca*), which by custom aim more at communal reconciliation than at revenge.

If Burundi's Hutu leaders had appealed for calm as the Rwanda genocide began, preventing a similar bloodbath there, that nation also faced troubles. Tutsi military commanders also seized power in Burundi, and this plunged the nation into eight years of civil warring that seemed to be solved with a power-sharing agreement worked out in 2001. However, two Hutu factions did not concur, and one of them turned to violent struggle not only against the Tutsis but also against the Hutus who were accommodationists (*The New York Times International*, Dec. 21, 2001, A–4).

If the underlying problem in both Rwanda and Burundi seems to be the growing population competing for access to land, it will remain insoluble until the growing labor force shifts out of the primary or extractive economic sector into secondary sector employment (manufacturing, transportation, construction) or tertiary sector employment (services, which by contrast account for most new jobs in economically advanced nations).

But there is also a political conundrum in that any purely majoritarian democracy will mean Hutus will dominate over the Tutsis, always tempting Tutsis to shift to a military regime where Tutsis will likely dominate over Hutus. It is unlikely that either group when in power would be very accommodative.

There seems little prospect of some vast and economically dislocative population exchange, as when Greece and Turkey exchanged their Muslims and Orthodox after World War I. If Tutsis and Hutus have to go on living side by side, only some sort of consociational arrangement would be in principle workable, perhaps something like that in Belgium. It would guarantee *some* protective voice in government for the Tutsis if democracy were restored, but the Tutsi minority in either Rwanda or Burundi is too small to demand parity as in Belgium. I would guess that a consociational arrangement of full minority veto would not be acceptable to Hutus. As I write, the Tutsi minority yet dominate Rwanda and Burundi with military regimes. One could imagine that the Tutsi militaries could consider going back to the barracks after themselves setting up a consociational regime generous to Tutsis, but reempowered Hutus would then attempt to remove any likely overrepresentation of Tutsis. Peaceful solution to the ethnic tensions of Rwanda and Burundi requires all powers of human invention.

The Arab-Israeli Conflict

The Arabs and Israelis have been in major shooting wars six times, in 1948, 1956, 1967, 1973, 1982, and 2002. One would think that nearly fifty-five years of mutual mayhem should be enough. At the heart of these conflicts, Palestinians and Jews have been killing each other over a zero-sum claim to the land currently occupied by the state of Israel. Each claims a historic right to the land. Understating considerable voluntary Jewish migration to Alexandria and elsewhere before the event, the Jews claim that they only left the land involuntarily after defeat by Rome in the Jewish Wars. This diaspora began 70 c.e.

As the British sought to displace the Ottoman Empire from Palestine during World War I, they sought to enlist Jewish support by issuing the 1917 Balfour Declaration, defending a Jewish "national home" within Palestine, without prejudice to the rights of other peoples there. The Turks withdrew from Palestine shortly thereafter.

If in 1880 there had been only 25,000 Jews in Palestine, this had risen by immigration to 50,000 by 1903. During the course of the Nazi persecutions in Europe, increasing waves of Jewish immigrants, many turned away, pressed on the Palestinian Muslim population already resident. After World War II, the United Nations in 1947 sought to define respective territories for the two national groups. The Jews found themselves in conflict with the British authorities, deploying some actions such as blowing up a hotel containing British troops, which could be called terroristic, and eventually fought their first major war with the Arabs in 1948.

The Arabs sought to deny any Jewish national home in Palestine. The Israelis were victorious, however, and although they lost some territories designated for them by the United Nations, they ended up with more territory than had been granted by the UN partition plan. A second war was fought in 1956, when Egypt's Nasser closed the Suez Canal to Israeli ships, but the United States pressed Israel as well as Britain and France to withdraw their forces from Egypt's territory. Another war in 1967, the Six-Day War, ended with the Israelis in control of the West Bank, Gaza, portions of Syria, and Egypt's Sinai peninsula. In 1968 a Labor government sponsored the first Jewish settlement in the added territories, but rightist Likud governments would sharply expand their numbers later. After another round of warring with Egypt and Syria in 1973, which involved threats of Soviet and U.S. direct involvement near the end, the Israelis were able in 1979 to settle a peace with Egypt's Anwar Sadat and returned nearly all of the Sinai peninsula. Israel by 2002 has not yet made peace with Syria, and it continues to occupy part of that nation's territory called the Golan Heights, which Israel has annexed.

A first Palestinian rising called the *intifada* (Arabic for "a shaking off") began in 1987, killing a thousand before ending in 1993. The Palestine Liberation Organization was given limited autonomy on the West Bank and Gaza, allowing police and security forces rather than a military. An Israeli prime minister, Yitzhak Rabin, was in 1995 assassinated by a militant Jew for having been too generous to the Palestinians. Yasser Arafat spurned peace proposals in 1999–2000 offered by prime minister Ehud Barak, on the stated ground that his own people would similarly kill him. But a second round of *intifada*, more mutually violent than the first, broke out in September 2000 after a provocative trip of Ariel Sharon to the Temple Mount, and it continued well into 2003. The violence was severe: Over sixty youthful Palestinians, eventually including some young women, became suicide bombers by strapping explosives under garments, and in choosing Jewish targets. Palestinians called them martyrs, and the Israeli Jews called them murderers. Especially when guided by Hamas, they often attacked purely civilian targets such as shopping centers or public dining spots. Ariel Sharon, who had become prime minister after Ehud Barak, sent tank brigades into Palestinian territories to capture or kill the leading Palestinian militants and alleged planners of such suicide bombings.

Each action-reaction cycle of violence seems to have grown worse, with each side claiming it is merely acting in self-defense. Each side complains that too many of their casualties are noncombatants, often women and children. Such conflicts can become especially nasty when militants become preoccupied in part with getting revenge for their past losses, rather than preventing new ones. Those preoccupied with settling old scores value their "justice" more than peace. Militant Islamic groups, arguably not controlled by Arafat with apparent funding from Syria and Iran, increasingly turned to the mentioned suicide bombings. While demanding that the Palestinian police get control of their terrorists, the Israelis counterattacked against police installations as well as private homes or cars of militant leaders. The Israelis also used helicopter rocket attacks to destroy Arafat's then unoccupied helicopter, thus confining him to the West Bank, isolating him from Gaza. They further used tanks to isolate him at his headquarters in Ramallah, then even forced him into a few rooms with one fetid toilet for several dozen persons so confined with him. A later Israeli attack exploded a shell alongside his own bedroom, but he was then elsewhere in the house. He had been allowed to emerge by May 2002, and the Israelis published allegedly captured documents apparently showing that Arafat was behind some of the suicide bombings. The Palestinians asserted these were forgeries.

Peace? One hopeful sign was the February 2002 announcement of Prince Abdullah of Saudi Arabia that if the settlements were abandoned and Gaza and the West Bank permitted to become a fully independent state, all Arab states should accept the existence of Israel within its 1967 borders. Israel is most unlikely to cede East Jerusalem, declared by Israeli governments to be a permanent accession, and where Arabs have been reduced to a minority.

One can foresee the ultimate exit of Jews from the West Bank and Gaza settlements. Some Palestinian refugees (of the some 3.8 million) could be housed in vacated settlements. But no Israeli state would permit refugee Palestinians a right of return to Israel proper, where there is already a Palestinian minority of about a million (of whom three quarters are Muslims, the others mostly Druze or Christian). Israel is roughly stratified in this order from higher to lower status: Jews born in Israel (sabras), Jews immigrated from Europe (Ashkenazics), Jews from Africa or Asia but principally elsewhere in the Middle East (Sephardics), and the non-Jews, mostly Arabs. The Jews are 82 percent of the population of Israel, and they have kept that ratio roughly constant by enough Jewish immigration (recently massive from the former Soviet Union) to offset higher Arab-Israeli fertility. Although by the 1950 Law of Return any Jew in the world can freely immigrate, even if ancestors left many centuries ago, return is not thus permitted for Palestinians, even if they left in fear in 1948. Less than 40 percent of all Jews of the world live in Israel (Goldscheider, 2002, 14).

Arab Israelis have rights to vote and support a political party, just like Jewish Israelis. They have the special group right to refuse military service, but at the price of losing many veterans' benefits available to those who serve. The Israeli national anthem is Zionist, and some Israeli holidays celebrate defeats of Arabs. On the other side, the Arab-Israeli celebration of Land Day is a reproach to Jewish takeovers of Arab land. Although informally residentially segregated (less than a tenth of neighborhoods mix Jews and Arabs), Arab Israelis seem more likely to have their properties taken by eminent domain, for such purposes as security corridors, or the like. (On the situation of Palestinians within Israel, cf. Fouzi, 1975; Goldscheider, 2002, 15–16; Kretzmer, 1990; Lustick, 1980).

In 2002 there were yet Muslim Palestinians who dreamed of totally abolishing the Jewish state of Israel. On the other side, recent surveys reported that between a third and nearly half of Israeli Jews, angry about suicide bombings and shootings, said that for peace Palestinians would have to leave the West Bank and Gaza. But they may know this is not feasible. For other surveys have shown that majorities of Jewish Israelis expect emergence of an independent Palestinian state in those territories. At least on this question, the United States concurs with Saudi Arabia. In 2003 the United States, Russia, and the European Union proposed what they called a "road map" toward peace to restart Arab-Israeli negotiations, which were underway as we went to press.

Solution will not come readily, because of the usual disparity between minimalist concessions by the Israelis and maximalist demands of the Palestinians, especially the mentioned groups of ultramilitants. At base this is a zero-sum contest for turf, which has historically been a very difficult kind of conflict to resolve (cf. Fraser, 1995; Goldscheider, 2002). But one can roughly predict what each side will have to give up in order to secure any stable peace.

The militant Palestinian dream of eliminating any Jewish state is out of the question. Palestinians will have to make do with a state consisting largely of the West Bank and Gaza, with but a token presence somewhere in East Jerusalem. Some parts of Jerusalem, perhaps including parts of the Temple Mount, may be made condominia, jointly controlled by Palestinians and Jews, perhaps with some UN arbitrator of any dispute. If Palestinians will not recover Israeli-annexed East Jerusalem, they will also have to give up the demand for the right of return of Palestinian refugees to Israel proper, because that would clearly swamp any Jewish majority. The 1948 Palestinian losses in land within Israel may be compensated in unusual ways, such as homes for some within abandoned Jewish settlements and scholarships for refugee youths.

On the other side, those who believe in Greater Israel will also have to abandon the notion of preventing any Palestinian state. They will restore the Golan Heights to Syria and offer some token presence of the Palestinian state in parts of East Jerusalem, including at least shared control of the Dome of the Rock. As noted, the ill-advised Jewish settlements on the West Bank and Gaza, which came to house some 200,000 Jews, will have to be abandoned, most likely in phases, with the smaller and most isolated settlements the first to revert to Palestinian control. The most obviously exposed situation consists of some 6,000 Jewish settlers in 22 settlements in the Gaza strip, where they are surrounded by about a million Palestinians (*The New York Times International*, Feb. 15, 2002, A–5). There would be few Jewish takers for any offer to remain in some settlements under Palestinian authority.

Also, Israel will have to retreat from its strong distrust of international organization, especially the UN, and permit temporarily some sort of neutral international monitors and peacekeeping forces between themselves and the Palestinian state territories. That would be better than the ugly fortified walls now rising between Israel and Palestinian territory.

If time heals over the old wounds, perhaps Arabs and Israelis could even move on to a mutually advantageous free trade area or common market. They could move from a negative-sum game situation (in both security and economic measures) to a positive-sum situation. Perhaps other options mentioned in the chapter 7 discussion of the similarly long-lived Kashmir conflict could help break the Arab-Israeli deadlock.

Afghanistan

In the chapter 3 discussion of the Taliban's aggressive assimilationism, I noted that Afghanistan has three principal ethnic categories of Pashtuns, Uzbeks, and Tajiks, with a weaker, religiously Shi'a minority of Hazaras, a trading people, only marginally involved in the political rivalries. If the Pashtuns were dominant under the Taliban, the Tajiks were militarily strongest in the Northern Alliance which the United States backed to overthrow the Taliban (2001–2002). The interim leader is an anti-Taliban Pashtun, Hamid Karzai. In alliance with the returned, aged monarch, Zahir Shah (who did not upon return from exile demand restoration of his throne), this interim government convened a traditional council *(loya jirga)*, which chose Karzai president for a two-year term, pending arrangement of a constitution by a constituent assembly. The immediate problem is that Karzai's 30 interim council members were

11 Pashtuns and 8 Tajiks, whereas the Uzbeks received only 3 posts and the weaker Hazaras, 5. Further, the Tajiks, long known to excel in civil service jobs, got the top cabinet posts of Foreign Affairs, Defense, and Interior, which further angered their Uzbek allies (*New York Times International*, Dec. 6, 2001, B–4; also, Dec. 17, 2001, A–1 and B–4). Karzai struggled to complete a cabinet. There is virtually no prospect of ethnically blind or meritocratic recruitment of top leadership in the future. As long as tribal identities are stronger than Afghan ones, any failure to follow an informal rule of population proportionality in all cabinets as well as the constituent assembly will cause future tribal rebellions. But the Pashtuns are the largest ethnic group, and many of them miss the Pashtun-dominated Taliban (cf. Goodson, 2001).

CONCLUSION

I have been asking all along how fears, if not driving people to the irrationality of either wholly random or rigid behavior, may cause people to support or oppose some specific ethnic minority policy. A successful accommodation requires a meeting of minds of the leaders of *both* the dominant ethnic group and the weaker ethnic group. One side can make a war, but short of a military victory of one side, it takes two sides to make a peace.

Several attributes of leaders of ethnic groups may make some difference. For one thing, Eric Nordlinger has suggested that a leader with an insecure hold on power may tend to project more aggressivity toward an opposed ethnic group, and be less likely to adapt toward conciliatory change: "Secure leaders are more likely to react to conflict situations in a manner commensurate with the actual level of the conflict, whereas insecure leaders tend to perceive and react to the conflict situation in exaggerated terms. They may even contribute to its escalation" (Nordlinger, 1972, 67–68). But I submit that what they are likely to do may depend on their specific coalition base within their ethnic group.

Chapter 5 noted that stable leaders tend to occupy the median issue space of their support base. But one could distinguish different medians by their distinctive bases, such as those of the militants only, a broad spectrum, and the moderates only. On each side, accommodation would be helped by leadership of centrists or moderates, roughly defining these last as those who feel no need to prove their own ethnic group identity by displays of hatred of the rival ethnic group.

The fears precluding accommodations are primarily those of the militants of each side, with the one thinking too much will be given away, the other, that not enough will be granted. A weaker ethnicity naturally tends to wish maximal concessions for accommodation, and its militants may continue to hold to that, even when moderates may be willing to cut a bargain with the other side. But the dominant ethnic group may start by thinking of a minimal accommodation, and their militants may oppose even that when moderates of the dominant ethnic group also turn to the idea of compromise.

Here borrowing and extending some thoughts about leadership styles from my colleague Tom Preston, often the militants on each side may be least *cognitively complex*, that is, least able to see the world as not all dichotomous, either-or, good versus evil. They cannot see intermediate shades of gray. They are not open to the kinds of information that could see the world that way.

Nor will they be open to multilateral approaches to a problem, because that would include many outlooks, including more moderate positions. Their cognitive horizons also make them reluctant to accept third party or neutral interveners, that is, conciliators, mediators, and arbitrators. After all, such outsiders would include intermediate policy positions, which militants are especially predisposed to think invalid. Hence the militants most in need of the richer views possible with multilateralism or third party interveners are least likely to accept either. This makes them less likely to succeed in negotiating any compromise. In late spring 2002, Egyptian president Hosni Mubarak saw the problem of getting the United States more involved in the Arab-Israeli conflict, saying, "To leave the problem of the Middle East to Arafat and Sharon alone, you will get nowhere" (on intervenors, cf. Fisher, Kopelman, and Schneider, 1994; Trachte-Huber and Huber, 1996).

Militants often make things worse in selecting advisers like themselves. If they ever do succeed, it usually is because they had not rejected from their entourage all of a more cognitively complex outlook on the world. Perhaps the 1972 Nixon-Mao accords between two hard-liners were possible only because more moderate Chou and Kissinger were involved, or the 1979 accord of hard-liner Menahem Begin with more moderate Anwar Sadat may have depended on Begin's more moderate foreign minister, Moshe Dayan (cf. Fraser, 1995, 119). Or some special pressures, such as actual or anticipated third party military action or economic boycott, can sometimes turn militant leaders about.

If one were to play the "if I were king" game, the problem may be one of cutting out the militants, for the more they matter in a coalition base, the further apart would be the *median* coalition positions. If militants are left out of the picture within each group, even if uttering cries of "sellout," "betrayal," "appeasement," the two medians would converge considerably, resulting in distance that could perhaps be closed with the assistance of intervenors who often take a stance of being at the anticipated midpoint of their accommodation.

I started the chapter by noting Alasdair MacIntyre's comment: "The costs of consensus are paid by those excluded from it." To get a consensus on a mutually acceptable accommodation, it becomes clear that these costs must be paid by the die-hard militants on each side. They must be somehow excluded from leadership if talks are to be concluded between leaders. Alternatively, they must be somehow gotten to accept the presence in negotiations of some views outside the narrow boxes of seeing only my side, which embodies all good, and enemy, which incarnates evil.

In Figure 6.2 I illustrate leadership coalitions on each side, the brackets illustrating coalition bases and the vertical dotted lines the medians or stable leadership lines. I show only three symmetrical cases, illustrating differing "accommodation distances," which could be called the gulf of distrust or the impasse. Arguably, case 2 best fits Yasser Arafat and Ariel Sharon as I write, although each likes to paint the other as based on militants only. Each would prefer to see his counterpart replaced by a more moderate leader.

What of asymmetrical models? I can only raise questions that I am not prepared to answer. Do they spontaneously tend to restored symmetry? That is, does a shift to a more militant leader on one side tend to elicit the same on the other side? Or does one group's change to a more moderate leader tend to help chances of a moderate emerging on the other side? Or can leaders often remain the same, merely changing their more militant or more moderate hats along with appropriate shifts in coalition bases, to adapt to changing conditions?

In another context I have warned against an exaggerated view of leader autonomy, emphasizing that most leaders are hemmed in by political coalition

Figure 6.2
Spans of Coalitions, Leadership Medians, and Accommodation Distances between Groups in Conflict

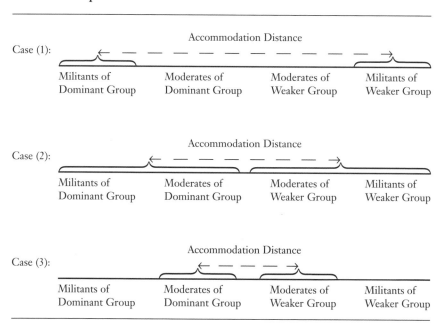

imperatives (Cook, 2002, 188–92). The important thing is to see that the coalition bases not wholly controlled by them constrain leaders' positions, and these positions define the gravity and nature of the problem in working out an accommodation. The greater the accommodation distance, the less likely is a successful accord, unless either existing leaders are subjected to third party pressures or the leaders themselves are somehow changed.

But it could also help to have creative invention of new solutions, as addressed in chapters 7 and 8. Those who are caught up in a mutually destructive game should be looking for every possible way out of it. I begin in chapter 7 with an illustration of that in terms of the Kashmir crisis, then in chapter 8 speculatively address the larger concept of where such thinking could go as part of the theory of conflict resolution.

How to Get Out of a Zero-sum Game: The Case of the Kashmir Conflict

All life is problem solving.

—Karl Popper, philosopher of science

I ended the previous chapter by reviewing some especially difficult ethnic conflicts in view of securing a mutual reconciliation in a stable, accommodative solution. Within this chapter I look at one more of these, but now shift attention to the question of how to get out of an especially dangerous kind of game, here taken in the game theoretic sense. This is the zero-sum game, especially when the competition is not bounded by any formal rules but is played primarily by Realpolitik or opportunistic rules only. If in zero-sum contests, by definition, any winnings of one side are directly matched by losings of the other, they often dive into negative-sum games, where any winnings of the winners are less than the losings to the loser. Indeed, in the most bleak outcome, sometimes called the Doomsday game, everyone is a loser. One could view any future nuclear war between Pakistan and India as precisely that. But as Karl Popper (1999) reminds us, living is problem solving, and there are reasons to believe people can get out of dangerous contests that cause mutual ruin. The larger significance of what is addressed within this chapter emerges in the subsequent chapter on transformational game theory.

BACKGROUND

The conflict between India and Pakistan over control of the Vale of Kashmir and Jammu has been festering for well over a half century, and it has been a contributory cause to three full-scale wars as well as the more limited war of 2001–2002.

In the Kashmir conflict, both states claimed to have all of the right on their side. Pakistan asserts that Mountbatten secretly connived with Nehru to get Kashmir into India, in part by intervening with a British arbitrator's division of an adjacent territory. India emphasizes the choice of the Hindu Maharaja Hari Singh to accede to India just after Pashtun (Pathan) tribesmen invaded the territory and threatened Srinigar. Pakistan denies, and India asserts, that the government of Pakistan aided and abetted that invasion. This was underway just before Indian troops were sent in, mistakenly thinking that Ali Jinnah was poised to go to Srinigar when he really was in Lahore. India's forces were most likely going in before the Maharaja signed the accession agreement, if he ever formally signed it at all (Lamb, 1994, 97; cf. also Bose, 1997). Denying Indian claims as to timing, Pakistan rather invoked popular sovereignty and the greater numbers of Muslims within the disputed territories, especially in the Vale of Kashmir (then some 70 percent Muslim) rather than Jammu (in 1947 just under 50 percent Muslim, with Hindus and Sikhs together making just over 50 percent). Currently as many as 77.5 percent in the Vale are Muslim. Pakistan, as noted, denies that it organized the Muslim tribals who invaded to rescue fellow Muslims from genocidal slaughter. Hindus and Sikhs probably did destroy about two-fifths (or some 200,000) of the Muslims in Jammu, the rest getting out to Pakistan-controlled West Punjab. Pakistanis note correctly that India did not accept princely discretion when absorbing Junagadh and Hyderabad, where Muslim rulers were in the minority position (Wirsing, 1994, 37). Yet they ask why India has not lived up to its clear 1949 commitment to the United Nations to permit a plebiscite within the region (Wirsing, 1994, 54–59). With neither side consistent in holding that princely or popular discretion should decide accessions, there is plenty of hypocrisy to go around. Apologists for each side may spin out further elaborations forever, but without any possibility of persuading their adversaries to their position.

The conflict remains heated. Officials of the Indian state of Jammu and Kashmir reported deaths in the year 2001 alone at 3,465, including 2,000 militant Muslims, 408 Indian soldiers of the army and paramilitary forces, 128 of the police force there, and 909 civilians.

One can define a set of games or problem situations ranging from those which are highly tractable to those which are most unforgiving. To grasp some of such possible game shifts, one needs at least basic definitions of some common game-theoretic models, and I list them in Figure 7.1.

The full purport of the discussions here are elaborated in chapter 8, where I describe a fresh conflict-resolution agenda. In the discussions that follow, it will be apparent I am exploring in the abstract, but often with some real-world examples, how the players of a dangerous zero-sum game could *possibly* get out of the game, shifting to less dangerous or more tractable kinds of games.

Although often bordering on negative-sum and now threatening nuclear

Figure 7.1
Type of Games or Problem Situations: Ordered by Typically Increasing Danger

---

(1) **Pure Coordination Problem:** Everyone wants an agreement, and that is more important than its content, so clear communication is enough to solve it, as meeting for lunch.

(2) **Collaboration Problem:** There is a good that is collective, that is, indivisible and nonexcludable. If anyone can enjoy it, all can do so. Problem: Most want to enjoy it without contributing, or free ride—let George or Georgina do it.

(3) **Impure Coordination Problem:** Everyone would like an agreement, but find it hard to agree on its terms, or who gives what and who gets what. A typical problem of reaching an accord on what is distributively just or fair.

(4) **Prisoner's Dilemma Problem:** The parties would like to collaborate, but out of the fear of being a sucker because the other will not deliver (will defect), each defects from the other, leaving a suboptimal outcome for both.

(5) **Zero-sum Game Problem:** Hard conflict of interest, whereby any winnings of winners precisely equal the losings of the others. Or, more for me must mean less for thee, as in conflicts of states to control territory.

(6) **Negative-sum Game Problem:** Harsher conflict of interest, whereby any winnings of the winners are less than the losings incurred by losers.

(7) **Doomsday Game Problem:** If one attacks, destroying the other, the other gets off a counterattack, destroying the aggressor, too. Everyone loses, and loses big.

Doomsday, the Kashmir crisis is a zero-sum game. But is every such zero-sum contest insoluble? Is it not possible to imagine change of that specific kind of game into another which is more tractable? Consider *in the abstract* eight possible ways to transform a zero-sum game contest into a more manageable one:

1. mutual renunciation of the object;
2. increasing the supply of the object of contest;
3. imposing a solution from without;
4. dividing up, partitioning, the object of contest;
5. alternating control over the object of contest;
6. simultaneously sharing control over the object of contest;
7. embedding the conflict within a larger, package negotiation of mutually advantageous exchanges;
8. shifting to new, encompassing identities such that parties in contest no longer see the contest as meaningful.

Perhaps my working list is not exhaustive. but it at least enables expanded comment on the practical obstacles or opportunities offered by some of such abstractly possible solutions to a zero-sum game situation.

I. MUTUAL RENUNCIATION OF THE OBJECT OF CONTEST

Against the common tendency to recommend renunciation only for one's adversary, sometimes those in a heated zero-sum contest may see the advantage of mutual renunciation of the object coveted by both. Indeed, this could be said to be central to conflict resolution in much of the spiritual wisdom of the East. Thus the Hindu teaches renunciation of the object of desire in that one *already* possesses it, because your view that it is separate being is *maya*, illusion. Or the Buddhist teaches renunciation in that maintenance of the desire, rather than not having the object, is what causes one's suffering. Indeed, Buddhism even recommends self-effacement (mentally erasing the self) as the ultimately correct path. The Christians believe love of others and many renunciations in this life could be recompensed in a next and eternal life. Although such strenuously spiritual forms may become elusive in an age of increased secularization, especially in the more economically developed societies, there are instances of reconciliations of antagonists by such renunciations in everyday life.

In late medieval Europe, the Roman Catholic Church experienced the scandal of the Great Schism, which involved two or even three rival popes during the years 1378 to 1417. The conciliarists Peter d'Ailly and John Gerson both proposed the solution of asking the two main contenders to both renounce their claim to the papacy in favor of a third figure, supported by the Council of Constance, which convened from 1414 to 1418. The two did resign, and the problem was permanently solved.

One finds other instances of mutual renunciations in the survival of microstates along the borders of larger powers that had often warred before. The frame of mind usually supposes the wars have been more costly than any gain possible, especially where no gain seems conceivable, because the adjacent powers can each block the goals of the other, or indeed, even destroy the other, as in mutually assured destruction by nuclear warfare. To suggest that both Pakistan and India withdraw from Kashmir seems preposterous, yet not inconceivable.

In the first place, Kashmir enjoyed formal independence under the Maharaja from the British renunciation of Paramountcy on August 15, 1947, to near the end of October, when he acceded to India. He was promised he could continue to rule, although India encouraged him to take a vacation outside his principality and then had him abdicate in favor of his son, who served for a time as the provincial chief of state.

Also, from the Islamic side, Sheikh Abdullah proposed independence for Kashmir just before the 1947 war, even if placed under confinement for talking that way. He kept returning to that idea but backed off toward autonomy within India by his death in 1982. Even the Maharaja Hari Singh may have contemplated the possibility of independence, which may explain why he kept postponing choice between India and Pakistan (Wirsing, 1994, 2). After the fighting was underway in 1947, the idea of independence from both neighboring states was also suggested by the British (Lamb, 1994, 140).

Even now mutual renunciation would surely be a wiser choice for each state than to have another full-scale war over Kashmir, especially should it go nuclear. Both states would, of course, demand guarantees that the state would not in the future merge with, or militarily ally with, the other. But an essentially neutral state could yet enjoy free trade with both Pakistan and India. Tourism, now ruined by the violence that keeps tourists away, would literally thrive in a pacified, independent state, even if including only the Indian-held portion of Kashmir. Referring to the whole of the original principality (Pakistan occupies about one-third, India, two-thirds), Victoria Schofield notes that its territory would be larger than that of 68 UN member nations, and its population would eclipse 90 (Schofield, 1996, 3). Once put into existence, such a state would develop its own dynamics toward continual sovereignty, especially in the self-interests of Kashmiri state leaders but also in some trade protections, and so on, of its business firms.

What makes this solution difficult is the background of commitments and infrastructure investments that makes a loss always look larger than the possible gain. Neither state would presently favor having a referendum on independence within the whole of Kashmir. Another formidable problem is the Muslim-Hindu-Sikh rivalries that would exist within an independent state, and the certainty that the Hindus as well as Sikhs would find themselves in a minority position. Hence the solution would have to include constitutional guarantees for the religious minorities. Would these guarantees be just leaves in the wind if Kashmiri Muslims turned to neo-Islamic fundamentalism comparable to the movements of Iran or Algeria? The Pakistani novelist Salman Rushdie has publicly proposed Kashmiri independence as a viable solution, but one recalls that Iran, a neo-Islamic revolutionary state, placed a bounty on Rushdie's life for an alleged blasphemy against Islam.

Note that if any actual mutual withdrawal were implemented, one may have just shifted from a zero-sum conflict into a Prisoner's Dilemma game (review Figure 7.1), in that, either because of no communications or else communications that are so untrustworthy to be tantamount, each would expect the other to later defect on their agreement, perhaps then taking the whole of Kashmir for themselves.

Even acceptances of buffer zones or "deterritorializing" (e.g., separation of trade rights from monopoly rights over territory) may not be feasible in very high-conflict situations, where the essentially zero-sum contest for turf reemerges (cf. Vasquez, 1983, esp. 148–52).

II. INCREASING THE SUPPLY

Most conflicts assume that the wants of the parties involved exceed the available supply, but if neither can renounce the want, another possible solution to *some* conflicts is to increase the supply of what is wanted. This is often applicable to other kinds of zero-sum contests. One may allay fights over market *share* by boosting overall market *size*. Historically, as already apparent in William Petty's *Political Arithmetik* or in Locke's *Second Treatise* chapter on property, capitalist economics imagines transcending conflict over wealth or income by expanding the supply of both. It is at least possible that *everyone* could become better off *without* making *anyone* worse off. A rising tide, the cliché goes, lifts all boats. In the real world it may not always work that way, either because no growth occurs or because the worst-off lose even their relative share, sometimes even becoming absolutely worse off during growth (as in the 1970s Brazilian economic miracle, which may have recurred in the 1990s).

Water rights have also tended to be regarded as zero-sum objects of dispute. But the availability of water supplies can sometimes be literally increased by such means as joint construction of dams to capture more rainwater or joint investment in desalinization plants.

Although unfixed zero-sum conflicts of interest can spontaneously game-shift into negative sum conflicts of interest, a modest increase of something in dispute could convert a negative sum game into some kind of positive-sum game, most likely remaining an impure coordination game, where, by definition, they want an agreement but find it difficult to agree on the terms of who bears what burdens or who gets what rewards. An extreme increase of something in dispute, however, could make it into a pure coordination game, where, again by definition, all want an agreement but are indifferent as to its content, as often illustrated by when good friends, both omnivores, are happy to meet just anywhere for lunch.

Alas, not everything can be increased. A contest of two persons for the affections of a third becomes a zero-sum contest if matrimony is involved, if only because of laws requiring monogamy. One has the imagined solution of cloning the beloved, but that would take a long time, and neither suitor would want to wait. Besides, the clone's nearly identical body would lack the same consciousness and hence might not be loved.

Increasing the supply is quite obviously least promising for the present case study. Unlike wealth or income or even water, land is a constant sum. Apart from petty cases of filled-in bays (Japan, Hong Kong), it is not normally increased. Hence the humorous investment advice of Mark Twain: "Buy land. They have stopped making it!" Leaving aside future colonizations of other planets and moons, the only feasible increase of a contested territory would involve theft of territory from some other state, not previously a party to the issue, as in taking territory from China to satisfy the territorial ambitions of both Pakistan and India. At least for small portions of each class, when the workers and the owners of an industry coalesce to support protectionism, they end zero-sum conflict between them (Gourevitch, 1986, 47). Yet their "solution" is really a *displacement* of the zero-sum conflict, now between their own coalition and foreign owners/laborers in the industry. So it would be if India and Pakistan settled their conflict over Kashmir by each taking a slice of China, an unlikely solution in any case unless China were to fall into complete warlordism, losing all control over Xianjiang or Tibet. After China in 1956–1957 built a road through a disputed area to link Tibet to Xianjiang, India in 1962 lost a war with China and the territory, the Aksai Chin slice of Ladakh.

Yet there are a few historical cases that approximate such a mutual solution of territorial demands at the price of some third party. One recalls the partitions of Poland by Russia, Prussia, and Austria in the eighteenth century. Also, Stalin increased the supply of Polish land for the Soviet Union by compensating Poland with a slice of defeated Germany: "As the Soviet Union grew, so Germany shrank: Poland was bodily shifted over one hundred miles west, exacting territory from Germany in the West in compensation for lands claimed by the Soviet Union in the east" (Pearson, 1998, 32).

There was in 1947 a foregone opportunity of bringing more land into the bargaining, because the princely state of Hyderabad provided a mirror case of a state ruled by a Muslim but with a largely Hindu population. Sir Conrad Cornfield in vain urged Mountbatten to introduce that in the bargaining over Kashmir. Perhaps Menon and Patel, negotiating for India, conceded in January 1947 a plebiscite for Jammu and Kashmir with the idea it would work for India in Hyderabad. But that came to nothing, because Nehru rejected a plebiscite in Jammu and Kashmir. He had earlier broached the stillborn idea of having such a plebiscite only if all outside Muslim forces withdrew, leaving India's army in place (Lamb, 1974, 150–51). Hyderabad was in the heart of India, and Nehru surely did not want equivalent consideration. He invaded the state in 1948 and deposed the Nizam (Schofield, 1996, 121, 158). Surely Nehru had expected any linkage to cost him the Vale of Kashmir, the much loved home of his own Brahmin ancestors. In a like case, the Muslim Nawab of Junagadh ruled a majority Hindu population and chose to accede to Pakistan. India prevented that by creating a puppet state and hinting at military intervention, causing the Nawab to flee to Pakistan.

Whatever its strategic military uses, disputants could be asked whether land and its possible produce (minerals, agricultural commodities) may be receding in importance relative to manufacturing and especially services, and services to services, in the postindustrial economy. I suspect the key to national economic prosperity for advanced nations is having tertiary or quaternary sector jobs grow faster than primary and secondary sector jobs decline. If so, possession of more rather than less land recedes in importance, at least economically. They could contest it for power or security. But the irony is this:

the contest over land (or perhaps the land with co-ethnics attached) may be the chief cause of the Indo-Pakistani insecurity.

If zero-sum conflicts of interest characteristically focus around some object in scarce supply, the zero-sum contests themselves can in some cases notoriously increase the scarcity. Thus if an economy stagnates due to other causes, the rise of zero-sum contests over jobs, public budget shares, and so on, can contribute to further stagnation of the economy. Exorbitant military spending has opportunity costs. Imagine what a great university could be built in Srinigar with all of the wealth squandered in regard to the military confrontations over Kashmir.

III. IMPOSITION OF A SOLUTION FROM WITHOUT

Some accommodations may involve third party interventions, which can include conciliation, mediation, arbitration, or outright imposition. Although the other forms of third party interventions can help secure voluntary accommodations, as noted in chapter 6, another possible solution of a zero-sum conflict is a third party imposition of a solution on two antagonists. If they mutually recognize that they *must* accept the agreement and hence could be said to more or less want it, if they each believe they could at all favorably influence on their own behalf the contents of the imposition, this would amount to a conversion of a zero-sum game into an impure coordination game.

The UN General Assembly in 1948–1949 was asking India and Pakistan to solve their problem with a plebiscite. Failing to secure India's consent, the UN in 1951 urged that the dispute go to arbitration, which Pakistan accepted, but India rejected. India later accepted an arbitration of the Rann of Kutch territorial dispute in the West, but it resulted in loss of much land to Pakistan. After defeating Pakistan in their 1971 war, India simply took back that land.

There are many historical examples of externally imposed resolution, not all of them successful. An imposed partition had been adopted for Palestine by the UN in 1947, but it failed, leaving that conflict, too, yet unresolved as I write. Another instance was most recently displayed in the NATO intervention of the Bosnian war. It stopped the warring and imminent threat of warring, even if final resolution remains elusive. A similar process occurred in Kosovo in 1999, with the Albanian Kosovars gaining but the Serb minority ultimately losing when NATO bombings forced withdrawal of Yugoslav troops. Possible agreed solutions of the other seven approaches normally suppose that the two sides talk, which can be difficult when one or even both of two states involved in a dispute will not go to a bargaining table (J. Stein, 1989). An imposition can quickly deal with that obstacle, whether by forcing the sides to talk or by giving them their terms.

An imposition could only work in the Kashmir crisis if key great powers became involved and worked in harmony. In the past, this has been unavailing, because China's foreign policy leaned in favor of Pakistan, whereas the USSR's was more favorable to India. The relevance of political changes in both Russia and China is hard to predict. Russia in October 2000 resumed major arms sales to India, including an aircraft carrier with 40 MiG-29's as well as 310 T-90 tanks. Pakistan looks toward China for missiles. Although seeking to keep doors open to both states, France, Britain, and the United States have shown no inclination to literally impose a resolution of the Kashmir crisis. Sanctions were launched to dissuade further nuclear arms testing by either side, but this ended when the United States needed Pakistan's support for the 2001 invasion of Afghanistan to break up the headquarters of al-Qaeda, which almost surely planned the September 11, 2001, destruction of the World Trade Center towers. But my point here is that if great powers had the will to intervene more extensively, they surely have the capacity. Unlike mediation and conciliation, they would not require the consent of one or both powers. But how many of us would be comfortable with such exertion of power in the world? What may work with small states such as fragments of the former Yugoslavia may be much resisted by larger states such as Pakistan and India.

IV. DIVIDING UP THE OBJECT OF CONTEST

Another possible solution for the zero-sum conflict is some kind of mutually agreed division of what is at issue, without the presence of any imposition. This would mean a conversion from a zero-sum contest into an impure co-ordination problem, in that each would want to slice the object of the contest to their own advantage.

One may note that arbitrated partitions had preceded 1947 independence in both Punjab and Bengal, but one must concede that, especially in the first case, this resulted in considerable communal killing as unfavorably located populations transferred to the separated sections.

Braving recurrence of the like, could India and Pakistan ever voluntarily get to the point of another, formalized partition of the territory? Without the complication of a princely will, they had been able before independence to divide the two provinces named above. Even after fighting broke out in Kashmir in 1947, the British favored partition, and the Maharaja seemed amenable if left in control of the original dynastic state of Jammu (Lamb, 1974, 143–45).

In a true zero-sum conflict of two parties, demands are incompatible: More for me means less for thee. Halfway measures between maximum demands would not work. It is most unlikely that India and Pakistan would accept each other as equal claimants.

Indeed, Kashmir is already in a de facto division from the war following the 1947 start of the partitioning of India. But Pakistan controls only about a third, yet the Muslim population in the two states combined was about twice that fraction (70 percent of some 3 million people in Kashmir, nearly

50 percent of 1 million in Jammu). Only India, which refuses to negotiate Kashmir, could see a plausible solution in the status quo, arguably not having any really serious claim on the Pakistani-occupied third of the original principality. Yet India still formally claims the whole, as does Pakistan. India yet fears any kind of referendum within Kashmir, knowing the large Muslim majority there. Pakistan could welcome one, expecting to win, but would not want that paired with the option of independence as well as merger with either Pakistan or India. It may seem that an over fifty-year division would be a de facto resolution of the conflict, but neither the Pakistanis nor many of the Kashmiri Muslims view it that way, nor are they likely to have a change of mind. In the twentieth century this conflict took 34,000 lives, of whom 20,000 were civilians (*New York Times International*, Sept. 7, 2000, A-10). Although not always equally intense, the conflict drags on, now as internal war and sometimes as external war. And a consequence of the unresolved situation is not only costly internal war in the Vale of Kashmir but the threat of yet another full-scale Indo-Pakistan war. As India and Pakistan further develop their nuclear war capabilities, the continuation of the status quo must be viewed as terribly unsatisfactory. There are no sure guarantees in nuclear deterrence, if only because of the possibilities of either accident or miscalculation in escalation from conventional war. Although India and those Hindus not refugees from Islamic terrorism within Kashmir (Sikh residents have more recently come under attack, apparently by Muslims) may implicitly think of an end of the conflict by Pakistani and Kashmiri Muslim acquiescence in the de facto division, Pakistanis and their Muslim allies within Kashmir may dream of a terminus in India's withdrawal. Any notion of division has not worked out and it probably will not succeed.

A study of conflicts since 1815 found that only one-seventh of them were solved by some kind of peaceable acquiescence, so it is not very promising (Bueno de Mesquita and Lalman, 1992, cited in K. Monroe, 1997). For what it is worth, Steven Brams and Alan Taylor have explored at length the possibilities of partitioning as a solution to conflicts, and they have invented a now patented algorithm for doing this (Brams and Taylor, 1996).

V. ALTERNATING CONTROL OVER THE OBJECT OF CONTEST

Another possible solution for some zero-sum contests is alternation of control. If both sides want the agreement, but if they have incompatible preferences as to who goes first, we have passed over into an impure coordination problem. But if both want the agreement and have no time preference, it becomes a collaboration problem (again, for definition, see Figure 7.1).

Alternated control sought to end *la violencia* in Colombia, a period of civil warring running from 1947 to 1958, culminating in a near military dictatorship of General Gustavo Rojas. Leaders of the Liberal and Conservative parties agreed to change the constitution to require (1) a twelve-year alternation of the presidency between them, and also (2) parity (absolute equality) in distribution of all other public offices (Needler, 1970, 239). However, initial agreements of leaders did not readily dominate their followers, and it took a long time for the shootings between parties to break down into mere banditry and individual settlements of scores before the guns went silent (Nordlinger, 1972, 76).

Other attempts at alternation have failed, including those of Benin and Yugoslavia. In Benin, the military in 1969 sought to bring an end to frictions among the somewhat ethnically distinctive followings of three civilian politicians surnamed Maga, Ahomadegbe, and Apithy. As Eades and Allen have described it, "A complex settlement was worked out which appeared to give something to everyone: the three old political rivals were appointed to a presidential council, with each of them scheduled to hold power for two years" (Eades and Allen, 1996, xxxvi). But while Maga did pass the torch after two years to Ahomadegbe, the military cut short the latter's term and excluded Apithy with a new coup d'état in 1972. The grand coalition alternation system failed, perhaps because tripolar systems tend to be notoriously unstable, especially amid high conflict of interest likely to encourage action by Realpolitik rules, culminating, as noted earlier, in a coalition of two against the third.

Before his death in 1980, the League of Communists leader Tito had attempted to secure the future of his federation of Yugoslavia (the national name means "south-slavs") by setting up a plural presidency somewhat like that of Switzerland. The chief position was alternated among the persons representing the six republics and the two autonomous regions. But the last to hold the position was the notorious Serb, Slobodan Milosevic, who managed to corral four of eight votes on the plural presidency, namely, those of Serbia, Vojvodina, Kosovo, and Montenegro (Kaufman, 2001, 181). He changed the constitution to permit him to dominate the position alone. Then he aided and abetted warring with other ethnic groups in Slovenia, Croatia, Bosnia-Herzegovina, and finally the Serbian province of Kosovo. Milosevic remained in power over the rump of Yugoslavia, consisting only of Serbia and Montenegro until mass demonstrations forced him out after the fraudulent election in 2001. He was later arrested and faced an international war crimes tribunal in the Netherlands.

In a related case in Bosnia, the Muslim, Serbian, and Croatian groups worked out a power-sharing agreement that includes an alternation of leadership among members of the troika presidency, beginning in 1998 with the Muslim leader Alija Izetbegovic, who in 2000 resigned his four-year term two years early for health reasons, with leadership shifted to a Bosnian Serb, Zivko Radisic. As in other tripolar systems, the prospects are not optimistic.

Because the Hazara minority, largely Shi'a Islam in a predominantly Sunni Islam nation, is weak in Afghanistan, its system is also tripolar, with the larger Pashtun tribals, and smaller Uzbeks and Tajiks. As noted in chapter 6, the post-Taliban grand coalition of the three underrepresented the Uzbeks in cabinet posts and military leadership, and the Uzbek military leader Rashid Dostum loudly protested. The interim leader while awaiting a constituent assembly to write a constitution is Hamid Karzai, who is Pashtu. It is difficult to imagine that Pashtuns will recognize equality of Uzbeks and Tajiks in any arrangement for a rotated presidency.

In Malaysia, the ceremonial kingship, a national chief of state role more honorific than important, is rotated among the nine state sultans every five years. If a sultan dies, the survivors elect the successor.

In 2003, the planned reunification of Cyprus included the alternation of its presidency between a Greek and a Turk, part of the plan already accepted by the Greeks as this book goes to press.

Alternations of leadership posts aside, I do not know of any alternation respecting a territorial conflict between states. Indeed, the solution does not appear at all likely in the case of Kashmir, especially in the current climate of ascendant religio-national movements. Pakistan has adopted much of the *shari'a*, which, aside from the Ottoman *millet* system, has been often imposed on the whole population governed by a Muslim ruler, a fact causing strife just now in the southern Sudan, as in the Hausa-Fulani region in northern Nigeria as addressed in chapter 6. In India, electoral gains of Bharatiya Janata, a Hindu nationalist party, also suggests that the spirit of exclusivity of religion could also be extended to Kashmir from India's side, inflamed by Hindu exiles from the fighting in Kashmir. In 1992 Hindu militants tore down a mosque on a hillock at Ayodhya, and Hindu-Muslim tensions remained electric for a time. I sensed the fear shortly afterward while visiting Varanasi as a column of Muslim demonstrators marched on the Ganges city, before being persuaded to stop short. After Hindus eventually declared they would build a Hindu temple to honor their god Rama at the Ayodhya site, angry Muslims in 2002 torched a train returning Hindu pilgrims from the site, and nearly fifty Hindus died. In revenge, the Gujarat province Hindus then killed 300 to 600 Muslims.

Given such tensions, alternation of control would only be possible in the implausible case of separation of religion and state, at least for governance of Kashmir. Indeed, even more than such a separation, perhaps it requires a secularization in elites, who would no longer regard either Islam or Hinduism as a way of life that must be sanctioned by the state. We know that in the long run, economic development correlates with most measures of secularization, but in the short run it also may bring out an intensified fanaticism in fundamentalists dislocated by development (Barber, 1995; Huntington, 1996).

The zealots of any one religion may emphasize that its universal extension would bring peace, but that there are similar zealots of *other* religions may mean in fact that it is a way to war. Indeed, notwithstanding claims made, none of the major religions of the earth has been able to secure peace even among states dominated by its own persuasion. Muslim states have not only fought non-Muslim ones, but Muslim states have fought other Muslim states.

The same is true of Hindu states. Nor does a shared economic system, whether feudalism, capitalism, or socialism, help discourage warring among the economically similar states. The *only* system of shared ideas and practices that has arguably pacified states is democracy, even if that only brings nearly certain peace between democratic dyads (Doyle, 1983a, 1983b; Rummel, 1983, 1997). Indeed, Rudolf Rummel is so strongly convinced of this, he would no doubt urge that only insistence on democracy within both India and Pakistan, and at all times, would bring peace between them (Rummel, 1997). But even the democratic peace has been challenged (Gowa, 1999). In the year before General Musharraf took power by coup in Pakistan, over a thousand died in fighting in sporadic warring in Kashmir, which is the conventional definition of a war as succinctly defined by Stuart Kaufman: "A war is organized armed conflict between at least two belligerent sides in which at least one thousand people are killed" (Kaufman, 2001, 17). Although that occurred when democracy had been evident in both Pakistan and India, defenders of the democratic peace could argue that democracy had not been fully installed in Pakistan, that the military there yet controlled this domain of policy (Maluka, 1995). Thus when the civilian national leader ordered withdrawal of Pakistani regulars from the disputed mountain area, he was ousted by a coup d'état.

VI. SIMULTANEOUSLY SHARING CONTROL

Rather than dreaming of alternated control, another possible solution is simultaneously sharing control. Perhaps this could convert a zero-sum game into a kind of collaboration problem, whereby both by definition want to enjoy a share of the indivisible, nonexcludable collective good, but the problem becomes free riding in that neither wants to incur real costs in the attainment of the good.

Perhaps some of the greatest obstacles to sharing control are conceptual rigidities. Thus in the dominant understanding of "property," one understands an exclusive set of rights over something, whereas there are concepts of property such as among many preliterate bands, among medieval populations, or even Muslims in North Africa who can conceive of a multiplicity of owners over one palm tree. Or again, the sixteenth-century term "sovereignty" is again not some essence with a correct definition somewhere in the clouds but a mere word formed for human purposes. Since articulation by Jean Bodin, *Six Books of the Commonwealth* (1576), its dominant meaning once again tends, even more than the concept of property, to imply an exclusive right of one person or assembly to have the last word over what the rules are and what they mean. Rigid concepts of "property" or "sovereignty" hence must be overcome.

A partial condominium exists in Andorra, where France and Spain jointly control security affairs. Each nation also has a right to appoint two of the

four members of Andorra's Constitutional Tribunal. Yet Andorra is nominally "sovereign," having been a member of the UN since 1993 (Krasner,
1999, 16).

There is a historical instance of shared rule in the Anglo-Egyptian Condominium over Sudan in the nineteenth century. However, Egypt at that time
was a de facto protectorate of the United Kingdom, lacking any real
autonomy.

In another case approximating conjoint control, shared access if not control
over the Ruhr resources was aimed to prevent yet another world war:

[T]he European Union was begun largely with the high statesmanship of Jean Monnet,
who proposed the founding of the European Coal and Steel Community, with the
rationale of putting the war-making capacities of historic enemies France and Germany
under the collective supervision and control of themselves, Italy, Belgium, Luxem-
bourg and the Netherlands. (Prager, 1998, 460)

Assertion of national sovereignly rights, argues Susan Woodward, can be
more dangerous than insistence on human rights for individuals (Woodward,
1995, 339). The language of sovereignty supposes *all or nothing*, but there is
abundant hypocrisy in use of the term to make some claims as over territory,
control of what passes borders, allocation of power within a state, and the like
(Krasner, 1999). To repeat, we often forget that "sovereignty" is not a natural
essence but an artificially created word, a word that can block any kind of
compromise of the claim. It would be better to dump the word than to abandon the possibility of compromise.

Looking at some long-festering territorial conflicts, conjoint control would
seem to be at least a possible solution in some cases. One thinks of potential
condominia in Gibraltar, in the Falklands (Malvinas), or in the contested part
of Sri Lanka. I presented these thoughts for the first time at a conference in
October 2000, and by May 2002 both the British and Spanish governments
began hinting that they intended to consider joint sovereignty as the solution
for their long conflict over Gibraltar. The Gibraltarians, however, are dis-
pleased by that, wanting to remain decidedly British. It is a case to watch, but
I assume any implementation would reveal few difficulties.

Consider the possibility of a like solution for control over at least parts of
Jerusalem now contested by Israeli Jews and Palestinians, perhaps with some
permanent co-sovereignties (e.g., the Temple Mount and some other parts of
Jerusalem) and other merely transitional co-sovereignties (even the larger Israeli settlements in the West Bank, one assumes, would eventually pass to a
Palestinian state). When yet prime minister, Ehud Barak was apparently talking of some zones of conjoint control, just as I had discussed with an Israeli
friend, Dan Avnon, several years earlier.

One could conceive of a somewhat similar arrangement for the whole of
Jammu and Kashmir, however improbable it may appear. It would be aided

by extensive English competence among elites of both Pakistan and India, permitting easy communication for any possible co-rule. A practical obstacle consists in incompatible demands of religious fundamentalisms. Economic development tends to reduce religiosity, with only a few outliers such as the United States (Wald, 1987, 2). Not even long-term secularization helped during the breakup of Yugoslavia, where even nonreligious persons were tagged with the religion of their grandparents. The solution could work if certain religious issues were kept out of the political arena by a system of constitutional guarantees. Both Pakistan and India would have to forego forever any wish to impose their religions (or cultures more broadly) on the whole population of the contested region. It is easy to say this would be possible given a certain kind of leadership of both states, inclined to tolerance if not also secularization at its base.

But those who talk too easily of the autonomy of leadership often forget to ask who wrote the rules for leadership selection, which leaders get selected, and the conditions of their hold on office. I repeat that coalition imperatives can constrain choices (cf. Cook, 2002, esp. 188–92). If ethnonational bigotries pervade the more structural side of political recruitment, any notion of better leadership as the solution conceals a shallow grasp of the problem. Yet there are many studies of power sharing as an approach to conflict resolution, with Arend Lijphart being the most cited (Lijphart, 1975, 1977, 1984; Sisk, 1997).

VII. SUBSUMPTION OF THE DISPUTE IN A LARGER PACKAGE OF MUTUAL ADVANTAGE

Perhaps a start toward another kind of solution would be the subsumption of the Kashmir issue within a larger set of issues, such as resolution of trade issues, management of the Ganges or other waters, and so on. One supposes here a shift into an impure coordination problem, in that the parties could sharply dispute the terms, even if finally reconcilable on the whole packages (Fisher, Ury, and Patton, 1991). But as Jon Elster notes, if having *two few* things on the negotiation floor can block agreement, so having *too many* alternatives in the air could also prevent anything being decided (Elster, 1989, 80). In any event, this approach would only make sense if resolution on other issues would be easier than resolution of the tough knot of authority over Jammu and Kashmir, taken in isolation. That is not obviously so. But this possible long-run solution is here stated just to be thorough, even if it does not look practicable in the near term.

Classic functionalist theorists such as David Mitrany, Amitai Etzioni, or the early Ernst Haas, Sr., held that cooperation in small matters is the way toward cooperation in the large. Confidence building measures (CBMs) are similar, if often understood as more episodic gestures of goodwill. Arguably, only deep environmental or economic cooperation will pave the way for ultimate co-

operation in the large sense, perhaps making use of one of the possible solutions named here. In questions related to war and peace, one must always
retain some measure of hope.

VIII. TRANSCENDING THE CONFLICT THROUGH LARGER IDENTITIES

Yet another logically possible solution to a zero-sum conflict is changing
the frame of reference to new, shared identity. Imagine that two cantankerous
neighbors, a man and a woman, have had a fifty-year quarrel over their lot
lines. But if the old dears shock everyone, even themselves, by falling in love
with each other and perhaps getting married, the lot line ceases to be a meaningful issue. They could want agreement so much that they are indifferent
about the boundary between their lots, although there could be another problem about which of their houses should be sold.

Short of a good marriage, which, as passions cool, often settles into an
elaborate friendship, other kinds of friendship could work the same magic. As
Arthur Stein has noted, some knotty problems are only really solved by development of a joint interest frame of mind (A. Stein, 1990, 152–4, 166). One
must lose the me to win through we.

This could work for issues of territorial conflict. Indeed, it seems to be
actually working in Europe, which was long bloodied by wars. At least one
may say that any residual territorial discontents among the fifteen states (with
more to come) of the European Union will tend to vanish as the sense of
being European transcends that of being part of a particular state. At least for
the governing elites of both London and Dublin, the Northern Ireland (Ulster) issue was in 1998 settled by a pact they deem fair. The problem is that
it has not yet been settled in the minds of the Protestant and Catholic zealots
of the province in question, with the IRA and some Protestant militants de-
laying in letting go of their arms and the other Protestants holding that this
suspends or even nullifies the agreement to share power.

Is a new, shared identity a hopeful solution to the Kashmir crisis? Is it
wholly out of the question that the Indian subcontinent could reunify (Bangladesh as well as India and Pakistan) as in 1947, before the partitions began?
So far the outlook looks bleak. Perhaps it is true, as Carl Schmitt argued in
1932, that most identities in the interstate system arise from a shared enmity
(Schmitt, 1932/1976). No friendship, let alone marriage, of Pakistan and India
seems plausible, short, perhaps of an attack of either Russia or China against
both of them at once. At both the popular and elite levels, the enmities between India and Pakistan continue, even if some intellectuals have sought to
rebuild the long-shattered bridges between them.

Often the very demand for justice for past offenses can for too many be the
primary obstacle for any present reconciliation. Each side wants to see "jus-

tice" done to the agents of horrors committed by the other side, while wanting exoneration of their own agents of similar crimes. Often a mutual amnesty in domestic political conflicts is a necessary condition for any further negotiated settlement of their conflict, and the like spirit may be necessary for international reconciliation.

CHAPTER 8

Transformational Game Theory in Conflict Resolution

> Where there is negotiation, there is hope for agreement.
>
> —a Somali proverb

Although laying no claim to expertise in game theory, not being mathematical enough, in this final chapter I indicate the larger meaning of the attempt to brainstorm possible solutions to the Kashmir problem as discussed within chapter 7. Game theorists know that mathematical development could be daunting, but it is sometimes useful to imagine tools yet to be created.

Within the present chapter I identify a very tentative research program that could be called either *transformational* or *transgenic* game theory. I have mentioned this concept only in passing in a prior book (Cook, 2002, 15–17). Its primary purpose is to promote those accommodations that could prevent or end civil or international wars.

I. A BRIEF HISTORY OF GAME THEORY

Game theory is a largely mathematical study of how choices of rational agents engender consequences by interaction with the choices of other agents. Although it can include cooperative games, it more often has been applied to competitive ones, especially in economic, military, or political life. It looks to define optimal solutions from within the definitional terms of the game.

Much of the following is drawn here and there from an anthology of essays entitled *Toward a History of Game Theory* (Weintraub, 1992; cf. also Poundstone, 1992). The theory has antecedents that some would trace all the way back to probability theorists from the late eighteenth century, including Condorcet, Borda, and Laplace. But more focused work of relevance was launched by the Paris mathematician, Emile Borel. For Borel it was primarily an exercise in pure mathematics, but his 1921 published work seems inspired in part by parlor games. Also, he explicitly suggested eventual practical applications of the theory of games in economics and military strategy. Leaving his work largely speculative, Borel eventually drifted away from further work, believing the subject could not find the equations to cope with the complexity of real-world choices.

Although eventually becoming acquainted with Borel's work, the more important developer of game theory, John von Neumann (1903–1957), rarely acknowledged any influence. Who was he? His father, Max Neumann, was of a leading Jewish banking family in Budapest, and for contributions to the economic development of his Hungarian kingdom, the Austro-Hungarian emperor Franz Joseph in 1913 ennobled him. This permitted his son to add the heritable "von" to his name. John was early recognized as a child prodigy, as in being able to memorize at a glance a page from a phone directory, and he had a special facility in mathematical intuition. While briefly enrolled at Budapest University, he was to do his major study at the University of Berlin, where, among other teachers, he heard Albert Einstein lecture on statistical mechanics. His own seminal paper on game theory emerged in 1928. He had some interest in applications of parlor games, even those of children, claiming to know how one could defeat an opponent through the children's game of scissors, paper, stone (use each gesture equally, but randomize occurrences). But within a few years he was forced to leave Germany, which in 1933 came under the control of the Nazis. He settled at Princeton University. Working there, von Neumann became generally regarded as the principal father of game theory and at least one of the main founders (along with Alan Turing and Norbert Weiner) of cybernetics as well.

In 1938 another figure came to Princeton, this time to its economics department. Oskar Morgenstern (1902–1977) fled the degenerating conditions of Vienna. With Hitler's *Anschluss*, in 1938, he knew he could not return. Although not himself a significant philosopher or innovating mathematician, he was interdisciplinary in spirit, attentive to how positivist philosophy (of Moritz Schlick and Rudolf Carnap of the Vienna Circle) or mathematical ideas such as game theory could have practical application in economics. He saw flaws in laissez-faire economic views of neoclassical economics. As someone rather from the Austrian school of economics, he did not regard the economy as one of individual utility-maximizers standing before an impersonal market flowing into a static equilibrium. Rather, there was action and reaction, with all strategic actors forced to anticipate behavior of each other. Among other observations, just because the consequences of their choices may be affected by the choices of other individuals, rational individuals favor some government regulation to reduce the range of unpredictability. Or they may instead do something privately, as in forming a cartel. In other words, new institutions may be formed that modify the market. When Morgenstern came to know von Neumann at Princeton, each found the other a complement (neither found much resonance with their own departments, and they spoke German rather than English between themselves, although Morgenstern called von Neumann "Johnny"). Von Neumann offered mathematical brilliance, and Morgenstern offered a practical domain with some arithmetical measures for application.

Initially intending to write just a paper together, by 1944 they published a large book called *Theory of Games and Economic Behavior.* Princeton University demanded an outside subvention to publish it, and the authors got the $4,000 from the Rockefeller Foundation. The book found its earliest popularity among military strategists (especially at the Santa Monica–based RAND Corporation), and it was slow to attract economists. But it emerged as a major methodology in economics by the 1970s and after. John Nash, the subject of the 2002 film, *A Beautiful Mind,* contributed important ideas, especially the Nash Equilibrium (a condition where neither adversary could rationally favor any option other than the one chosen). Morgenstern's student Martin Shubik, as well as the late William Riker, were central in introducing game theory to political scientists (Riker, 1992).

Political science made use of the cooperative side of game theory, not just the competitive angle. The field over time has broadened from simple two-person games to n-person games, while also shifting from one-shot (i.e., one round) to iterated (i.e., repeated) games, as in work by the late Robert Axelrod (Axelrod, 1984, 1997a, 1997b). But they kept to their original focus on definition of game and subgame types and their original mathematical interest in (1) proving the existence of an equilibrium, and (2) identifying the solution(s).

II. ONE-SHOT GAME THEORY, EVOLUTIONARY GAME THEORY, TRANSFORMATIONAL GAME THEORY

Among other distinctions, games could be analyzed as either nonshifting (whether one-shot or iterated) or shifting (whether spontaneous or transgenic), as in Figure 8.1.

Whereas von Neumann and Morgenstern in 1944 emphasized one-round play, others have developed what is called "evolutionary game theory." Unlike one-shot games, it studies what happens to the play of a game (usually Prisoner's Dilemma) over many iterations, when variables such as information about prior moves of rivals or the range of strategic options, and so on, are experimentally manipulated, often by way of computer simulations, or what I like to call "simductive reasoning." In iterated Prisoner's Dilemma, researchers have found that, apart from the final round, the advantage may shift over time from the defectors (or noncooperators) to the cooperators, which can be good news for chances of peace. Although many parameters of a game may

Figure 8.1
Four Types of Game Theory

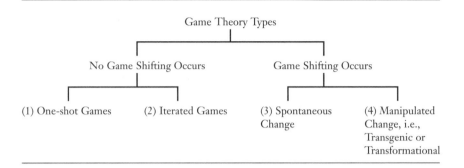

be experimentally modified, including shifts in strategies of the players, evolutionary game theory stops short of changing what at root defines the game (e.g., Axelrod, 1984, 1997a, 1997b; Lomborg, 1995; Weibull, 1995). It has not entertained strategies of players or of outside actors that could intentionally change the game from one kind into another.

Iterations may "evolve" (perhaps even undergo "mutations" if keeping to the same "species"), and some mixed motive games may become more manageable thereby, but in the real world it may take too long to get a wanted result. Thus Hobbes, self-avowedly of timid disposition, would prefer to see a fast change from his state of nature/war negative-sum contests to merely zero-sum ones, then quickly move on to a resolved Prisoner's Dilemma game. This would be through the supposedly rational acceptance of the Hobbes's absolutist sovereign as "King of the Proud." Yet in noting long periods of comparable anarchy in recent Somalia, Sierra Leone, or Congo, we know that *spontaneous* game changing may fail to appear, or it may not last.

Yet in other contexts it somehow happens. One could describe developments of interstate regional rules climates as well as domestic political regimes through Martin Wight's Machiavellian, Grotian, and Kantian phases and then reversing sequence through three more phases, while showing more or less spontaneous game shifting along the way (Cook, 2000). Such analysis of institutional development and disintegration reveals that relatively spontaneous game shifting can cut either way, into either more cooperation or into less of it.

Often a highly cooperative kind of game can change into a more competitive one, truistically simply by adjusting the assumptions that define the game. By definition, a pure coordination game becomes an impure one if players are not indifferent (or become not indifferent) as to the alternative on which they could agree. A zero-sum conflict of interest could spontaneously arise for food or even living spaces (indeed, even sitting spaces!) if the population of a small island kept growing beyond some point. Even with ostensibly successful economic development, which is normally correlated with greater subjective happiness, secularization, and political stability, comparable "crowding effects" can arise (Hirsch, 1976).

In evolutionary biology, we know that some mutations can lead to "speciation," a biologist's term for spontaneous emergence of a new species, an organism that no longer interbreeds with its antecedent. Also, a molecular biologist friend, Michael Kahn, tells me that biologists recognize other non-manipulated if rarely occurring boundary crossings, such as "horizontal gene exchange" or "trans-kingdom gene exchange."

Spontaneous game shifting aside, let us turn to the idea of engineered game changing. Following up on the biological metaphor of "evolutionary" game theory, *manipulated* game changing could not employ the image of a "metamorphosis"—as pupa, chrysalis, butterfly. Metamorphosis lacks both human manipulation and change from one species to another. Although acknowledging that recombinant DNA researchers normally change only a portion of the genome, their term "transgenic engineering" comes closest to what I have in mind.

What I indifferently called either *transformational* or *transgenic* game theory is focused on engineered change of kind, a crossing over from one game to another, a qualitative rather than merely quantitative change. Quite obviously, it does not await spontaneous speciation but asks how one could *create* it, and in the very *direction* wanted.

I contrast the conceptions of evolutionary game theory and transgenic game theory in Figure 8.2.

In evolutionary game theory focused on Prisoner's Dilemma, there is a conscious intention to get from a mixed motive game with suboptimal outcomes due to defections to a more tractable play of the same game. If analysts such as Axelrod and Lomborg are correct, it may be expectable in the real world rather than only in their simulated worlds for nice guys to finish first rather than last. Yet they concede that noncooperation (defection) becomes the optimal strategy in a final round of play, if known to be such. Short of their last round, after many iterations, they assume that players can recognize how specific others acted in prior encounters: In such conditions, the nastiest strategists would go on being nasty to each other, the moderate strategists such as "tit-for-tat" players (try initial cooperation, but if the other defects, do the same to that other next round) would increasingly defect from the nasties, and these would increasingly cooperate with the nice strategists, who also typically cooperate when recognizing each other. The last round aside, the nasties become isolated targets of defection from just about everyone, and the nice guys get cooperation from everyone but the nasties (Axelrod, 1997b; Lomborg, 1995).

That more benevolent objective is shared with transgenic game theory, although it differs in not just domesticating the same kind of game but rather

Figure 8.2
Evolutionary Game Theory Contrasted with Transgenic Game Theory

Evolutionary Game Theory	Transgenic Game Theory
Arguably, for many analysts the mathematical interest eclipses the practical interest.	The practical interest in conflict-diversion or conflict-resolution eclipses any mathematical interest.
Relative to one-shot games, theory of an iterated game is open to more complex development. Yet not unlike earliest game theory, it loves rigorous assumptions that may not always be realistic.	Not stinting on possible complexity, it wants to use assumptions close to real-world conditions. It looks for historical cases that are close to the conflict problem now in view.
One does not change the essential game. That is to say, one keeps within its rules. As if changing the rules while playing chess, that would be cheating rather than commendable creativity.	Rule changing and game changing can be commendable. This is creativity, not cheating. In any politics, artful change of the rules of the game while playing is part of the game.
Any evolutions will be normally slow self-generations from additional rounds of play. Assuming a computer simulation rather than small-group research, the initial programming of the simulation assures that the game will remain recognizably the same (there is no "speciation" by mutations that survive to reproduce, but not with the original stem). Yet both choices of players and their outcomes may change if programs allow for new learning, especially from prior moves of specific players. But the learning is cognitive rather than affective, because the players in such a "simuductive" study are cold computer constructs.	Transgenic game theory looks for fruitful change, as in recombinant DNA work. Altering a species or even changing the species is wanted. One wants to get real-world people out of their more dangerous kinds of games into more tractable ones, already recognizable from game theory definitions. This theory must recognize not only cognitive framings of problems but also fears and hates of real-world actors as often part of the problem to be solved. Gandhi would remind us that strategies and tactics should look to ultimate restoration of community between adversaries.
There seems to be little interest in the application or creation of sidegames or subgames, such as when Mutual Assurance could change the equilibrium outcome of Stag Hunt.	Transgenic game theory would try to identify or invent sidegames or subgames that could aid in game-shifting. Again, it looks for historical examples.
There is no place in evolutionary game theory for third party interveners who could guide a destructive competition into more tractable directions.	Third party conciliators, mediators, arbitrators, or other interveners can be central and should be incorporated into game theory analysis, because they do become involved in real-world conflicts.

crossing over from an often nastier kind of game to the normally nicer ones, with greater inclinations to cooperate, often without any need for iterations. Although Axelrod or Lomborg will say that noncooperation becomes again the optimal strategy in the last round of Prisoner's Dilemma, I suggest that this need not be so if one anticipates a shift of players into a more tractable kind of game.

Forgiving an earlier list for those who have read chapter 7, for those who come in here one can consider a rough spectrum ranging as follows across game types, which are really problem forms recognizable in many real-world cases: Ignoring the Doomsday game where everyone loses, one can define the *negative-sum game* as when any winnings of the winners are less than the losings of the losers. The *zero-sum game*, as in classic contests for territory as illustrated in chapter 7 by the Kashmir conflict, any winnings of winners exactly equal losings of the losers.

In the *Prisoner's Dilemma game*, as already noted, two agents have an optimal interest in cooperation but make the suboptimal choice of defecting in anticipation that the other side will do that first. If they only had communication and more trust they could have made a choice better for both.

In an *impure coordination problem game*, perhaps central in many issues of "justice," as I argued in chapter 5, both parties want an agreement and could communicate to get it, but they disagree regarding contents, such as who gets what in the way of benefits, or also who gives what in the way of contributions.

In a *collaboration game*, all recognize a collective good, such that if anyone gets the benefit, they all can do so, but the collective good may not be attained if too many people are free riders, wanting to get a share of the good without making any contribution of their own.

In a *pure coordination game*, all value getting an agreement more than any specific contents, being as if indifferent as to the content, as when all they have to do is to communicate to concur on a place for a meeting or lunch (for the most readable definitions and contrasts of the mentioned games, see A. Stein, 1990; for more mathematical precision, see Gintis, 2000, or the more difficult Shubik, 1984).

In transformational game theory, one would normally want to move oneself and friends from the negative-sum, zero-sum, or Prisoner's Dilemma games toward the often more tractable impure coordination, collaboration, and the conflict-free pure coordination games.

Transgenic engineering in the life sciences surely entails some risks, although it does not appear to be true that thuringia-laced cornfields are more dangerous than those laden with pesticides for monarch butterflies. Survey researchers have found that publics worry less about plant research than about tinkering with the genes of nonhuman animals, perhaps because that could bring more immediate harm to humans. And so transgenic game changing (in this like spontaneous game changing) need not always have uniquely benign outcomes.

Thus some would want to transcend, in a more bounded way, the more severe forms of conflict only to better unify their group for more effective abuse of outsiders. Shubik notes in economic life, "An underlying problem in the control of oligopoly is that actions that are jointly optimal from the viewpoint of the competing firms may be regarded by society as a whole as highly undesirable" (Shubik, 1984, 63). Or again, a nation may solve a collaboration problem by recourse to coercive taxation or the draft to better fight a zero-sum war with an enemy. That war need not necessarily be a "just war" in its means and end, even if declared by an appropriate authority. On the contrary, it could be most unjust.

If not unifying one's side for a bad end, bad people could abuse things in bringing disunity to those they would defeat. As illustrated by the arrow on the right side of Figure 8.3, someone may want to reverse directions. Thus a revolutionary wants to shift a society in apparent concord into one of zero-sum class conflict. Or again, those fighting a terrorist group such as al-Qaeda would want to do the same for their enemies. Not like other tools, engineered game shifting could cut two ways, toward more cooperation or toward less of it.

My interest in conflict resolution obviously dwells on the benign rather than malign direction of game shifting. Game theorist friends tell me that the mathematics of transformational game theory could be quite demanding, especially when one player wants to remain with one game while the other looks to a shift to another. Although I do not doubt my friends are right in this, I suspect I am right in suggesting that much could be learned by at least attempting such an extension of the game theoretic tool.

It is simply true that real-world actors do *not* always play the same game, with some refusing to admit their real game. It is arguably true that shifting

Figure 8.3
Transforming Games, Benevolent vs. Malevolent Directions

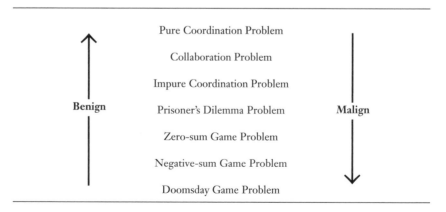

Pure Coordination Problem

Collaboration Problem

Impure Coordination Problem

Benign   Prisoner's Dilemma Problem   Malign

Zero-sum Game Problem

Negative-sum Game Problem

Doomsday Game Problem

actors to less deadly games would be usually beneficial, *at least if we could get them into the same more tractable game that is not aimed against third party victims.*

However, realist theorists of international relations could warn that it could be dangerous if some were covertly playing a negative-sum or zero-sum game while inducing their suckers to play some more tractable game such as a collaboration game or even an impure coordination game. When Metternich was about to attack Napoleon at the Battle of Nations, he assured his so-called ally that he was sending Austro-Hungarian forces to aid their common defense, as if helping solve their collective action problem in collaborating. When Hitler perhaps already knew he would eventually attack Stalin's USSR, in part by means of a nonaggression pact, he and Stalin settled their impure coordination problem of carving up Poland between themselves. Alas, deceptive playing certainly happens in the real world, and at least some of the outcomes can be ugly. It adds to the complexity of transgenic game theory.

Hereafter assuming the players move together to the same game page, a shift of subjectivity alone can sometimes alter the nature of a game. If individuals on an island look for hut sites and agree they do not want their huts piggybacked on each other, the nature of the game would change if a diabolical publicist convinced some that only one site had a beautiful view of the sea, or that certain others aimed to bring in more people like themselves and eventually control the whole island. The inventors of the TV series *Survivor* engineered zero-sum conflicts among their islanders by creating "immunity" games and offering grand prizes of $100,000 and $1 million for the second from the last and the last one standing.

Thus although some could pursue cooperation only to further deadly competition or to change cooperative games into nastily competitive ones, I prefer to frame the problem toward light rather than darkness, of building higher and higher levels of human cooperation, culminating with the view of our species as potentially one community. One can hear Nietzsche sneer in his *Will to Power*, "Mankind does not advance, it does not even exist." Of course we are far from that community, because even the unity of a nation-state may often have little substance but for shared enmities toward other peoples, as shown in my study comparing four usually nested coalitions focused about country, constitution, credo, and cabinet. These differ in appearance and size, like the nested Russian dolls (Cook, 2002).

Conceived as a project to curb nastier forms of human conflict, especially civil and international wars, the research program of transgenic game theory would have three phases of development:

In *Phase I*, one would look closely at each of the less cooperative games, analyzing its definitional properties. Then one asks what would *logically* have to change to literally transform the game into more tractable games: I will not here address the Doomsday game where all are fated to destroy each other, nor the game of Chicken, which is mutually disastrous unless one or both turn out. But I would ask how to convert a negative-sum game into a zero-sum game. Or again, how can one convert the zero-sum game into Prisoner's Dilemma? How can we change either of those into an impure coordination game, a collaboration game, or even a pure coordination game?

At each point there could be found several alternative sets of logically possible changes that could effect a transformation. The whole point of Phase I will be to specify them clearly, in principle, exhaustively. How could one change one kind of game into another? Having explored the definitional properties of the game, one can see both what is *necessary* to its continuance and also what alternative moves could make it into another game, preferably less conflictual.

Part of Phase I is a search for subgames or sidegames, which could in principle ease the transformation of one major kind of game into another. Thus someone has noted that a Stag Hunt problem, the problem of securing collaboration to bag the stag over the temptation of any hunter to chase a rabbit, may be better managed if one added an Assurance Game. In part such bridging games may be identified from history. But perhaps here best fitting use of "transgenic," one would also expect *invention* of new bridging games. Much of invention is but an unfamiliar combination of familiar things, but sometimes only new questions raise new insights.

Most students of practical negotiation have emphasized the importance of creativity, of invention of new options. They urge an uninhibited brainstorming where everyone suggests new options, with the process not curtailed by any premature criticisms of what is suggested: "Nothing is so harmful to inventing as a critical sense waiting to pounce on the drawbacks of any idea. Judgment hinders imagination" (Fisher, Ury, and Patton, 1991, 100, 58).

Game theorists know that sometimes real-world actors deal with a competitive game problem by setting up an illicit or licit cooperative game alongside it. Thus firms (or even nations, as in OPEC) facing price wars may turn to a cartel, as an example of a usually illicit game. Or as an example of a lawful game, the European states, which had in part warred over control of Rhineland coal and iron, set up the European Coal and Steel Community to minimize any future recurrence.

In *Phase II*, the research program shifts from identifying *abstract* possibilities (largely an armchair exploration) to searching out *empirical instances* of those devices of transgenic change. In such a search, one would want to mine all literatures of conflict resolution, such as those of the Harvard negotiation project (Fisher and Ury, 1981; Fisher, Ury, and Patton, 1991; Fisher, Kopelman, and Schneider, 1994; Trachte-Huber and Huber, 1996). But even more, Phase II requires a broad review of human history for clear, relevant cases of a kind of conflict as well as any use of the devices in an attempt to resolve it. Often this would suppose special attention to circumstances that, by both contemporary observers' judgments and those analysts would make now, came close to communal violence or civil war (or international war in another application) but surprised everyone by some sort of accommodation. But one can also learn from cases where things degenerated into violence, avoiding the usual tendency of historians with clear hindsight to write as if it were predetermined or inevitable that it turned out that way. As Tetlock and Belkin have noted, historical hindsight too often tends into a "creeping determinism," an insistence that whatever happened was inevitable, refusing to recognize that often different outcomes were expected by those involved and could be judged by us to have been even possible (Tetlock and Belkin, 1996, 15).

In the spirit of Thucydides or Machiavelli, for a given case of conflict, one would want to know what was tried and with what result. One must concede the Guicciardini/Hegel retort that sometimes even small shifts in circumstances or even small shifts in actors' motives may change to frustrate our quest for really useful lessons from history. Yet just as two "similar" historical cases are not wholly identical, so they are never wholly "different"or unique. Because purposively selected by the criterion of game form, or abstract problem type, the gathered evidence would surely help expand thinking about our contemporary conflict problems.

Turning now to *Phase III* of this research program, an attempt would be made to apply plausibly valid findings to specific real-world problems, such as illustrated in the prior chapter in terms of the Kashmir conflict, which many believe now poses more danger of nuclear war than any other conflict of our time. We may be blindsided in not recognizing that most wars of recent decades come at us from domestic group conflicts, largely ethnic ones. Although they could now add the second war in Afghanistan fought in 2001–2002, David Carment and Patrick James have written, "While conflicts such as those in Nigeria and India have been around for decades, both the volume and geographic range of cases represent significant increases. States, by contrast, rarely go to war with each other anymore. Since 1980, the only true interstate wars have been with Britain and Argentina over the Falklands/Malvinas, Iraq with Iran, China's border skirmish with Vietnam, and the Gulf War" (Carment and James, 1999, 14). One could add the Afghanistan War of 2001 and the Second Gulf War of early 2003. Phase III would recognize that there are several possible intervention angles to change the game being played from a less cooperative to a more cooperative form, as illustrated in Figure 8.4.

Although some tactics could be worked out by the parties in conflict themselves, often this could be facilitated by outside or third party interveners in a local dispute, as in conciliation, mediation, arbitration, or imposition. One wonders whether an increased presence of women, known by extensive research to be less inclined to violent political solutions than are men, and arguably often more subtle with verbal skills, could help, especially when conciliation and mediation are vital. We need research on actual involvement of women as principal interveners in disputes.

Sometimes it may be possible to get those involved in a conflict into a fresh

Figure 8.4
Four Ways Third Parties May Help Transform a High-Conflict Game into a More Tractable Situation

	Subtracting Something from the Present Situation	Adding Something New to the Present Situation
Using Sheer Persuasion to Effect Changes in Beliefs or Preferences	Getting each side to tone down the rhetorical attacks on each other. Or persuading each side to bracket aside certain of their favored options that cannot possibly win acceptance from the other side, or that have been tried with failure in comparable past historical cases.	Brainstorm with the disputants to enlarge the range of possible alternative solutions, as illustrated within this book regarding Kashmir in chapter 7. Do anything to make continued talking attractive to both sides, perhaps by getting a "no walkout" agreement from the outset.
Manipulating the Objective Situation of Parties in Dispute	Illustrated by working to cut off outside assistance to one or both of the parties who are recalcitrant.	Introduce some positive inducements of both parties to come to agreement, as when the United States offered generous aid packages to facilitate peace between Israel and Egypt. Or one could add the opposite, such as external economic sanctions against the belligerent parties.

cognitive framing of their problem, recognizing it could in fact be converted into another game more readily solved without mayhem. Although it is arguable that enmities of parties in conflict are less the cause of the problem than the consequence, once formed, perceptions of adversaries tend to feed continuation of a conflict, in part by blocking perceptions of any nonviolent ways out. Social psychological insights of such thinkers as William Zartman (Zartman, 1997; Zartman and Berman, 1982) are important aids to any rhetorical strategies to effect changes in cognitions and valuations. Perhaps the chief contribution of social psychology since the 1970s has been its enrichment of our attention to cognitive frames of problems. But I said in my preface that we also need to dwell on the situational framing of problems, which can select or shape psychological repertoires. Certainly third party facilitators—conciliators, mediators, arbitrators—need to focus attention on that to help two other parties transcend a negative-sum or zero-sum conflict of interest situation that is near war or even into war.

If psychological states must be viewed as variables rather than constants, so it is with the objective situations underlying conflicts. As apparent from Figure 8.4, the other approach to accommodation may involve feasible changes in the world to facilitate the shift of competing agents into actually more cooperative behavior. Any outside interveners here may be manipulating *resources* rather than *words* alone. Some of their inducements or sanctions may indirectly change cognitive frames of the parties in conflict.

It has been complained that the Harvard negotiation project trivializes things by not dealing with a really hard conflict of interest situation where more for one side means less for the other. Fisher and Ury (1981) originally took the mixed motive nature of some negotiations as if the cooperative potential were the whole of it, such that mere "problem-solving" processes will work. Fisher counters that their approach is relevant to hard bargaining situations, as when two people are in a small lifeboat and one threatens to smash it if not permitted to enjoy it alone. Of course the option ignored is simply pushing that destructive person over the side. Even a revised edition of *Getting to Yes* retained the idea of a lifeboat where if they may quarrel over food, both could conceivably get to shore alive (Fisher, Ury, and Patton, 1991, 73). But what if they could starve because there was only food enough for one? Or what if the boat were too overloaded to float?

Although not enamored of such extreme cases, perhaps the research program suggested here is best illustrated with examples such as the Kashmir crisis, a hard conflict of interest problem, a negative-sum game that has cost many lives and has lasted over a half century without solution.

The practical application of the analysis here concerns research to prevent or end domestic or international wars. Not surprisingly, historians give most attention to wars that happen. As Peter Kropotkin in his *Mutual Aid* once noted, history dwells too much on the bad news of total breakdowns, which gives us a bleak outlook on human nature. It could rather give more attention to successful cooperation and avoidance of conflicts in most of human life. But given the present tendency of historians to put most attention on the warring, they often face a difficult counterfactual reasoning in attempting to conclude what could have been done to avoid the war. Unfortunately, such "whatiffery" has too many possible directions, as readily obvious when one considers the roster of proposed war preventives. It becomes a challenge to create plausible counterfactual argument, but it is possible to state some criteria that would warrant confidence in such judgments (Tetlock and Belkin, 1996).

The opposite approach would attempt to exploit regional or local history specialists to identify past cases where wars *were fully expected* due to hard conflicts of interest, yet they never happened. Further, we are far enough beyond the cases to assume that the wars, or at least the wars for the past reasons, will never occur. We mention "hard conflict of interest." This means not just a Prisoner's Dilemma sort of defection from peace as a suboptimal choice due to failed trust that the other would act on elements of common interest. Hard conflicts of interest would rather be zero-sum or even negative-sum game situations, not unlike the Kashmir case as reviewed in chapter 7, especially when at least one antagonist could expect utility in attacking.

Once we have identified such cases of expected wars that never happened, we can help history teach us how to get out of any similar near-war circumstances in our time. For a given case, the only counterfactual is the war-that-never-happened, because we can know precisely what, if anything, was done to prevent the expected war. One cannot exclude the possibility that nothing other than mutual deterrence occurred, and the antagonists thus gave up the game. Although there may be cases of overdetermination, of several peace efforts, where we cannot say which one mattered most, in more cases one would find some single initiative that plausibly prevented the war.

A companion study would only seem to be more pessimistic. It would look at the agreements that fail to get implemented or that break down, perhaps expressing the kind of malign transformations of games such as those illustrated in Figure 8.3. But even there we may find the patterns that could permit corrections, returning us to an optimistic note.

We need to learn how to get actors out of games that can be not only mutually destructive but dangerous to others. Clashes such as the Kashmir conflict or the Arab-Israeli conflict are a threat to far more than the immediately involved parties. We need to find ways to exit such games before they may expel too many of us from life. Although admittedly left at a speculative level, the concept of transgenic or transformational game theory is just that. From this suggested research program, we could improve on relatively impoverished abstract analysis of possible escapes from zero- or negative-sum situations bordering on war. We could enrich the study of conflict-resolution by deep mining of many regional histories. As if mocking the idea of progress of the two preceding centuries, the twentieth century involved more human slaughter of fellow humans than any prior century. Let us hope that the twenty-first century will be far better, even if we are only wise enough to act to prevent it from being worse.

By the kind of strategic analysis offered by this book, we can better understand the forms of human ethnic conflict, and in principle we can act to prevent their descent into violence. If all life is problem solving, as Karl Popper said, an excess of pessimism never helped solve any human problem.

References

Adam, Herbert. 1971. *Modernizing Racial Domination: South Africa's Political Dynamics.* Berkeley: University of California Press.

———. 1985. "Legitimacy and the Institutionalization of Ethnicity: Comparing South Africa." In *Ethnic Groups and the State,* ed. P. Brass, pp. 264–302. London and Sydney: Croom Helm.

Adams, Henry. 1974. *The Education of Henry Adams.* Boston: Houghton Mifflin.

Adelman, Howard, and Astri Suhrke, eds. 1999. *The Path of a Genocide: The Rwanda Crisis from Uganda to Zaire.* New Brunswick, N.J.: Transaction Publishers.

Armstrong, Karen. 2000. *The Battle for God.* New York: Ballantine Books.

Axelrod, Robert. 1984. *The Evolution of Cooperation.* New York: Basic Books.

———. 1997a. *The Complexity of Cooperation: Agent-Based Models of Competition and Collaboration.* Princeton, N.J.: Princeton University Press.

———. 1997b. "The Evolution of Strategies in the Iterated Prisoner's Dilemma." In *The Dynamics of Norms,* Cristina Bicchieri, Richard Jeffrey, and Brian Skyrms, eds., pp. 1–15. Cambridge, England: Cambridge University Press.

Bain, David Howard. 1986. *Sitting in Darkness: Americans in the Philippines.* Boston: Houghton Mifflin.

Barber, Benjamin. 1995. *Jihad vs. McWorld.* New York: New York Times Books.

Barkley, Henri, and Graham Fuller. 1998. *Turkey's Kurdish Question.* New York: Rowman and Littlefield. The epigraph to chapter 3 cites their page 10.

Bartkus, Viva Ona. 1999. *The Dynamic of Secession.* Cambridge, England: Cambridge University Press.

Bauer, Yehuda. 1982. *A History of the Holocaust.* New York: Franklin Watts.

Beamish, Bob. 1992. *Marx, Method, and the Division of Labor.* Chicago: University of Chicago Press.

Bennett, Scott. 1999. *White Politics and Black Australians.* St. Leonards, New South Wales: Allen and Unwin.

Berresford, Ellis P. 1968. *Wales a Nation Again: The Nationalist Struggle for Freedom.* London: Tandem Books.

Bialer, Seweryn. 1980. *Stalin's Successors: Leadership, Stability and Change in the Soviet Union.* Cambridge, England: Cambridge University Press.

Bodley, John H. 1982. *Victims of Progress.* 2nd ed. Palo Alto, Calif.: Mayfield.

Bogardus, E. S. 1959. *Social Distance.* Yellow Springs, Ohio: Antioch Press.

Bookman, Milica Z. 1993. *The Economics of Secession.* New York: St. Martin's Press.

———. 1998. "The Economics of Secession." In *Separatism: Democracy and Disintegration*, M. Spencer, ed., pp. 69–95. Lanham, Md.: Rowman and Littlefield.

Borowiec, Andrew. 2000. *Cyprus: A Troubled Island.* Westport, Conn.: Praeger.

Bose, Sumantra. 1997. *The Challenge in Kashmir: Democracy, Self-Determination, and a Just Peace.* Thousand Oaks, Calif.: Sage Publications

Brams, Steven J., and Alan D. Taylor. 1996. *Fair Division: From Cake-Cutting to Dispute Resolution.* Cambridge, England: Cambridge University Press.

Brand, Josh. 1978. *The National Movement in Scotland.* London: Routledge & Kegan Paul.

Brass, Paul, ed. 1985. *Ethnic Groups and the State.* London & Sydney: Croom Helm.

Brinton, Crane. 1958. *Anatomy of Revolution.* New York: Prentice-Hall.

Buchanan, Allen. 1991. *Secession: The Morality of Political Divorce from Fort Sumter to Lithuania and Quebec.* Boulder, Colo.: Westview Press.

Bueno de Mesquita, Bruce, and David Lalman. 1992. *War and Reason: Domestic and International Implications.* New Haven, Conn.: Yale University Press.

Bunge, Mario. 1996. *Finding Philosophy in Social Science.* New Haven, Conn.: Yale University Press.

Calic, Edouard, ed. 1971. *Secret Conversations with Hitler.* New York: John Day.

Cameron, Kirk, and Graham White. 1995. *Northern Governments in Transition: Political and Constitutional Development in the Yukon, Nunavut and the Northwest Territories.* Quebec: Institute for Research on Public Policy.

Carment, David, and Peter James. 1999. "International Ethnopolitics: Theory, Peacekeeping, and Policy." In *The Ethnic Entanglement: Conflict and Intervention in World Politics*, J. E. Stack and L. Hebron, eds., pp. 13–31. Westport, Conn.: Praeger.

Carment, David, John F. Stack, Jr., and Frank Harvey, eds. 2001. *The International Politics of Quebec Secession: State Making and State Breaking in North America.* Westport, Conn.: Praeger.

Chadda, Maya. 1997. *Ethnicity, Security and Separatism in India.* New York: Columbia University Press.

Chaliland, Gerard, ed. 1980. *People without a Country: The Kurds and Kurdistan.* London: Zed Press.

Chennels, David. 2001. *The Politics of Nationalism in Canada: Cultural Conflict since 1760.* Toronto: University of Toronto Press.

Cheong, Ching. 2001. *Will Taiwan Break Away? The Rise of Taiwanese Nationalism.* River Edge, N.J.: World Scientific Publishing.

Ciment, James. 1996. *The Kurds: State and Minority in Turkey, Iraq, and Iran.* New York: Facts on File.

Cole, K. C. 1997. *The Universe and the Teacup: The Mathematics of Truth and Beauty.* New York: Harcourt Brace.

Colley, Linda. 1992. *Britons: Forging the Nation 1707–1837.* New Haven, Conn.: Yale University Press.

Collins, Roger. 1990. *The Basques.* Oxford, England: Basil Blackwell.

Connor, Walker. 1972. "Nation-Building or Nation-Destroying." *World Politics* 24, no. 3: 319–55.

———. 1994. *Ethnonationalism: The Quest for Understanding.* Princeton, N.J.: Princeton University Press.

Conquest, Robert. 1986. *Harvest of Sorrow: Soviet Collectivization and the Terror-Famine.* New York: Oxford University Press.

Cook, Terrence. 1983. "'Misbegotten Males'? Innate Differences and Stratified Choice in the Subjection of Women." *The Western Political Quarterly* 36, no. 2: 194–220.

———. 1991. *The Great Alternatives of Social Thought: Aristocrat, Saint, Capitalist, Socialist.* Savage, Md.: Rowman & Littlefield.

———. 1994. *Criteria of Social Scientific Knowledge: Interpretation, Prediction, Praxis.* Lanham, Md.: Rowman & Littlefield.

———. 2000. *The Rise and Fall of Regimes: Toward Grand Theory of Politics.* New York: Peter Lang.

———. 2002. *Nested Political Coalitions: Political Community, Regime, Program and Cabinet.* Westport, Conn.: Praeger.

Copper, John F. 1990. *Taiwan: Nation-State or Province?* Boulder, Colo.: Westview Press.

Covell, Maureen. 1985. "Ethnic Conflict in Belgium." In *Ethnic Groups and the State,* ed. P. Brass, pp. 230–61. London and Sydney: Croom Helm.

Cronon, Edmund, ed. 1973. *Marcus Garvey.* Englewood Cliffs, N.J.: Prentice-Hall.

Dahl, Robert. 1971. *After the Revolution: Authority in a Good Society.* New Haven, Conn.: Yale University Press.

Darby, John. 1995. *Northern Ireland: Managing Difference.* London: Minority Rights Group.

Davies, Charlotte Aull. 1989. *Welsh Nationalism in the Twentieth Century: The Ethnic Option and the Modern State.* New York: Praeger.

Dawidowicz, Lucy S. 1975. *The War against the Jews 1933–1945.* New York: Holt, Rinehart and Winston.

Deloria, Vine, Jr., and Clifford Lytle. 1984. *The Nations Within: The Past and Future of American Indian Sovereignty.* New York: Pantheon.

Demko, George, Agel Jerome, and Eugene Boe. 1992. *Why in the World: Adventures in Geography.* New York: Anchor Books.

De Vos, George. 1973. "Japan's Outcastes: The Problem of the Burakumin." In *The Fourth World: Victims of Group Oppression,* Ben Whitaker, ed., pp. 308–27. New York: Schocken Books.

———, and Hiroshi Wagtsuma, eds. 1966. *Japan's Invisible Race: Caste in Culture and Personality.* Berkeley and Los Angeles: University of California Press.

Dewey, John. 1929. *The Quest for Certainty: A Study in the Relation of Knowledge and Action.* New York: Minton, Balch and Co.

De Winter, Lieven, Arco Timmermans, and Patrick Dumont. 2000. "Belgium: Of Government Agreements, Evangelists, Followers and Heretics." In *Coalition Governments in Western Europe,* W. C. Müller and K. Strom, eds., pp. 300–55. Oxford, England: Oxford University Press.

Donnet, Pierre-Antoine. 1994. *Tibet: Survival in Question*. Atlantic Highlands, N.J.: Zed Books.

Doran, Charles F. 2001. "Will Canada Unravel?" In *The International Politics of Quebec Secession: State Making and State Breaking in North America*, D. Carment, J. F. Stack, Jr., and F. Harvey, eds., pp. 57–66. Westport, Conn.: Praeger.

Doyle, Michael W. 1983a. "Kant, Liberal Legacies, and Foreign Affairs: Part I." *Philosophy and Public Affairs* 12, no. 3: 205–36.

———. 1983b. "Kant, Liberal Legacies, and Foreign Affairs: Part II." *Philosophy and Public Affairs* 12, no. 4: 323–53.

Du Bois, W. E. B. 1968. *The Autobiography of W. E. B. Du Bois: A Soliloquy on Viewing my Life from the Last Decade of Its First Century*. New York: International Publishers.

Duffy, R. Quinn. 1988. *The Road to Nunavut*. Canada: McGill-Queen's University Press.

Dunn, Seamus, ed. 1995. *Facets of the Conflict in Northern Ireland*. London: Macmillan Press.

Durkheim, Emile. 1933. *The Division of Labor in Society*. New York: The Free Press.

Eades, J. S., and Chris Allen. 1996. *Benin*. Denver, Colo.: CLIO.

Eckstein, Harry, and Tedd Robert Gurr. 1975. *Patterns of Authority: A Structural Basis for Political Inquiry*. New York: Wiley.

Edelman, Murray J. 1964. *The Symbolic Uses of Politics*. Urbana: University of Illinois.

Edwards, Lyford. 1927. *The Natural History of Revolution*. Chicago: University of Chicago Press.

Ekman, Paul. 1985. *Telling Lies: Clues to Deceit in the Marketplace, Politics, and Marriage*. New York: W. W. Norton.

Elster, Jon. 1989. *The Cement of Society: Studies in Rationality and Social Change*. Cambridge, England: Cambridge University Press.

———. 1993. *Political Psychology*. Cambridge, England: Cambridge University Press.

Fanon, Frantz. 1968. *The Wretched of the Earth*. Constance Farrington, trans. New York: Grove Press. (Original work published 1963)

Fest, Joachim. 1974. *Hitler*. New York: Harcourt, Brace, Jovanovich.

Finer, S. E. 1999. *The History of Government from the Earliest Times*, Vol. III: *Empires, Monarchies, and the Modern State*. New York: Oxford University Press.

Finlay, Richard J. 1994. *Independent and Free: Scottish Politics and the Origins of the Scottish National Party, 1918–45*. Edinburgh: John Donald.

Fisher, Roger, Elizabeth Kopelman, and Andrea Kupfer Schneider. 1994. *Beyond Machiavelli: Tools for Coping with Conflict*. Cambridge, Mass.: Harvard University Press.

Fisher, Roger, and William Ury. 1981. *Getting to Yes: Negotiating Agreement without Giving In*. Boston: Houghton Mifflin.

Fisher, Roger, William Ury, and Brace Patton. 1991. *Getting to Yes: Negotiating Agreement without Giving In*. 2nd ed. Boston: Houghton Mifflin.

Fonseca, Isabel. 1995. *Bury Me Standing: The Gypsies and Their Journey*. New York: Random House/Vintage.

Foucault, Michel. 1980. *Power/Knowledge*. Colin Gordon, trans. New York: Pantheon Books.

Fouzi, El-Asmar. 1975. *To Be an Arab in Israel*. London: Frances Publishing.

Fraser, T. G. 1995. *The Arab-Israeli Conflict*. New York: St. Martin's Press.

Fuchs, Lawrence H. 1968. *American Ethnic Politics.* New York: Harper & Row.

Geen, Russell G. 2001. *Human Aggression.* 2nd ed. Buckingham, England: Open University Press.

Gellner, Ernest. 1983. *Nations and Nationalism.* Ithaca, N.Y.: Cornell University.

Gilliam, Reginald Earl. 1975. *Black Political Development: An Advocacy Analysis.* New York: Dunellen/Kennikat Press.

Gilpin, Robert. 1975. *U.S. Power and the Multinational Corporation: The Political Economy of Foreign Direct Investment.* New York: Basic Books.

Gintis, Herbert. 2000. *Game Theory Evolving: A Problem-Centered Introduction to Modeling Strategic Behavior.* Princeton, N.J.: Princeton University Press.

Goldhagen, Daniel J. 1996. *Hitler's Willing Executioners: Ordinary Germans and the Holocaust.* New York: Vintage.

Goldscheider, Calvin. 2002. *Cultures in Conflict: The Arab-Israeli Conflict.* Westport, Conn.: Greenwood Press.

Goldstein, Melvyn C. 1997. *The Snow Lion and the Dragon.* Berkeley and Los Angeles: University of California Press.

Goodson, Larry P. 2001. *Afghanistan's Endless War.* Seattle: University of Washington Press.

Gourevitch, Peter. 1986. *Politics in Hard Times: Comparative Responses to International Economic Crises.* Ithaca, N.Y.: Cornell University Press.

Gourevitch, Philip, ed. 1998. *We Wish to Inform You That Tomorrow We Will Be Killed with Our Families: Stories from Rwanda.* New York: Farrar, Straus, and Giroux.

Gowa, Joanne. 1999. *Ballots and Bullets: The Elusive Democratic Peace.* Princeton, N.J.: Princeton University Press.

Graham, Carol, and Stefano Pettinato. 2002. *Happiness and Hardship: Opportunity and Insecurity in New Market Economies.* Washington, D.C.: Brookings Institution.

Green, Peter. 1970. *Alexander the Great.* New York: Praeger.

Griffith, Cyril E. 1975. *The African Dream: Martin R. Delany and the Emergence of Pan-African Thought.* University Park: Pennsylvania State University.

Grossman, Mark. 1993. *The ABC-CLIO Companion to the Civil Rights Movement.* Santa Barbara, Calif.: ABC-CLIO.

Gurr, Ted. 1993. *Minorities at Risk: A Global View of Ethnopolitical Conflicts.* Washington, D.C.: United States Institute of Peace.

———. 2000. *Peoples versus States: Minorities at Risk in the New Century.* Washington, D.C.: United States Institute of Peace.

———, and Barbara Harff. 1994. *Ethnic Conflict in World Politics.* Boulder, Colo.: Westview Press.

Halliday, Fred. 1999. *Revolution and World Politics: The Rise and Fall of the Sixth Great Power.* Durham, N.C.: Duke University Press.

Halpern, Manfred. 1963. *The Politics of Social Change in the Middle East and North Africa.* Princeton, N.J.: Princeton University Press.

Hampshire, Stuart. 2000. *Justice Is Conflict.* Princeton, N.J.: Princeton University Press.

Hardin, Russell. 1995. *One for All: The Logic of Group Conflict.* Princeton, N.J.: Princeton University Press.

Hardt, Michael, and Antonio Negri. 2000. *Empire.* Cambridge, Mass.: Harvard University Press.

Hechter, Michael. 1999. Revised ed. of original 1975. *Internal Colonialism: The Celtic*

Fringe in British National Development. New Brunswick, N.J.: Transaction Publishers.

Heidenrich, John G. 2001. *How to Prevent Genocide: A Guide for Policymakers, Scholars, and the Concerned Citizen.* Westport, Conn.: Praeger.

Hentoff, Nat. 1992. *Free Speech for Me But Not for Thee: How the American Left and Right Relentlessly Censor Each Other.* New York: HarperCollins.

Hewitt, George. 1998. *The Abkhazians.* New York: St. Martin's Press.

Hicks, George. 1997. *Japan's Hidden Apartheid.* Sydney, Australia: Ashgate.

Hill, Christopher. 1972. *The World Turned Upside Down: Radical Ideas during the English Revolution.* New York: Viking Press.

Hill, Robert A., and Barbara Bair, eds. 1987. *Marcus Garvey: Life and Learning.* Berkeley: University of California Press.

Hirsch, Fred. 1976. *Social Limits to Growth.* Cambridge, Mass.: Harvard University Press.

Hirschman, Albert O. 1970. *Exit, Voice and Loyalty: Responses to Decline in Firms, Organizations, and States.* Cambridge, Mass.: Harvard University Press.

———. 1981. *Essays in Trespassing: Economics in Politics and Beyond.* Cambridge, England: Cambridge University Press.

Hitler, Adolf. 1961. *Hitler's Secret Book.* New York: Grove Press.

Hoffman, Stanley. 1970. "Participation in Perspective?" *Daedalus* (Winter): 177–220.

Horowitz, Donald L. 1980. *Coup Theories and Officers' Motives: Sri Lanka in Comparative Perspective.* Princeton, N.J.: Princeton University Press.

———. 1985. *Ethnic Groups in Conflict.* Berkeley: University of California Press.

Huntington, Samuel P. 1996. *The Clash of Civilizations and the Remaking of World Order.* New York: Simon & Schuster.

Ibrahim, Ferhad, and Gülistan Gürbey. 2000. *The Kurdish Conflict: Obstacles and Chances for Peace and Democracy.* New York: St. Martin's Press.

Inglehart, Ronald. 1977. *The Silent Revolution: Changing Values and Political Styles in Western Publics.* Princeton, N.J.: Princeton University Press.

———. 1990. *Culture Shift in Advanced Industrial Society.* Princeton, N.J.: Princeton University Press.

Ingram, David. 1995. *Reason, History, and Politics: The Communitarian Grounds of Legitimacy in the Modern Age.* Albany, N.Y.: State University Press.

———. 2000. *Group Rights: Reconciling Equality and Difference.* Lawrence: University of Kansas Press.

Jaffa, Harry. 1959. *Crisis in the House Divided: An Interpretation of the Issues in the Lincoln-Douglas Debates.* Garden City, N.Y.: Doubleday.

Jennings, Christian. 2000. *Across the Red River: Rwanda, Burundi and the Heart of Darkness.* London: Victor Gollanz.

Johannson, Warren, and William Perry. 1990. *Homosexuals in Nazi Germany.* Vienna: Simon Wiesenthal Center Annual, Vol. 7.

Jordan, Terry, and Bella Jordan-Bychkova. 1998. *Siberian Village: Land and Life in the Sakha Republic.* Minneapolis: University of Minnesota Press.

Joseph, Joseph S. 1997. *Cyprus: Ethnic Conflict and International Politics.* New York: St. Martin's Press.

Karpat, Kemal H. 1985. "The Ethnicity Problem in a Multi-Ethnic Anational Islamic State: Continuity and Recasting of Ethnic Identity in the Ottoman State." In

Ethnic Groups and the State, ed. P. Brass, pp. 95–116. London and Sydney: Croom Helm.

Kaufman, Stuart J. 2001. *Modern Hatreds: The Symbolic Politics of Ethnic War.* Ithaca, N.Y.: Cornell University Press.

Kautilya, Vishnagupta. 1992. *The Arthashastra.* L. N. Rangarajan, trans. New Delhi: Penguin Books

Kautsky, Karl. 1959. *Foundations of Christianity.* New York: S. A. Russell.

Khaldun, Ibn. 1963. Prolegomena. Excerpted in *An Arab Philosophy of History*, Charles Issawi, trans. London: John Murray Ltd.

Kincaid, Dennis. 1971. *British Social Life in India, 1608–1937.* Port Washington, N.Y.: Kennikat.

Kírící, Kamal, and Gareth M. Windrow. 1997. *The Kurdish Question and Turkey: An Example of a Trans-State Ethnic Conflict.* London: Frank Cass.

Koenigsberg, Richard A. 1975. *Hitler's Ideology: A Study in Psychoanalytic Sociology.* New York: The Library of Social Science.

Krasner, Stephen D. 1999. *Sovereignty: Organized Hypocrisy.* Princeton, N.J.: Princeton University Press.

Kretzmer, David. 1990. *The Legal Status of Arabs in Israel.* Boulder, Colo.: Westview Press.

Kuper, Leo. 1981. *Genocide.* New Haven, Conn.: Yale University.

Laitin, David. 1998. *Identity in Formation: The Russian-Speaking Population in the Near Abroad.* Ithaca, N.Y.: Cornell University Press.

Lamb, Alastair. 1994. *Birth of a Tragedy: Kashmir 1947.* Hertingfordbury, England: Roxford Books.

Landau, Jacob M. 1993. *The Arab Minority in Israel, 1967–1991: Political Aspects.* Oxford, England: Clarendon Press.

Langer, Walter C. 1972. *The Mind of Adolf Hitler: The Secret Wartime Report.* New York: Basic Books.

Laver, Michael, and Norman Schofield. 1990. *Multiparty Government: The Politics of Coalition in Europe.* New York: Oxford University Press.

Laver, Michael, and Kenneth Shepsle. 1996. *Making and Breaking Governments: Cabinets and Legislatures in Parliamentary Democracies.* Cambridge, England: Cambridge University.

Le Bon, Gustave. 1968. *The Crowd: A Study of the Popular Mind.* 2nd ed. Dunwoody, Ga.: Norman S. Berg.

Lee, Changsoo, and George De Vos. 1981. *Koreans in Japan.* Los Angeles: University of California Press.

Lee, Lai To. 1991. *The Reunification of China: PRC-Taiwan Relations in Flux.* New York: Praeger.

Leites, Nathan, and Charles Wolf, Jr. 1970. *Rebellion and Authority: An Analytic Essay on Insurgent Conflicts.* Chicago: Markham.

Levin, Nora. 1968. *The Holocaust: The Destruction of European Jewry 1933–1945.* New York: Thomas Crowell.

Lewis, Rupert, and Maureen Warner-Lewis. 1994. *Garvey: Africa, Europe, the Americas.* Trenton, N.J.: Africa World Press.

Liechty, Daniel. 1994. *Early Anabaptist Spirituality: Selected Writings.* New York: Paulist Press.

Lievan, Dominic. 2000. *Empire: The Russian Empire and Its Rivals*. New Haven, Conn.: Yale University Press.

Lilienthal, David E. 1953. *TVA: Democracy on the March*. New York: Harper.

Lijphart, Arend. 1975. *The Politics of Accommodation: Pluralism and Democracy in the Netherlands*. 2nd ed. Berkeley: University of California Press.

———. 1977. *Democracy in Plural Societies: A Comparative Exploration*. New Haven. Conn.: Yale University Press.

———. 1984. *Democracies: Patterns of Majoritarian and Consensus Government in Twenty-One Countries*. New Haven, Conn.: Yale University Press.

———. 1989. "Consociational or Adversarial Democracy in the Netherlands." In *Politics in the Netherlands: How Much Change?* Hans Daalder and Galen A. Irwin, eds. London: J. Cass.

———. 1999. *Patterns of Democracy: Government Forms and Performance in Thirty-Six Countries*. New Haven, Conn.: Yale University Press.

Loew, Patty. 2001. *Indian Nations of Wisconsin: Histories of Endurance and Renewal*. Madison: Wisconsin Historical Society.

Lomborg, Bjorn. 1995. "The Evolution of Social Structure in the Iterated Prisoner's Dilemma." Santa Fe Institute, Nov. 15, 1999 (a videotape of the presentation).

Lovejoy, Arthur O. 1936. *The Great Chain of Being*. Cambridge, Mass.: Harvard University Press.

Lustick, Ian. 1980. *Arabs in the Jewish State: Israel's Control of a National Minority*. Austin: University of Texas Press.

McDowall, David. 1985. *The Kurds*. London: Minority Rights Group.

McGarry, John, and Brendan O'Leary. 1995. *Explaining Northern Ireland*. Oxford: Basil Blackwell.

Machtan, Lothar. 2001. *The Hidden Hitler*. New York: Basic Books.

MacIntyre, Alasdair. 1971. *Against the Self-Images of the Age*. New York: Schocken Books. The epigraph to chapter 6 here cites his page 10.

MacKinnon, Catherine A. 1987. *Feminism Unmodified: Discourses on Life and Law*. Cambridge, Mass.: Harvard University Press.

———. 1989. *Toward a Feminist Theory of the State*. Cambridge, Mass.: Harvard University Press.

———. 1993. *Only Words*. Cambridge, Mass.: Harvard University Press.

McRoberts, Kenneth. 2001. *Catalonia: Nation Building without a State*. Ontario, Canada: Oxford University Press.

Mallie, Eamon. 2001. *Endgame in Ireland*. London: Hodder and Stoughton.

Maluka, Zulfikar Khalid. 1995. *The Myth of Constitutionalism in Pakistan*. Oxford, England: Oxford University Press.

Marsden, Peter. 1998. *The Taliban: War, Religion and the New Order in Afghanistan*. Karachi and London: Oxford University Press.

Meadwell, Hudson. 2001. "Institutional Design and State Breaking in North America." In *The International Politics of Quebec Secession: State Making and State Breaking in North America*, D. Carment, J. F. Stack, Jr., and F. Harvey, eds., pp. 11–32. Westport, Conn.: Praeger.

Middle East Watch. 1993. *Genocide in Iraq: The Anfal Campaign against the Kurds*. New York: Middle East Watch.

Milne, R. S. 1981. *Politics in Ethnically Bipolar States: Guyana, Malaysia, Fiji*. Vancouver, B.C.: University of British Columbia Press.

Minns, Amina, and Nadia Hijab. 1990. *Citizens Apart: A Portrait of the Palestinians in Israel.* London: I. B. Tauris.

Mitra, Subrata K. 1987. "The Perils of Promoting Equality." *Journal of Commonwealth and Comparative Politics* 25, no. 3: 291–312.

Monroe, Kristen, ed. 1997. *Contemporary Empirical Political Theory.* Berkeley and Los Angeles: University of California Press.

Mousavi, Syed Askar. 1997. *The Hazaras of Afghanistan.* New York: St. Martin's Press.

Müller, Wolfgang C., and Kaare Strom. 2000. *Coalition Governments in Western Europe.* Oxford, England: Oxford University Press.

Nardin, Terry. 1971. *Violence and the State: A Critique of Empirical Political Theory.* Beverly Hills, Calif.: Sage Publications.

Needler, Martin C. 1970. *Political Systems of Latin America.* 2nd ed. New York: Van Nostrand.

Newman, Graeme. 1978. *The Punishment Response.* Philadelphia: Lippincott.

Nietzsche, Friedrich. 1914. *The Will to Power.* Anthony M. Ludovici, trans. London: T. N. Foulis. (Original work published 1901)

Nordlinger, Eric A. 1972. *Conflict Regulation in Divided Societies.* Cambridge, Mass.: Center for International Affairs of Harvard University.

Norton, Anne. 1988. *Reflections on Political Identity.* Baltimore: Johns Hopkins University Press.

Nyankanzi, Edward L. 1998. *Genocide: Rwanda and Burundi.* Rochester, Vt.: Schenkman Books.

O'Ballance, Edgar. 1996. *The Kurdish Struggle.* New York: St. Martin's Press.

O'Donnell, James. 1999. *A Coming of Age: Albania under Enver Hoxha.* New York: Columbia University Press/East European Monographs.

Okladnikov, A. P. 1970. *Yakutia before Its Incorporation to the Russian State.* Montreal: McGill-Queen's University Press.

Parkin, Frank. 1971. *Class Inequality and Political Order.* London: MacGibbon and Kee.

Pearson, Raymond. 1998. *The Rise and Fall of the Soviet Empire.* New York: St. Martin's Press.

Perdue, Theda. 1993. *Nations Remembered: An Oral History of the Cherokees, Chickasaws, Choctaws, Creeks, and Seminoles in Oklahoma, 1865–1907.* Norman: University of Oklahoma Press. (Original work published 1980)

Peterson, Scott. 2000. *Me against My Brother: At War in Somalia, Sudan, and Rwanda: A Journalist Reports from the Battlefields of Africa.* New York: Routledge.

Pipa, Arshi. 1990. *Albanian Stalinism: Ideo-Political Aspects.* New York: Columbia University Press/East European Monographs.

Pittock, A. Barrie. 1979. *Australian Aborigines: The Common Struggle for Humanity.* Copenhagen: International Work Group for Indigenous Affairs.

Plato. 1980. *The Laws.* Tom Pangle, trans. New York: Basic Books. (Original work published c. 355 B.C.)

Pohl, J. Otto. 1999. *Ethnic Cleansing in the USSR, 1937–1949.* Westport, Conn.: Greenwood Press.

Popper, Karl. 1999. *All Life Is Problem Solving.* New York: Routledge.

Portes, Alejandro, and Robert L. Bach. 1985. *Latin Journey: Cuban and Mexican Immigrants in the United States.* Berkeley: University of California Press.

Posen, Barry R. 1993. "The Security Dilemma and Ethnic Conflict." *Survival* 35, no. 1: 27–47.

Poundstone, William. 1992. *Prisoner's Dilemma*. New York: Doubleday/Anchor.

Prager, Carol A. L. 1998. "Barbarous Nationalism and the Liberal International Order." In *Rethinking Nationalism*, J. Couture, K. Nielsen, and M. Seymour, eds., pp. 441–62. Calgary: University of Calgary Press.

Pressman, Jeffrey L., and Aaron Wildavsky. 1979. *Implementation: How Great Expectations in Washington Are Dashed in Oakland*. Berkeley: University of California Press.

Prunier, Gerard. 1995. *The Rwanda Crisis: History of a Genocide*. New York: Columbia University Press.

Racklin, Howard. 1980. "Economics and Behavioral Psychology." In *Limits to Action: The Allocation of Individual Behavior*, J. E. R. Staddon, ed., pp. 205–36. New York: Academic Press.

Rattansi, Ali. 1982. *Marx and the Division of Labor*. London: Macmillan.

Reilly, Kevin A. 1992. *Readings in World Civilization*, Vol. II. New York: St. Martin's Press.

Reno, William. 1998. *Warlord Politics in Africa*. Boulder, Colo.: Lynne Rienner.

Rescher, Nicholas. 1966. *Distributive Justice: A Constructive Critique of the Utilitarian Theory of Distribution*. New York: Bobbs-Merrill.

Riker, William. 1992. "The Entry of Game Theory into Political Science." In *Toward a History of Game Theory*, E. Roy Weintraub, ed., pp. 207–23. Durham, N.C.: Duke University Press.

Roshwald, Ariel. 2001. *Ethnic Nationalism and the Fall of Empires: Central Europe, Russia and the Middle East, 1914–1923*. London and New York: Routledge.

Rothschild, Joseph. 1981. *Ethnopolitics: A Conceptual Framework*. New York: Columbia University Press.

Roy, Olivier. 1994. *The Failure of Political Islam*. Cambridge, Mass.: Harvard University Press.

Rummel, R. J. 1983. "Libertarianism and International Violence." *Journal of Conflict Resolution* 27, no. 1: 27–71.

———. 1997. *Power Kills: Democracy as a Method of Nonviolence*. New Brunswick, N.J.: Transaction Publishers.

Saideman, Stephen M. 2001. *The Ties That Divide: Ethnic Politics, Foreign Policy, and International Conflict*. New York: Columbia University Press.

———. David J. Lanoue, Michael Campenni, and Samuel Stanton. 2002. "Democratization, Institutions, and Conflict: A Pooled Time Series Analysis 1985–1998. *Comparative Political Studies* 35, no. 1: 103–29.

Sandberg, Neil C. 1981. *Identity and Assimilation: The Welsh-English Dichotomy: A Case Study*. Washington, D.C.: University Press of America.

Schmitt, Carl. 1976. *The Concept of the Political*. New Brunswick, N.J.: Rutgers University. (Original work published 1932)

Schofield, Victoria. 1996. *Kashmir in the Crossfire*. London: I. B. Tauris.

Schroeder, Manfred. 1991. *Fractals, Chaos, Power Laws: Minutes from an Infinite Paradise*. New York: W. H. Freeman.

Schwartz, Ronald D. 1994. *Circle of Protest*. New York: Columbia University Press.

Scott, James C. 1986. *Weapons of the Weak: Everyday Forms of Peasant Resistance*. New Haven, Conn.: Yale University Press.

———. 1989. "Everyday Forms of Resistance." In *Everyday Forms of Peasant Resistance*, Forrest D. Colburn, ed., pp. 3–33. London: M. E. Sharpe.

———. 1990. *Domination and the Arts of Resistance*. New Haven, Conn.: Yale University.

Shryock, Henry. 1964. *Population Mobility in the United States*. Chicago: University of Chicago Press.

Shubik, Martin. 1984. *Game Theory in the Social Sciences*, Vol. 2: *A Game Theoretic Approach to Political Economy*. Cambridge, Mass.: MIT Press.

Sisk, Timothy. 1997. *Power Sharing and International Mediation in Ethnic Conflicts*. Washington, D.C.: Carnegie Commission and United States Institute of Peace.

Smith, Anthony. 1986. *The Ethnic Origins of Nations*. Oxford: Basil Blackwell.

Spencer, Metta. 1998. *Separatism: Democracy and Disintegration*. Lanham, Md.: Rowman & Littlefield.

Stack, John E., Jr., and Lui Hebron, eds. 1999. *The Ethnic Entanglement: Conflict and Intervention in World Politics*. Westport, Conn.: Praeger.

Stein, Arthur A. 1990. *Why Nations Cooperate: Circumstance and Choice in International Relations*. Ithaca, N.Y.: Cornell University Press.

Stein, Janice Gross., ed. 1989. *Getting to the Table: The Process of International Prenegotiation*. Baltimore, Md.: Johns Hopkins University Press.

Strossen, Nadine. 1995. *Defending Pornography: Free Speech, Sex, and the Fight for Women's Rights*. New York: Scribner's.

Taras, Raymond C., and Rajat Ganguly. 2002. *Understanding Ethnic Conflict: The International Dimension*. 2nd ed. New York: London.

Taylor, Peter. 1999. *Behind the Mask: The IRA and Sinn Fein*. New York: TV Books.

———. 2001. *Brits: The War against the IRA*. London: Bloomsbury.

Tetlock, Philip E., and Aaron Belkin, eds. 1996. *Counterfactual Thought Experiments in World Politics: Logical, Methodological and Psychological Perspectives*. Princeton, N.J.: Princeton University Press.

Theophylactou, Demetrios A. 1995. *Security, Identity and Nation-Building: Cyprus and the European Union in Comparative Perspective*. London: Aldershot.

Thomas, Ned. 1971. *The Welsh Extremist: A Culture in Crisis*. London: Victor Gollancz.

Tocqueville, Alexis de. 1945. *Democracy in America*, Vol. 1. New York: Vintage Library.

———. 1970. *Recollections (Souvenirs)*. George Lawrence, trans. Garden City, N.Y.: Doubleday.

Tonge, Jon. 2002. *Northern Ireland: Conflict and Change*. Harlow, England: Longman.

Tourval, Shadia, and William Zartman, eds. 1995. *International Mediation: Theory and Practice*. Boulder, Colo.: Westview Press.

Trachte-Huber, E. Wendy, and Stephen K. Huber. 1996. *Alternative Dispute Resolution: Strategies for Law and Business*. Cincinnati, Ohio: Anderson Publishing.

Tumin, Melvin. 1967. *Social Stratification*. Englewood Cliffs, N.J.: Prentice-Hall.

Vasquez, John. 1983. *The Power of Power Politics: A Critique*. New Brunswick, N.J.: Rutgers University Press.

Vasta, Ellie, and Stephen Castles. 1996. *The Teeth Are Smiling: The Persistence of Racism in Multicultural Australia*. London: Allen & Unwin.

Veenhoven, Ruut. 1984. *Conditions of Happiness*. Dordrecht, Holland: D. Reidel.

Wald, Kenneth D. 1987. *Religion and Politics in the United States*. New York: St. Martin's Press.

Walzer, Michael. 1986. "The Reform of the International System." In *Studies of War and Peace*, Oyvind Osterud, ed. Oslo: Norwegian University Press.

———. 1997. *On Tolerance*. New Haven, Conn.: Yale University.

Washington, Booker T. 1970. *The Story of My life and Work.* New York: New American Library. (Original work published 1900)

Weber, Max. 1946. "Politics as a Vocation." In *From Max Weber,* Hans H. Gerth and C. Wright Mills, eds., pp. 77–128. New York: Oxford University Press.

Weibull, Jorgen. 1995. *Evolutionary Game Theory.* Cambridge, Mass.: MIT Press.

Weintraub, E. Roy. 1992. *Toward a History of Game Theory.* Durham, N.C.: Duke University Press.

Went, Robert. 2000. *Globalization: Neoliberal Challenge, Radical Responses.* London: Pluto.

Willard, William. 1998. "The Bureau of Indian Affairs and the Reservation System" (pp. 34–55) and "The Termination Policy" (pp. 56–68), both in his course packet, "Intro to American Indian Study," Pullman, Washington.

Williams, George Huntson. 1962. *The Radical Reformation.* Philadelphia: Westminster Press.

Wirsing, Robert G. 1994. *India, Pakistan and the Kashmir Dispute.* New York: St. Martin's Press.

Wolf, Eric. 1969. *Peasant Wars in the Twentieth Century.* New York: Harper & Row.

Woodward, C. Vann. 1974. *The Strange Career of Jim Crow.* 3rd rev. ed. New York: Oxford University Press.

Woodward, Susan L. 1995. *Balkan Tragedy: Chaos and Dissolution after the Cold War.* Washington, D.C.: Brookings Institution.

Young, Crawford. 1976. *The Politics of Cultural Pluralism.* Madison: University of Wisconsin Press.

Younis, Najib Nicholas. 1978. *The Breakdown of Lebanese Consociationalism.* Unpublished Ph.D. dissertation, Department of Political Science, Washington State University.

Zartman, William I., ed. 1997. *Governance as Conflict Management: Politics and Violence in West Africa.* Washington, D.C.: Brookings Institution.

Zartman, William I., and Maureen R. Berman. 1982. *The Practical Negotiator.* New Haven: Yale University Press.

Index

About the Author

TERRENCE E. COOK is Professor of Political Science at Washington State University, Pullman. He is the author of *Nested Political Coalitions: Nation, Regime, Program, Cabinet* (Praeger, 2002).